Dear Dudley

Dear Dudley

A celebration of the much-loved comedy legend

Barbra Paskin

JB
JOHN BLAKE

First published in Great Britain by John Blake Publishing,
an imprint of Bonnier Books UK
Suite 2.25 The Plaza
535 Kings Road
London SW10 0SZ

www.johnblakebooks.com

www.facebook.com/johnblakebooks
twitter.com/jblakebooks

First published in hardback in 2018

Hardback ISBN: 978 1 78606 965 8
Ebook: 978 1 78946 019 3

British Library Cataloguing-in-Publication Data:
A catalogue record for this book is available from the British Library.

Design by www.envydesign.co.uk

Printed and bound in Great Britain by Clays Ltd, Elcograf S p. A

1 3 5 7 9 10 8 6 4 2

This book contains text previously published in *Dudley Moore: The Authorised Biography* by Barbra Paskin (Sidgwick & Jackson, 1997)

Papers used by John Blake Publishing are natural, recyclable products made from wood grown in sustainable forests. The manufacturing processes conform to the environmental regulations of the country of origin.

John Blake Publishing is an imprint of Bonnier Books UK
www.bonnierbooks.co.uk

To Simon

A brother whose support, encouragement and brilliance I cherish.

Contents

PART THREE

PART FOUR

Preface

In early 1999, when Dudley was approaching his sixty-fourth birthday, he was feeling acutely depressed. For four years it had become increasingly clear that something was neurologically wrong. For most of that time, his doctors were mystified by negative test results. Only one doctor ventured a diagnosis but Dudley didn't accept it and the uncertainty left him deeply despondent. To cheer him up, I approached hundreds of his friends and colleagues from the world of entertainment, telling them only that he was unwell, and asked them to write him letters which I would assemble in a massive album for his April birthday. I thought he might be heartened by such a vivid expression of what he meant to his friends. I had no idea what a mammoth undertaking it would be, entailing many months of locating everyone and contacting them in various corners of the planet.

I was blown away by the response. Over the next four months, letters poured in from all over the world. Even from some who hadn't known Dudley but wanted to be part of this mammoth expression of affection for the star who was loved by millions. Fan letters from Emma Thompson, Billy Joel, Phil Collins and others. People who'd never worked with Dudley but who wanted to express their appreciation of his infinite talents. The letters carried messages of love and devotion, many of them bearing words of comfort, and I was touched by the degree of humility shown by so many of these star performers.

Finding the right albums in which to assemble all the letters was a challenge. Not too small but not too big. David Hockney rang me several times to ask if I'd selected the album because he needed the exact measurements. I didn't know why until he sent over a painting of a birthday card that fitted exactly onto one of the pages. During all this time I was bombarded by phone calls from concerned friends. 'I didn't know he was ill,' Kelsey Grammer fretted. 'What's wrong with him?' This was a question that nobody could answer. Quincy Jones rang me one night after I'd started to run a bath. I answered the phone in my office and for the next fifteen minutes Quincy talked about the magic of Dudley, his wonderful spirit and how much he loved him. Only when I hung up did I remember the bath. I spent the next half-hour mopping up the flood.

By the time I'd assembled all the letters they filled two massive albums, which I packaged and sent to Dudley in New Jersey. He was living next door to the family of his classical musical partner and closest friend, Rena Fruchter, who had been caring for him for the last few years.

Dudley was overwhelmed when he saw all the letters. Accompanied by Rena, he flew to Los Angeles the following month and came to see me. He shuffled into my apartment with the aid of Rena and 'Maurice', his wooden cane. Reclining on a couch with one of my birds perched on his fingers, it felt like so many other occasions when he'd hung out with me in the apartment to share a lifetime's memories. He was deeply touched that so many of his colleagues had written him such loving and expressive letters. 'It gave me some encouragement to think a bit more pleasantly about myself,' he reflected, 'and to think more positively about myself.'

Just a few weeks later, he was given the confirmed diagnosis of progressive supranuclear palsy (PSP), a distant cousin of Parkinson's, which attacks the brain's motor functions. At last he could silence those critics who had blamed his slurred voice and imbalance on being drunk. For Dudley, it was almost a relief to be able to put a name to his illness.

It was, he told me, like having something on the tip of his tongue but unable to express it. Thought processes were incomplete. Sentences begun were left unfinished. Worst was his increasing unreliability at the piano when his fingers wouldn't go where he told them to.

For a long time he had said he would give me an exclusive interview once he knew for certain what was wrong with him. He never forgot that promise and in October 1999 I joined him in New Jersey.

I stayed in his house and when I woke the following morning I found him sitting on the end of my bed, smiling at me. It reminded me of so many times when I'd slept on sofas in his hotel suites while he played concerts across America. But this time was sadly different and the next few days were heart-wrenching as I saw the full devastation of Dudley's illness.

My interview ran in *The Times* and I was flooded afterwards with phone calls and letters that poured in from Dudley's friends in the UK and America who had been greatly touched to learn of the extent of Dudley's illness. 'I was moved to tears,' wrote Mel Brooks. 'Moved by the sadness of it and by Dudley's courage.' And Jack Lemmon, himself a credible pianist, admitted he'd been deeply affected by Dudley's interview. 'I can't imagine his pain of not being able to play the piano any more.' It was, as he rightly perceived, 'the cruellest blow of all'.

My relationship with Dudley began when, as the BBC's Hollywood correspondent, I took my film crew into his beachside home to interview him about his new movie *10* for Barry Norman's weekly film programme, *Film 79*. The film had just been released and America had become captivated by his humour and his charm. Overnight he became a sex symbol. After that, I interviewed him many times at his home, or mine, and on the set of many of his films. It was that long association that led him, many years later, to sanction me as his authorised biographer.

In 1994 I began working on Dudley's biography. I'd known him since that first television interview in 1979 when he stood on the threshold of mega-fame with *10*. Over the years, he'd been approached many times by journalists wanting to write his biography but he'd always refused permission. Now he gave it, not only willingly but wholeheartedly endorsing my biography. The timing, he said, was right. 'To coincide with my sixty naughty years, as Errol Flynn would say!'

Little did I know how all-encompassing would be his involvement. He began visiting me on a regular basis, leaning back on the sofa, drinking coffee and eating his favourite imported digestive biscuits, cheerfully sharing them with my birds – two cockatiels, two budgies and their offspring – as he ruminated on his life. Often, our biographical explorations were interspersed with personal injections, usually of the avian kind:

BARBRA: Tell me if you want Papillon to get off your shoulder.
DUDLEY: No, he's okay. Unless he pecks eyes! Ouch . . . what did he just do?
BARBRA: That was only a little nip on your cheek. He's

having a fit of pique because you're not paying attention to him.

DUDLEY: He's just like a child, for crying out loud! Mind you, not that my son ever bit me when I ignored him! He just sulked instead.

In the biography I wrote about Dudley's entire life, all it encompassed and the melancholic streak that always dogged him from a painful childhood. But in this book I want to celebrate his special gifts: his legacy that's survived through his films, the numerous jazz recordings and the remastering of his old albums. Fifteen years after his death, audiences are still entertained by his old movies. And more than fifty years after he recorded them, his jazz compositions continue to be played and be the focus of concerts by today's musicians. This is how Dudley would want to be remembered – through his movies, his comedy and especially through his music. And much of it here is in his own words from our many conversations over the years.

He had a wonderful gift of making people laugh and I can still hear his *Arthur* cackle in my ears. Many was the time when I'd play my telephone messages and find some from him, which invariably ended with his contagiously raucous laugh.

This, then, is not a book about sadness. It is a book about triumph and achievement and a cherished legacy we continue to enjoy today. It is above all a celebration of the man who became one of Britain's national treasures.

Part One

CHAPTER 1

Childhood
1935–46

Where does one start to celebrate the life of Dudley Moore? Would it be in the early sixties when he became one of the famous four to immortalise *Beyond the Fringe* and change the face of British comedy? Would it be in the late sixties when he joined with Peter Cook to bring us the landmark TV series *Not Only . . . But Also* and several movies that have become classics, like *The Wrong Box* and *Bedazzled*? Would it be in 1979 when, on a billboard on Sunset Boulevard for the movie *10*, his cut-out figure dangled from a pendant in Bo Derek's cleavage and turned him overnight into an unlikely sex symbol? Or was it two years later when he brought us his unforgettable drunken clown *Arthur*? Yet to focus on any one of those landmarks and jump over the interim achievements would be to do him a monstrous disservice. For Dudley was that rare commodity – a multitalented genius. Great not at one thing, but at several.

His was a life that began in the lower-class suburbs of London and reached the glittering heights of Hollywood. On the surface he didn't look like a movie star. He was short, had one thin leg and a club foot and a huge inferiority complex. But Dudley Moore also had the world's most endearing smile, a whopping gift for comedy, and a superlative talent as a pianist and composer. Not to mention a cackle of a laugh that was irrepressibly contagious.

Over the twenty years that I knew him I watched him run the gamut of emotions. From sadness to pleasure. From desperation to hope. From insecurity to confidence. And through it all there was the man who viewed his life with no small measure of astonishment and even more gratitude. He was married four times but the greatest and longest love affair of his life was shared with his public and his music.

We're told that suffering, especially in childhood, can lead to phenomenal efforts to bury the pain under layers of artistic brilliance. Perhaps if Dudley's youth had not been so traumatic, if he hadn't suffered deformities which he felt bound to hide through humour, we may never have known his comedic skill. If he hadn't clambered onto his mother's piano stool when he was five and loved the sound when he pounded the keys, we may never have enjoyed his musical genius.

To understand the journey that led to his phenomenal success, we need to go back to the beginning of Dudley's life where it all began. Only then can we begin to understand the background that moulded him and against which he spent a lifetime fighting to overcome his inner turmoil to reach the sparkling pinnacle of an extraordinarily multifaceted career.

Dudley's early years bore no hint that he was destined for greatness. Certainly there was no clue when as a baby he joined five-year-old sister Barbara in their modest Dagenham council home in spring 1935. He had been born with club feet and a withered, skinny, shorter left leg. Both his feet had been turned in and were clubbed, although the right one would naturally correct itself in time, and the left leg was shorter and misshapen. His mother felt guilty. She was shocked that her baby had been born with a deformities and found it frightening and shameful. Sadly, she would instil in her son the same deep shame she herself felt about it.

Dudley's physical problems led to endless operations on his leg from the age of two weeks old until he was seven. For his later operations, with his parents not easily able to travel in war-torn London, his stays in the hospital were lived out in isolation with the visions and sounds of war all around him. These were traumatic times, when he was the only boy in a ward full of badly wounded soldiers – for whom he played watchdog when they wanted to sneak a smoke – and his lengthy lonely sojourns would lead in adult life to a propensity for isolation.

There were lighter occasions, but at the time he was too young to recognise the humour in a dire situation. One of them, which sounds like it came out of a sketch with Peter Cook, occurred when he'd been wheeled into a darkened operating room and left alone for what seemed like hours.

> **DUDLEY:** Finally, this doctor came in and said, 'It's the right leg to come off, isn't it?' And I squeaked, 'No, no! You've got to do something to the left leg!' It turned out he was trying to be funny, but I thought he meant it! I thought he was going to take off my leg!

In many ways the Moores were a typical suburban working-class family. Though they were poor, there was little difference between them and others nearby. Dudley didn't recognise poverty. He only knew they weren't rich, since to him wealth meant owning a bike with three speeds rather than a fixed wheel.

Father Jock was an electrician for Stratford East Railway, earning five pounds a week. He was quiet and passive. Mother Ada, was a shorthand typist who supplemented their meagre income with rudimentary piano lessons. Both parents were reticent and undemonstrative, although Ada was 'very merry sometimes and loved to laugh', and they never hugged or kissed their children. Both were very repressed individuals, not given to expressing their emotions, and the young Dudley's mind erroneously translated that to not being loved.

DUDLEY: They created an aura of repression and suppression around themselves. They were two of a kind. I don't know that either of them could express love very well, either to each other or to us. My mother's excuse sometimes was that I shouldn't be touched because the plaster might break on my leg. So I often felt as if I were stuck on the mantel with a sign reading, 'Don't Touch Him'.

Christmas in the Moore household was austere. There was no tree and no decorations save for paper chains that Barbara and Dudley cut from coloured pieces of paper and hung from wall to wall. Presents were restricted to one apiece, and even Christmas lunch was a simple affair consisting of a small chicken.

When Dudley was five, the family was evacuated to Norfolk, an event recorded in his mother's diary, which only came to light in 1994 when he and I sifted through the masses of memorabilia he'd collected over the years.

DUDLEY: I'm reading bits of what my mother wrote in her diary: 'We were evacuated on the 3rd day, got up early at 3.30 w/packs on our backs, had to walk to Dagenham docks, 4 mums with children, got lift w/Dudley and Barbara . . . this place is a chicken and fruit farm . . . letter from Jock . . . Dudley and Barbara out to play, all week is Easter holiday'. I must tell you this is the most I've ever read of this diary! There's more: 'Getting ready for Dudley

> to start school April 1940' – this must have been when I was five, there's no date – 'Dudley likes the school but not the teacher! Ha ha!! . . . Dudley whistled in church . . . am anxious to get home . . . been evacuee for 4 months now . . . saw masseuse about Dudley . . . no letters at all, feel unsettled'. This is all an unknown side to my mother. It was very private. I don't think I even realised I had this. It's extraordinary!

Dudley's passion for music began when he was still a toddler. His mother's side of the family was very musical and they all played different instruments, particularly the piano, violin and organ. His early years were lived in the shadow of war, but it was then, as German bombs screeched overhead, that little Dudley clambered up to the family's battered brown upright. When he touched the keys for the first time of the piano that his third wife would later track down and import to Los Angeles, it left an indelible mark. He loved it and was an eager and fast learner. He enjoyed the sound and thought it 'made a nice noise'. His mother must have thought so too, and she enrolled him in music lessons when he turned six. By the age of seven he had graduated to the organ and violin, an instrument he longed to master but never felt he did.

The operations on his foot had been relatively successful in straightening his left leg, but nature turned off Dudley's growth clock when he reached five feet two and a half inches, although he had yet to realise it. He kept asking his mother if he would grow taller and he spent years perceiving his height and his clubfoot as inadequacies. The piano became his emotional refuge. Music was an outlet for the dwarfish boy to vent the increasing aggressions he was feeling about his foot and the thin leg that was so often either strapped into irons or encased in plaster after yet another operation. His education was being continually interrupted by operations and lengthy hospital incarcerations.

At eight, Dudley began choral singing at St Thomas's, Dagenham. He loved church music, loved the ethereal sound of angelic voices, and in time he would sing the entire range from soprano and alto through to tenor and bass. That love would remain with him all his life. As would another.

> **DUDLEY:** I loved hearing Mado Robin, the coloratura soprano, and I remember this one time . . . I was quietly having a grope on the sofa with my sister on my left and my father on the left of her and my mother to my right. We were listening to her singing on the radio and my mother said, 'This woman is singing the highest note that's ever been sung, don't do that, dear,' and the two moments were fused in my mind! For many years I was fixated with coloratura singing!

By the age of eleven, Dudley's musical acuity was acutely evident. But another side to his persona was about to open up. One that would prove to be his saviour in times of self-doubt.

CHAPTER 2

School Days 1946–54

It was at grammar school that Dudley discovered his comedic bent. The other children were cruel and hostile, bullying him for his lack of height, his wizened leg and his club foot. Kids would shout 'Hopalong!' behind him and mimic his limping gait. He felt unworthy of anything – 'Like a little runt with a twisted foot.' But at thirteen, a psychic switch flipped in his head. Tired of feeling constantly surrounded by the enemy, one day in class he made a crass joke to his teacher. It was entirely out of character, and his classmates stared at him in astonishment – but not without an admiration that instantly conveyed itself to Dudley. It was the turning point in his young life.

Forced to develop a classic defence, he discovered that playing the fool could go a long way towards self-preservation. Dudley found that comedy diverted his peers' aggression. His humour was a strong weapon and he wielded it with vengeance. Almost overnight he metamorphosed from class bookworm to class clown and his grades plummeted.

> **DUDLEY:** I remember that day when I decided not to be bullied any more and gravitated towards fooling. I said goodbye to my teachers and hello to my peers as it were. It wasn't until I was about forty that I discovered why I'd wanted to entertain and I didn't like it. I learned that you entertain to deflect hostility. I never realised it before then and it made me so angry. Angry that I'd turned my back on an academic life when I'd been fooling around, and I felt tremendous regret at not keeping up my studies.

A month after his thirteenth birthday, Dudley won a violin scholarship to attend weekly lessons at the prestigious Guildhall School of Music. He also won a scholarship to the Royal Academy of Music, but his mother opted for the Guildhall because it was a few stations closer on the underground. Every Saturday, the youngster trotted off to the Guildhall, violin case under his arm, where he studied Musical Theory and Composition along with piano and violin. His parents had scraped up the money to buy Dudley his first violin, an instrument he adored passionately, 'but I was so desperate to play it really well that I wasn't any good at it'. He was proficient enough to entertain family and friends and gave impromptu concerts in the garden, playing the violin for family and neighbours, his sheet music held up by clothes pegs on the line.

By then he'd also started composing. The previous year had seen his first musical composition, 'Anxiety', a testament to his early angst. Years later one of his wives, Brogan Lane, discovered the score, across which in his neat schoolboy hand he had written '*allegretto moderato misterioso sostenuto*', and had it blown up to poster size and hung on the landing in his house.

His talent soon became recognised by outsiders. The Stratford Music Festival held a competition and Dudley entered. 'He was in bed one day with the flu,' his sister Barbara remembered, 'and this letter arrived. I took it up to him, and when he opened it, they told him he'd won first prize for composing a carol. He was very excited and felt better immediately!'

As if the violin and piano weren't enough, Dudley had also now discovered the organ. He found it a natural progression from the piano and for some time he'd been 'messing about' with the organ in church. Under the guidance of Leslie Taylor, head of the Guildhall, he took it up seriously and became highly proficient, earning money at church functions. As the church organist he liked the feeling of sitting higher up than the congregation and looking down on them. 'I enjoyed feeling sort of isolated, as well as very feted.'

The pedals presented a problem, as his bad foot needed still more elevation, and he used to spend hours in the organ loft at St Thomas's trying to get his foot to work more efficiently. His answer was to build an extra rubber heel onto one of his mother's old right court shoes – right, because it made up for his inability to turn the left foot outwards – and cut a groove in the sole so he could strap on the shoe and wind the lace round the back of his leg. This had the effect of pulling his toes up to an angle that allowed him to match the agility of his right foot.

His music tutor, Peter Cork, was struck vividly by his pupil's musical prowess from the first moment of hearing him play. 'He had incredible musicality,' he remembered, 'which was astounding in a boy of his age. It was an amazing ability and, aside from playing the piano, violin and organ, he also composed and became my choir accompanist at school. His musical talents overflowed in all directions, but his capability on the organ was incredible.'

Although Dudley couldn't memorise very much, he astounded his teacher with his extraordinary talent for sight-reading. Cork once gave him a six-part Bach fugue and was dumbfounded when Dudley played it perfectly on sight. 'He was very self-assured as far as his music was concerned. It always used to annoy me a little bit that he never seemed to work at anything and then he'd turn up with something quite brilliant, having worked on it at the last moment.'

Dudley became friendly with thirteen-year-old Teifion Griffiths, who lived up the street from the Moores. Dudley persuaded him to join the choir at his church; by then he had become the assistant organist and choirmaster. The young Welsh boy was deeply impressed. 'He used to practise a lot,' recalled Teifion, 'and I would turn pages for him in the organ loft while he played pretty heavy stuff like Handel and Bach. He was also brilliant at extemporising on modern tunes. He'd take a simple tune like "Baa, Baa, Black Sheep" and play it in the style of Schubert or Beethoven! It was brilliant. He was an indefatigable and dedicated clown, but at the same time he was also very introspective, much more than most kids at that age.'

Now one of the most popular boys in his school, Dudley was in great demand at parties where he would sing silly songs at the piano in his highest squeaky soprano, a portent of things to come. His young friend Teifion remembered Dudley being very excited whenever he discovered something new and interesting. 'He wanted to share it with people, and he'd say, "Come and listen to this," and then play some wonderful Bach piece that he'd latched on to.'

Teifion's own parents were outgoing, and loved having Dudley around to their house. Mrs Griffiths adored him, which sometimes irritated her son. 'I used to find it pretty annoying. Whenever we had run-ins, she'd say, "Why can't you be a nice boy like Dudley?" He had extraordinary charm and that used to get up my nose a bit. Not only was I in his shadow as far as the fact that he was skilful, but also my parents thought he was a well-behaved, charming lad, while I was pictured as a naughty boy.'

Dudley probably got a few giggles out of that, because he was very much the ringleader in their antics, which led him into trouble on more than one occasion. The two boys used to annoy the locals with their habit of running around shrieking, 'It can't go on! It can't go on!' in high, squeaky tones. 'Dudley was a big one for shouting out crazy things in funny voices,' laughed Teifion. 'I think he was practising for later years.'

Dudley's social life was packed; he had become one of the leading lights of his small community. His music tutor was constantly amazed at Dudley's capacity to make everybody laugh. 'I would just get the choir to a serious moment when Dudley, who was my piano accompanist, would twinkle with something and the whole thing would collapse. I used to get so angry about it, but it was typical of him.'

Occasionally Dudley played the piano for the old people at Kingsley Hall, a local community centre. On one occasion, Dame Sybil Thorndike visited and two boys were invited to perform solo there. Dudley was one of them. He played the violin and, according to Peter Cork, 'Dame Sybil was very taken with him. He thinks he never mastered the violin, but he really was very good, and I remember writing something for him that he performed with the orchestra.'

Jim Johnson was a star pianist, playing regularly in religious services. He was a year younger than Dudley and the two had met when Dudley's school choir went to Kingsley Hall to sing Handel's *Messiah*. Dudley accompanied on the piano, and Johnson, who was standing at the back of the hall, remembers being 'absolutely gobsmacked by his playing. And I was a bit put out, too. It was a wonderful and definitive performance, and I was teased unmercifully about it afterwards.'

Church music became a central part of Dudley's existence, and he eagerly looked forward to choir practice on Thursday nights and the serious choir singing on Sundays in a full church. He had never lost his pleasure in looking down on the congregation. Perhaps, given his sensitivity about his height, it made him feel taller. He was so enveloped by his zeal that, as adulthood loomed, he discarded his ideas of becoming a violinist and thought instead of becoming a church organist and choirmaster.

But his musical horizons were about to widen. Drastically. Still playing classical music on the piano, violin and organ, one day he heard a record of jazz pianist Erroll Garner playing 'The Way You Look Tonight' and in it he discovered a whole new arena that would for ever become his metier. Jazz.

He was fascinated by Garner's style – 'the steady beat in the left hand and the way the melody sort of wriggled around inside that rhythm' – and he became a frequent visitor to the local music shop, where he would pick up whatever he could find by the jazz great.

There was a jazz record club in Dagenham, and Dudley began dropping in on the sessions. Gradually he learned to appreciate the virtuosity of Oscar Peterson and George Shearing (both of whom would later become his friends), and Fats Waller and Stan Kenton. But Erroll Garner remained a massive influence. Dudley wallowed in his sound and began experimenting with it himself on the piano.

Along with his music, Dudley was passionate to go to university and he applied to Oxford. When their letter arrived, he could barely open it. His heart was in his mouth; he wanted so badly to be accepted.

> **DUDLEY:** I opened the envelope and it said they were pleased to announce I'd won an organ scholarship to Magdalen College. I couldn't believe it! I was so excited! My mother snatched up that letter and went running down the street shouting, "My son's going to college!" It didn't impress anybody in Dagenham at the time. I was highly embarrassed. I just froze up there in the bedroom as I heard her screaming down the street! But that was a thrill to her.

> And to me. I wanted to be an organist and choirmaster, something very respectable to do with the church.

His headmaster was delighted too. So much that he gave the whole school a half-day holiday in honour of the occasion.

In Dudley's last year at school, his musical talents were constantly in demand. 'He did a Schubert parody, *Die Flabbergast*,' Peter Cork remembered, 'and the reaction was of tremendous amusement. Everybody loved it. I used to improvise around the tunes of the day, and Dudley once said, "I wish I could play chords like you." Which was a bit rich, really, when you consider what he went on to do!'

CHAPTER 3

Oxford

1954–58

Dudley had vaulted over the class barrier by winning a scholarship to the university, but he was acutely aware of his working-class background. Surrounded by upper-class accents in Magdalen College, he felt intimidated by the other students and worked at trying to sound more like them.

Magdalen was one of three Oxford colleges with the strongest choral tradition. It had its own choir, and organ scholars were also cathedral organists who played at daily services. The chapel at Magdalen was one of the most exquisite in Oxford, and Dudley found its beauty quite overwhelming.

> **DUDLEY:** There I was, this club-footed wanker sitting on the organ seat, playing this beautiful organ in this stunning chapel. I felt I really didn't deserve to be there.

In spite of his anxiety, every now and then his penchant for humour would break through. One of his music teachers had a stammer and, meeting his new students for the first time, he addressed Dudley. 'What's your na-na-name?' he asked. Dudley looked at him innocently. 'Mo-Mo-Moore!' he replied, and a titter ran round the classroom.

Academically he worked hard, his days an organised blend of tutorials and research. He sang in the choir and played violin and piano in the orchestra and the organ at chapel services. Formal education was confined to the academic theory of music.

His tutor, Dr Bernard Rose, found his young student very appealing. 'He was a very cuddly sort of a chap with a great sense of humour. He used to come to tutorials with another student and between them they were extremely amusing and good fun. Our tutorials were never terribly serious affairs.'

Dudley had discovered in a music shop in Oxford a record by Mado Robin, the French coloratura soprano who had years earlier been such a source of inspiration for his early ineluctable sexual activities whenever he heard her on the radio. On this record, Robin sang the highest note ever recorded, and, just like years before, Dudley's whole body trembled when he heard it. He didn't dare buy the record because he knew it would keep him from studying; instead, he took to frequenting the music shop. There, wearing his father's raincoat, he would slip into a glass booth and play certain tracks to which he would masturbate. 'The owners of the shop always wondered why I never bought the record!' Eventually he did. And he didn't leave his room for a week.

Dudley's music was paramount in his life and, in addition to his musical studies, he also belonged to several music societies. Theatre director Anthony Page was a fellow student and he regarded Dudley as a considerable talent. He spent many hours discussing music with him and cast him in some of the plays he directed.

Despite a lack of funds, Dudley was surviving well enough. He kept on hand a good stock of jam, marmalade, Marmite and fish paste and tried to allay his mother's worries that he wasn't eating enough. Indeed, in a letter to his parents in October 1956, he proudly told them of a recent evening when he had chipped in with some other students. 'We bought bread, butter, corned beef, tomatoes and cheese for dinner. It was very cheap and, boy, was it filling! We could hardly move after such a banquet!'

One of his few luxuries was to allow himself the *Radio Times* every week, so that he could schedule concerts to listen to on his tiny radio. Occasionally there was a gift of a couple of pounds from someone in Dagenham, and this would carry him through the next several weeks. As meticulous as his mother in such matters, he would take his couple of banknotes and deposit them in the bank, carefully logging such entries in his diary.

Whenever she could, Ada Moore sent care packages to her son, and she even managed to do his washing through the mail. Dudley recalls sending her his dirty clothes, which within the week would return all neatly laundered and wrapped up with a bag of his favourite sherbet lemons.

It was around this time that Dudley met fellow student John Bassett and began a lifelong friendship. John Bassett had his own jazz band at Oxford, the Bassett Hounds. 'Dudley loved jazz but didn't really know a thing about it. He wanted to know how jazz was made, and he cracked the code in five seconds flat! After that, he began playing with us regularly and he soon became very popular.'

By day Dudley studied classical music; by night he played jazz in the student nightclubs. The applause he heard boosted his self-esteem and his confidence soared.

By his third year, his penchant for humour had become well known. Through his attachment to the Bassett Hounds, he had begun writing sketches and performing outrageously comic and bold improvisations. And his hilarious musical parodies were like nothing heard before. He found himself increasingly being asked to perform for cabarets. No longer did he feel out of place. He had rediscovered comedy. He felt like the school clown all over again – 'a guy who improvised and generally made a fool of himself'.

Dudley was enjoying comedy more and more. It was becoming an obsession alongside his music. He was intoxicated. Once again, he had found the acceptance he craved by making people laugh. Dudley Moore had become Oxford University's Clown Prince.

Theatre director Patrick Garland was at Oxford and remembers being very struck by Dudley's performing capabilities and charm. 'He had become one of the most prominent humorists in Oxford. He was unquestionably the star and was gifted with immense spontaneity. Some people are natural clowns, and Dudley had that clown quality about him. Much of his later works were based very much on what he was doing in Oxford in the mid-fifties. What was particularly sweet was his tremendously affectionate nature, and it seems to me he never really altered.

'The name "Cuddly Dudley" began at Oxford, and stuck with him. But he was called that with good reason. He had an unforced, unpretentious wit that was very appealing, and people genuinely admired and liked him very much.'

Dudley was now so much in demand that the diaries he kept while at Oxford, at first so sparse on the social side, became a jumble of engagements from organ practices and orchestral recitals to jazz concerts and cabaret. And there were innumerable dinners with fellow students.

In three years he had come a long way from the day he first walked so nervously through the majestic portals of Magdalen College. No longer was he condemned as the runt of the litter, the boy everyone picked on because of his height and his foot. Now they picked on him for entirely different reasons. He may have been short, but his quick wit, cherubic features and brilliance at the piano made him a hugely romantic target.

His last few months at Oxford were packed solid with university cabarets and concerts. So crammed now was his time that the diary note of his treatise deadline had to be squeezed in between masses of engagements and countless scribbled notes for sketch ideas.

> **DUDLEY:** I was so busy having fun and being highly sociable that I was doing all my academic work at the last moment. I had to write a string quartet for my Bachelor of Music and I did it in a very short time. Talk about doing stuff by candlelight! There was me doing stuff literally by candlelight into the early hours and trying to finish this damned quartet that I'd said I'd write and was committed to doing.

When Magdalen College held its traditional Commemorative May Ball, John Dankworth's band and Cleo Laine were hired as the main attraction. While they were taking a dinner break, they heard someone playing 'the most wonderful jazz'. They thought it was a record until they realised the music was coming from the other side of an upright piano.

'We listened for about fifteen minutes then went around the piano,' Dankworth recalled, 'and there was Dudley playing. He knew who we were and was pleased to be noticed, and I told him, "If you're ever short of a job, let me know, because you'd make a good pianist for the band."'

Dudley's tutor, Bernard Rose, reflected, 'I could never tell whether he'd go the classical music route or the jazz route. In the end, he did both.' To Dudley's astonishment, Dr Rose offered him the post of organist to Queen's College, also tutor and choirmaster. Dudley was overwhelmed. It was what he'd always dreamed of. But no longer. In the most momentous decision of his life, he told his disappointed tutor, 'I don't think this would be the life for me.'

It was July 1958, and the world of entertainment had already beckoned. And so it was that Dudley Moore at last blew out the flames of his long-smouldering desire to be an organist and choirmaster. Whatever it would take, he was heading for show business, determined to be a comedy and musical entertainer.

But who could ever have imagined the heights to which he would ascend in his new career?

CHAPTER 4

Before The Fringe 1958–59

After Dudley graduated from Oxford in 1958, he found work immediately. Continual auditions landed him gigs up and down the country. There were dates in nightclubs and cabarets, often playing his now clearly defined Erroll Garner style of jazz, or combining his comic sketches with parodies of classical music.

London at this time was a thriving centre of jazz. Dudley flooded the clubs with pleas to play and one of his first Soho engagements was at Ronnie Scott's jazz club, a key hotspot. These were exciting times for him. His piano-playing thrilled the club audiences, and his adrenaline was in overdrive. Even though he was living on cornflakes, he never felt deprived. He was having a great time and felt certain he could always earn his living playing in a bar or a club, earning ten shillings a night to pay the rent. He considered himself very lucky. He had felt greatly imprisoned within the orbit of his family and Dagenham. His music was like a jumbo jet carrying him off to another world. No wonder he felt lucky. He was free.

He still played occasionally with John Bassett's band, and the Bassett Hounds became a regular sight in London hotels, particularly the Dorchester and the Savoy. And Dudley had now assembled a part-time trio with Hugo Boyd on bass and Derek Hogg on drums.

His Oxford contemporary Anthony Page was now a director at the Royal Court Theatre, and Dudley landed the lofty position of resident composer, writing incidental music for plays for five pounds a week. 'Dudley tended to work at the last moment,' rued Page, 'and I had the task of getting the music out of him. Usually I'd get it by having to stand over him or sit there with him. But the music he came out with was brilliant.'

By day, Dudley worked in the theatre. Come night-time it was jazz that engrossed him. He was convinced that as a jazz musician he would win not only the status he yearned for but also women, whom he was attracting in earnest. Besides which, jazz appealed to his emotional nature.

He was now an accomplished jazz pianist and, on a recommendation from John Dankworth, he was hired to join Vic Lewis's band. Lewis recognised that Dudley played 'a bit like Erroll Garner' and told him he could only do that when it came time for his solo. But to the chagrin of the other players, Dudley continued as before, and he recalled that some of the band players 'would get really pissed off, and tell me so to my face'.

> **DUDLEY:** A guy named Roy East who played the alto saxophone *hated* my guts. And then on the plane to somewhere I fooled around and he laughed at me for the first time. And I thought, 'Oh God, this is a repetition of what happened in school when I used humour to stop the bullies!' And so I became the clown of the band. It was very unconscious. It just happened.

After playing throughout England, the band landed an American tour. Dudley was thrilled and when they reached New York he instantly fell in love with the city.

> **DUDLEY:** I was so excited to be there. We went to Birdland and we heard Lennie Tristano, the blind pianist who was very favoured by the band, and I heard Dwike Mitchell and Willie Ruff play piano and French horn. I was very excited by these new experiences. I remember coming out into Times Square and seeing the steam coming out of the middle of the road, and the smell of New York has remained uppermost in my mind.

He was captivated by the jazz artists and the music that he heard and when the band returned to England, Dudley decided to remain.

New York in the late 1950s was a mecca for aspiring jazz musicians, and Dudley sought every opportunity to play. Amid sporadic unemployment and having digs at the YMCA, 'where I almost got punched up by some bloke who wanted to use the phone while I was on it', he landed odd gigs at some of the seedier clubs.

The Duplex was a popular nightclub in Greenwich Village, and he won a brief engagement in its downstairs bar. It was there that Ahmet Ertegun, president of Atlantic Records, encountered him.

Ertegun was dumbstruck. 'He played a little bit in the style of Erroll Garner, though he also had his own style about him. He was terrific!' Ertegun introduced himself and said he'd like to make an album with him. But Dudley said he was returning the next day to England. Although he did not take up the offer then, years later he would eventually record albums for the Atlantic label.

He would have liked to have stayed in New York, but he was unbearably homesick. And so, in early 1959 at the age of twenty-three, he passed up the opportunity he'd just been offered and flew back home. As it turned out, his timing was perfect. John Dankworth's pianist was leaving and Dudley was thrilled when Dankworth invited him to join his band.

The band kept Dudley busy at least four nights a week, for which Dankworth paid him five pounds a gig, and he began making television appearances with them, as well as having occasional spots of his own or with his new trio. Dudley had always found it hard to accompany other musicians.

> **DUDLEY:** I started up a trio because it was very hard to accompany people and know exactly what they wanted. I remember being threatened with dismissal by John Dankworth because I wasn't playing enough with the others but there was a lot of disagreement between me and the others as to what chords I should be playing. So I started the trio out of despair that I could ever play what anybody else ever wanted me to. I got a lot of bad looks from the saxophone section in John's band. They just didn't like this little guy who'd joined them.

The trio allowed Dudley the freedom to play whatever he liked and he was ecstatic when they landed their own concert at the Royal Festival Hall.

His earlier work at the Royal Court had brought him a widespread reputation for writing incidental music for plays; he was also writing jingles for his friend, ad-agency director Francis Megahy. Megahy had persuaded him to write the music for commercials, among them Persil detergent and Pepsodent toothpaste. And he was scoring Megahy's first film as a director.

Dudley, alone or with the trio, was often to be found playing at London's Cool Elephant and the Blue Angel, where he became a popular draw. It was now that he made his first record, 'Strictly for the Birds', for future Beatles producer George Martin, a jazz rendition of a lullaby he'd performed at Oxford for a production of Aristophanes' *The Birds*.

And then John Bassett came along with a proposition that was to change the entire direction of Dudley's life.

CHAPTER 5

Beyond the Fringe and All That Jazz 1960–62

The Edinburgh Festival was, as it still is, an annual showcase for the arts. John Bassett had left Oxford and now worked for Festival director Robert Ponsonby. Charged with organising a late-night comedy revue as part of the Festival, he proposed it be made up of two graduates from Oxford and two from Cambridge.

His first choice for his Oxbridge quartet was Dudley, who then suggested Alan Bennett, who had been in one of his Oxford cabarets and had performed in a Festival fringe revue the previous year. Bassett next went to Jonathan Miller, whose comic mimicry had made him famous in Cambridge's Footlights Club and who had earlier performed in two Footlights revues in London. Miller, in turn, suggested Peter Cook, who had already written two revues for West End clubs.

The first meeting of the four took place in an Italian restaurant close to the hospital where Jonathan Miller was now a junior doctor. 'Dudley had a reticent puckishness about him,' recalled Miller, but the overall feeling was of wariness between them all. 'We instantly disliked one another and decided that it might be a profitable enterprise.' They settled on the title *Beyond the Fringe*, because, according to Dudley, 'We couldn't think of anything else and it had a lunatic ring to it.'

John Bassett recalled everyone being rather cautious and quiet. 'Nobody said anything at first, because no one wanted to tell a joke that might not prove funny to the others. Alan was particularly quiet, because he was very shy. But I do remember Dudley doing a Groucho Marx and following an attractive waitress in through one swing door and out of another!'

Dudley, now under contract to John Dankworth, asked for a few weeks off so he could perform in the revue. Dankworth gave it to him, 'but I had a feeling that he wouldn't be back'.

He was right. When *Beyond the Fringe* opened in August 1960 at Edinburgh's Lyceum Theatre, it became an immediate draw for the Festival. Dudley's friend, jazz singer Barbara Moore, has always remembered that exciting first night. 'It was an amazing atmosphere! Absolutely electric. The ladies were leaping on to their seats and throwing their fur coats in the air! It was brilliant, and the next day there were about eight or nine offers from the West End.'

Critical reaction was excellent, although major public acclaim would not come until later. When it did, *Beyond the Fringe* would become one of the West End's greatest-ever attractions and go on to repeat its triumph on Broadway, with both the Queen and President Kennedy in attendance on each side of the Atlantic.

DUDLEY: I couldn't believe the reaction to *Fringe*. It was startling, like overnight something had changed. I suppose I was aware at the time that we were part of a whole new breed of English comedy but it was also the time that the Beatles came along. So it was slightly irksome when these four other guys made more of a public success than we did!

While in Edinburgh, the post of conductor of the Edinburgh Festival Ballet became vacant and Dudley auditioned for the job. His classical bent was still very strong. He conducted a couple of modern works but lacked the requisite ease and authority that he would later acquire. He was also still writing occasional music for theatre productions and he composed the score for Chekhov's *Platanov*, to star Rex Harrison and Rachel Roberts.

He was now earning more money than ever. When he told his parents he was earning a hundred pounds a week, their jaws dropped in astonishment. It had taken them twenty years to save that amount. 'But they didn't make me feel guilty in any way,' Dudley assured me, 'because they were so delighted and thrilled.' Still, it must have required a huge adjustment for them to accept that a son who had grown up with so many emotional and physical disabilities was about to become part of a West End show.

It opened in London on 10 May 1961 at the Fortune Theatre in the West End to a rousing reception. The show was an instant wild success. It would become a cult classic and the forerunner of an entirely new wave of comedy in Britain. Irreverent, daring, unashamedly offensive, it turned theatre upside down. In theatre critic Kenneth Tynan's estimation, this was when English comedy 'took its first decisive step into the second half of the twentieth century'.

Britain at that time was still largely smothered by a cloak of Victorian puritanism. Revues until then had been light-hearted offerings that took great care not to give offence. *Beyond the Fringe* changed all that. Underneath the national mood of apathetic acceptance of the status quo there was an uneasy discontent. Particularly among the university generation, there was a feeling of disenchantment and a stirring of a more cynical social awareness.

Fringe was a cocktail of silly, funny sketches blended with others that were satirical and biting. They dealt topically with political and world issues and poked fun at the prevailing sexual hypocrisy. As Alan Bennett reflected, 'We dealt with things that young people made jokes about in private but never publicly, like politics and the monarchy. It was very daring and wasn't like any other revue that had been seen before, so it was a breath of fresh air.'

> **DUDLEY:** I was always afraid we would get done because the political content of the show was very controversial. I was terrified that we'd get arrested for everything we did. I was very timid. And Jonathan, Alan and Peter treated that fear with total scorn, thinly disguised.

Jonathan Miller believed audiences had been waiting for something like *Fringe* without being aware of it. And from the moment they opened, all four men knew that something unusual was taking place. 'There was an intensity of laughter that made us feel that something strange and rather special had happened.'

Though Dudley himself only wrote a few of the twenty-two sketches in *Beyond the Fringe*, his working-class irreverence inspired some of the others. But his most brilliant contributions were at the keyboard, where he exhibited a zany and innovative skill. As Jonathan Miller put it, 'He secreted music like sweat.'

Dudley's musical parodies were extraordinary. A Brechtian opera was sung in ersatz German, there was an amazing rendering of 'Little Miss Muffet' as might have been arranged by Benjamin Britten and sung by Peter Pears, and the classic was his wildly witty arrangement of 'Colonel Bogey' that couldn't seem to come to an end but instead went on and on.

They were parody at its cleverest, and probably the finest of their kind since Victor Borge. They required an intimate classical knowledge, and Dudley's clowning added to their strength.

Still, Peter Cook, detailing his memories in *Esquire* years later, wrote:

> Apart from his musical contributions, Dudley's suggestions were treated with benign contempt by the rest of us. He rarely voiced an opinion during the years we performed in London. He was in awe of Jonathan Miller's spectacular ability to speak at length on everything under the sun. Alan Bennett also inhibited Dudley, mainly with his scholarly demeanour. And I wore a cloak of precocious urbanity, which did little to encourage friendships.

Dudley felt vastly inferior to the others. Some of that was the inner demons of the English class system at work. Cook and Miller were sons of the more privileged middle class; Dudley and Alan Bennett were scholarship boys from the sticks. He felt intellectually and physically dominated by the others.

> **DUDLEY:** I found them extraordinarily out of my reach. I didn't contribute much to the writing, because I was so intimidated by them. Their thrust was every area I knew nothing about. Psychology, philosophy and current events weren't up my alley, it seems, so how could I contribute in those areas?

Jonathan Miller denied that Dudley had any cause to feel inferior. 'We all had our different interests; that's all. I felt very inferior to Dudley with respect to his music. I felt he had an astonishing, almost promiscuous skill at playing the piano that to me seemed very enviable. His presence in the show was indispensable. He may not have written much, but it didn't matter. The whole character of the writing was determined by who was present. I know his height bothered him, and I do understand that short people can feel diminished in some way to people who are tall, but he more than made up for it.'

Meanwhile, Dudley was in continual demand as an entertainer

in his own right. After performances of *Fringe* he would jazz it up until the early hours, either alone or with Hugo Boyd and Derek Hogg, who made up his trio, and every Sunday night they played opposite John Dankworth, who had been such an integral part of his career ('We only kept the wolves away from the door,' Dankworth disclaimed to me modestly).

Music was a vital part of Dudley's life. Especially jazz, which he found deeply expressive.

> **DUDLEY:** I wanted love but wasn't able to ask for it. And jazz was a passive way of making my feelings available to whomever might pick up on it. It became nostalgia for the love I wanted as a kid.

Enjoying his new celebrity, the string of beautiful blondes that always seemed to flock around him helped to boost his self-esteem and revived the Oxford tag of 'Cuddly Dudley'. Women found his warmth and humour immensely attractive and responded accordingly. They wanted either to mother him or to love him. Often both at the same time. Coupled with his vulnerability, there was a potently engaging charm. It was a combination hard to resist. As Alan Bennett noted, 'He had a lot of sex appeal, and that gave him a very busy love life, which was highly enviable to all of us.'

Girls seemed to pour out of the woodwork when he was around, and his three *Fringe* colleagues were perpetually amazed at the stream of females that paraded in and out of his dressing room. 'He was very playful,' Jonathan Miller recalled, 'a bit like a cherub, with a Pan-like capacity to enchant ladies who always seemed to be very tall, with long legs.'

Dudley met tall, blonde model Celia Hammond when he was playing at The Establishment one night and they fast became a couple. 'He was very shy and I found that deeply attractive,' she reflected. 'Dudley had a vulnerability about him that to me was utterly endearing. I watched him play at the nightclub and I fell in love with his music. He was irresistible.'

Club jazz wasn't Dudley's only solo excursion away from *Fringe*. He was also appearing in Southern Television's weekly variety series, *Strictly for the Birds*, which had as its signature tune his own earlier recording of the same title. Every Friday when the curtain came down on *Fringe* he drove down to Southampton in his Mini to host the show and perform with his trio.

Dudley's composing achievements had led to his being asked to score a ballet for Gillian Lynne, later to become a renowned film and stage choreographer and a lifelong friend. She suggested a jazz version of 'The Owl and the Pussycat'. 'I used to meet him backstage at the Fortune or hang out where he was playing at Ronnie Scott's or the Establishment so I could grab him when he was finished. He was a brilliant composer but quite reluctant, and I'd have to sit him down and make him write.'

During the day, Gillian worked with Dudley at his Maida Vale flat. But it was a wonder that any work ever got done there, as she soon discovered, 'Everybody wanted to get in his bed. He had a window where you could climb out onto the roof, and there were a few times when I'd be holding on to a girl who was about to come in through the front door while he smuggled somebody else out of the back window!'

Dudley's sexual antics did not hamper his reputation and he was heartened to be asked to score Gillian's next production, a musical revue, *England, Our England*. He'd also just been named Britain's top jazz pianist, so it was no surprise that, at twenty-six, he was now being talked about as a brilliant success.

Writing the music for the revue meant that Dudley had to work round the clock. As soon as the curtain went down on *Fringe* each night, he drove to Wolverhampton or Hull where the dance company was rehearsing.

> **DUDLEY:** I'd write and rehearse all the next morning, then drive back to London for the next show. It was ridiculous. It was an amazing time. I couldn't believe it was all happening. I had boundless energy and didn't seem to need much sleep. Although I did finally collapse from exhaustion, which Jonathan diagnosed and ordered me to rest.

Dudley still played jazz at Peter Cook's club, the Establishment, many nights a week, and now he recorded the first of more than a dozen jazz albums. *Theme from Beyond the Fringe and All That Jazz* included Dudley's theme tune for the stage show together with a collection of jazz favourites, all performed with his new trio – Chris Karan who replaced Derek Hogg on drums and bassist Pete McGurk, who had replaced Hugo Boyd when he was tragically killed in a car accident.

Dave Green, a leading bassist who worked with such legends as Coleman Hawkins and Ben Webster, played a few times with the trio. 'Dudley's bass player Peter McGurk invited me to sit in. He was very kind and encouraging to me at that time and he began calling me and asking me to come in to do the last set with Dudley. I enjoyed playing with him. I think his playing was influenced by Oscar Peterson. A very good, busy – what I would call a two-handed style. And of course he was hilarious when he did his vocal numbers!'

Beyond the Fringe ran in London for over a year. It had widened the scope of contemporary British humour, influencing a new breed of comic performer, and was the precursor for a satire boom that would include the BBC's iconic *That Was The Week That Was*, which made David Frost an overnight star, and *Monty Python's Flying Circus*.

And it launched what would become four of the most famous names in British entertainment.

CHAPTER 6

New York

1962–64

When it opened on Broadway in October 1962, *Beyond the Fringe* was greeted with tumultuous applause. Alistair Cooke, writing in the *Guardian,* noted that 'the four irascibles of the non-establishment have come to New York to present their clownish commentary of the world before Cuba'.

It played to sell-out crowds, which included many transatlantic *Fringe* fans who, according to Cooke, turned out in sufficient numbers to cue the Americans when the accents grew unintelligible. One of the theatregoers was President Kennedy. He'd already seen the show in London, now he came back for more.

DUDLEY: President Kennedy came upstairs with Jackie to our dressing room, the green room, where we all sat around and exchanged words. I liked him and didn't find him at all intimidating. At one point he went in to use the bog. We really had no facilities at all – just the most disgraceful-looking broom closet on the first-floor landing – but the President didn't seem put off. While he was in there, Hildy Parks, the producer's wife, guarded the door. And afterwards Alan scrawled on the wall 'John F. Kennedy pee'd here' and the date.

Off stage, Dudley hung out with Alan Bennett. Despite his bespectacled scholarly demeanour, the shy, soft-spoken Yorkshireman who took to chewing his tie when he was nervous had a warmth and humour that matched Dudley's own. 'Jonathan and Peter were both married,' Alan told me, 'so Dudley and I tended to be together. Also, I didn't know anyone in New York and I was quite lonely. Sometimes I watched him play jazz, although I usually didn't like clubs.'

Beyond the Fringe became the toast of Broadway and the four performers were lionised in New York. The show's success allowed Dudley to play his music around Greenwich Village once the curtain came down after the night's performance, and he was a frequent attraction at local clubs. At the prestigious Village Vanguard, Dudley was persuaded to join Gerry Mulligan on stage. Mulligan, said John Bassett, 'obviously respected Dudley as a musician but fell about at the way he was accompanying him in an Errol Garner style. Garner was a musician who rarely accompanied anyone, and Mulligan was collapsing with hysterics at the contradistinction of style.'

> **DUDLEY:** I did once get the chance to meet Garner. He came to a club where I was working but when I saw him I was so eager and nervous to impress him that I dropped a bottle of Coke on the keyboard! Everything from middle C down to G was ruined. I looked at this mess and tried to play. And then when I looked up, he was gone! Years later I tried to make a documentary about him but I couldn't get it off the ground.

Dudley's scores for Gillian Lynne had won him many plaudits and now she asked him to write the music for *Collages*, an innovative series of small ballets combining modern and classical dance. 'We had to do it for nothing,' Gillian remembered. 'There was no money at all and Dudley wrote the most wonderful opening ballet called *Symbol*.'

In an early example of Dudley's inordinate generosity towards his friends, Gillian found herself flying every Friday night to New York on tickets that Dudley sent her, and staying in a room that he rented for her in Washington Square. There, they worked all weekend until she returned to London on the Monday.

During the Broadway run of *Fringe*, Celia Hammond flew to New York a few times to be with Dudley. Jonathan Miller found her 'a rather aphrodisiac presence – a long-legged blonde figure, very much out of that sixties world of miniskirts and ravishing legs'. But Celia's last visit was to break the news that their romance was over, and she returned to London leaving Dudley engulfed in sadness at the loss of his first adult love.

He sought solace in his music and threw himself into working on *Collages*. It seemed the only balm for his bruised soul. Meanwhile, in Britain, Gillian Lynne found herself facing major problems. With *Collages* just days away from its opening at the Edinburgh Festival, the lack of finance was acute. 'We ran out of costumes and had no money to buy more,' she explained, 'so Dudley went out and bought some in New York and put them on the plane. There was now a steady stream of people driving to Prestwick to receive money from Dudley and costumes from Dudley. He was incredible. Such a buddy; such an inspiration. Some years later I tried to pay him back and kept sending him cheques. Finally, he said, "If you do this any more I shall wipe my bottom on the cheque, tear it up, put it in an envelope, and send it back to you!"'

Not surprisingly, the *Fringe* foursome were now starting to get on each other's nerves. Jonathan had a row with Alan Bennett one night and flipped over a table in his anger, and Peter Cook upset Jonathan by improvising a walk-on during his philosophy sketch. One by one they left the show to be replaced by other actors. By March 1964, Dudley was the sole survivor of the original cast.

The famous quartet had done for American comedy what they had done earlier in Britain: inspired a new generation of comedians. They had also won a prestigious Tony Award and put British comedy firmly on the Broadway map.

Despite their mild disagreements, Dudley missed his cohorts very much when they were gone. They'd been like a family for almost four years. He assuaged his sorrows nightly after the curtain went down by playing with a trio at the Village Vanguard. And with Dizzy Gillespie he recorded a mostly improvised script and score for *The Hat*, a short animated film in aid of world peace.

He was still feeling down after Celia's departure and when his friend Peter Bellwood recommended he go for psychotherapy, he agreed. He'd already tried it for some time in London. Maybe New York would help more.

> **DUDLEY:** I was reading books on philosophy and God knows what else that Jonathan had given me and I suppose I felt there must be something to help the greyness I was feeling. Psychology was a fairly new area for me although I'd been seeing a couple of different therapists in London at different times. When Peter suggested it in New York I thought it was worth a try.

A letter from Alan Bennett cheered him up immensely. 'I had my first driving lesson today,' Alan informed him from the Isle of Man in his broad Yorkshire phraseology. 'Bowling along I was like ninepence. And right enjoyed it I did.' He had just seen *The V.I.P.s* with Elizabeth Taylor and Richard Burton, which he strongly recommended to Dudley. 'Burton is so good. It's the eyes that do it, scorch marks they are or pissholes in the snow.' He opined to Dudley that the success of *Fringe* had been because 'it was true when we did it and some of it true always. So it could stand by itself and made for itself a place in which it could stand.'

In April 1964 Dudley left *Beyond the Fringe*. He had been asked by the BBC to join the others in filming the show for television. With no other work on offer and now feeling very homesick, he returned to London.

Ahead of him lay an extraordinary working relationship that would span more than a dozen years and produce one of the most famous comedy duos in English history.

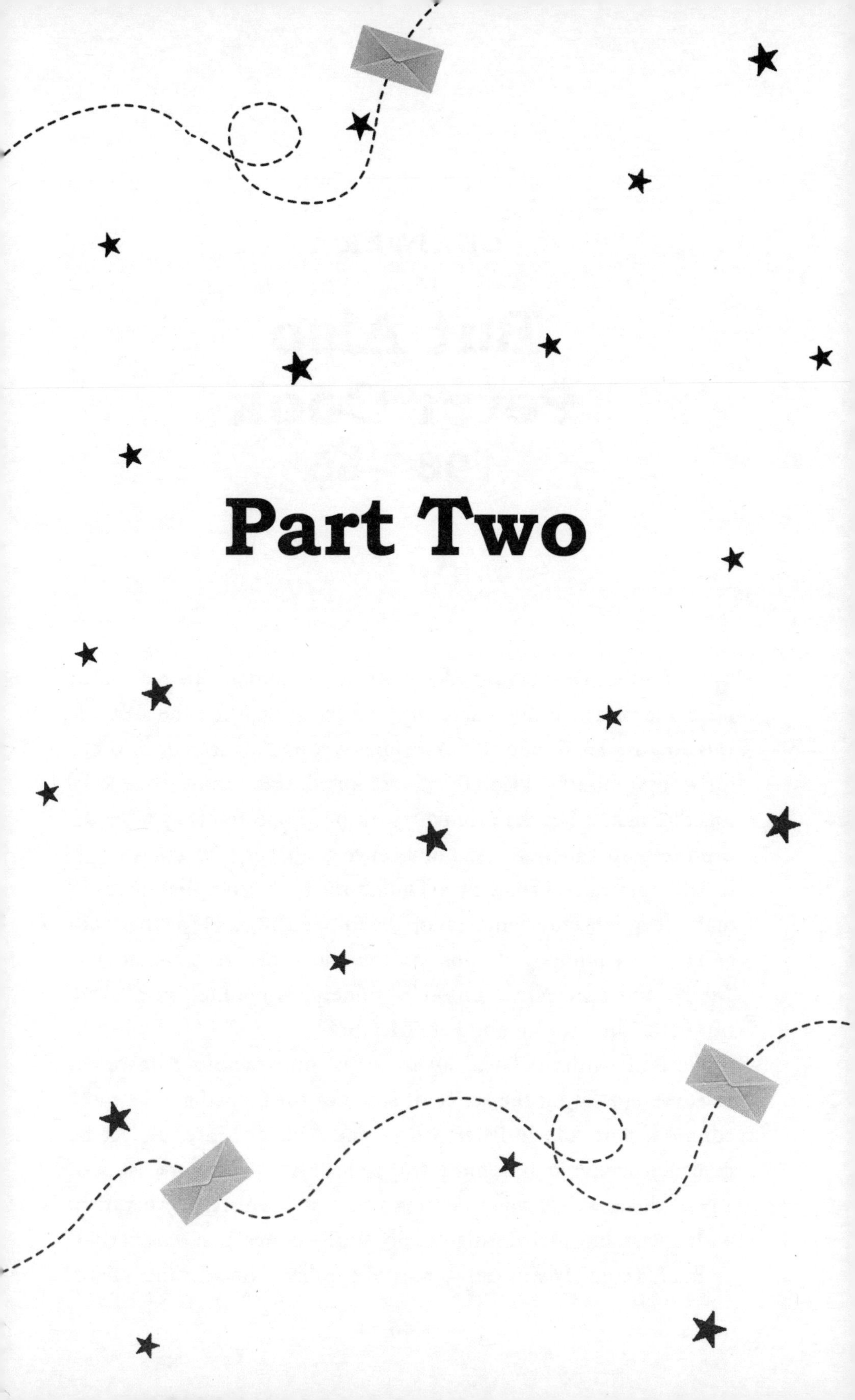

Part Two

CHAPTER 7

But Also Peter Cook

1964–65

In London, Dudley joined his former teammates to record, in front of a live audience, *Beyond the Fringe* for the BBC. It was August 1964, and the first time they had all seen each other for several months. Pleased to be reunited, they enjoyed working together again, but the original spark had gone and they failed to capture quite the magic and innocence of earlier *Fringe* days.

Still, their success had given Dudley the confidence that he could make it as an entertainer and, determined to achieve this end, he landed a number of spots on the television arts programmes *Tempo* and *Late Night Line-Up*, sometimes reunited in his jazz trio with Chris Karan and Pete McGurk.

He had, without being aware of it, unconsciously absorbed and was emulating the styles of some of the comedians he most admired, particularly Peter Sellers and Marcel Marceau, yet he managed to avoid becoming trapped within the mannerisms of any of them. What was emerging was a style entirely of his own, with a vast and varied range as physically comic as it was verbal.

But his comedy was only a part of Dudley's considerable talent.

Jazz was still the dominant passion in his life, and his trio soon became a regular fixture in the main clubs around Soho.

Around that time, broadcaster and jazz trombonist Michael Pointon saw Dudley with his trio in concert at the Queen's Theatre in Hornchurch. 'I'd already seen Erroll Garner performing in London,' he recalled, 'and I was impressed by Dudley's similarity of touch: that occasionally loping left hand and innate ability to bring out the best qualities of a melody and swing, all without losing the underlying tenderness of a ballad.'

Jazz pianist Chris Ingham was a devotee of Dudley's jazz, and a few years ago he began transcribing Dudley's compositions and performing them in his stage tribute, 'The Jazz of Dudley Moore'. The Chris Ingham Quartet is today a popular draw in clubs and concert venues, and in 2017 enjoyed a sell-out audience at the Royal Albert Hall.

'I was so excited and moved by the richness of Dudley's compositions,' Chris explained of his work. 'Some intricate pieces need specialised arrangements, but there are some wonderful tunes that should be in the standard jazz repertoire. My quartet made a CD (*Dudley*) and we perform Dudley's jazz all over the UK. I'm thrilled at the reception we get. And fifty years after he composed some of them, it shows how Dudley's work remains gloriously timeless.'

Though the reteaming of the *Fringe* players had been unexceptional, it was notable for having brought Dudley and Peter Cook back together. Dudley, who admired enormously Peter's comedy inventiveness, was keen to work with him again. The seeds had been planted in New York when, towards the end of *Fringe*, they began improvising together. 'I could see they had something,' avowed Alan Bennett. 'They sparked each other off, and they knew it, too, because even then they were talking about doing things together.'

Peter Cook, a majority shareholder in the satirical weekly

Private Eye, enlisted Dudley to add his voice to those of Richard Ingrams, John Wells and Willie Rushton, in recording the EP *Private Eye Sings*. It was followed almost immediately by a LP, *Private Eye's Blue Record*. Dudley's legendary partnership with Peter Cook was on its way.

The BBC had hired Joseph McGrath, a jolly Scotsman for whom Dudley had worked on *Tempo*, to direct a one-hour television variety special and McGrath asked Dudley to star in it. Dudley suggested adding Peter Cook to the mix and in 1964 *The Dudley Moore Show* went into production with two stars instead of one.

The programme worked so well that the BBC commissioned the duo to a regular fortnightly series with Joe McGrath holding the reins. And so was born *Not Only . . . But Also*, which so far exceeded the expectations of the BBC hierarchy that, after its transmission on BBC2 in January 1965, it was immediately repeated on BBC1.

The first programme went out as *The Dudley Moore Show Starring Not Only Dudley Moore But Also Peter Cook and John Lennon*. In one sketch, filmed on Wimbledon Common, John Lennon was seen in slow motion swaying back and forth on the children's swings. Dudley was pushing him but he pushed so hard that John's contact lenses fell out and were lost in the grass. McGrath had to stop filming while everyone got down on their hands and knees and searched frantically among the tall blades. 'Luckily,' he recalled, 'John had another pair on him. Because we never found the first ones.'

Not Only . . . But Also had a loose concept based on a series of sketches which ran the comedy gamut from descriptions of imaginary adventures involving famous film stars to an upper-class twit whose life's work consisted of teaching ravens to fly underwater. Many lunatic characters emerged from this lopsided view of life; the most famous of all were their cloth-capped idiots. 'Pete' and 'Dud' were two brainless, self-indulgent, bigoted men who, besides fantasising wildly about women and sex, discussed universal issues of life and philosophy with breathtaking inanity. They became cult heroes to millions of viewers and years later these Pete and Dud sketches were issued on an LP as *The Dagenham Dialogues*.

> **DUDLEY:** I based the Dud character on a guy who used to go to my church. I never knew his name. He struck me as mildly pathetic. This odd sort of creature who was obviously very down on himself. He walked into the church and he almost made me cry, he was so pathetic. A strange cloth-capped individual who didn't know anything about anything.

Nothing like this had ever been seen before. The show became a milestone in British television and established Cook and Moore as a brilliant comedy team whose names were being mentioned in the same breath as the historic Goons. Everyone wanted to be on the show. Long before *Monty Python* was devised, John Cleese found his way onto the programme in a bit part as a waiter. And Joe McGrath received a passionate phone call from Peter Sellers. 'He told me, "I'm absolutely hysterical with laughter after watching the show. Please can I be on it because those guys are what comedy's all about at this moment. I have to be part of it!"'

Dudley was thrilled to work with Sellers, who was his idol. But it wasn't the easiest of shows to pull together. 'Sellers was always difficult to work with,' explained McGrath, 'because he was a great giggler and he laughed all the time. It was to hide the nervousness, but it reached the stage where they were all doing it and I had to say, "You've got to stop the laughing and really get down to work, because this is live television!"'

Occasionally, Pete and Dud's ribald ramblings provoked the ire of some people. But the BBC was fairly lenient in censoring the material and they got away with much that had never been said on television before.

> **DUDLEY:** Peter loved it when we got away with things. Like the time he talked about a bottle of wine, which instead of being called Châteauneuf-du-Pape was called 'Shat All Over the Carpet'! We got away with an awful lot. Words I was never allowed to use at home, like 'bloody'. We used 'bloody' and got away with it, but we were criticised for it. I should think my mother must have had kittens when she heard that!

Terry Jones, one of the Pythons, who later substituted for Dudley in some Amnesty International stage appearances, was vastly influenced by what he saw in *Not Only . . . But Also*. 'Those shows had a big effect on the way I thought about comedy. They had wonderful visual puns and visual jokes. One of the best was "The Order of Leaping Nuns", where all these nuns were leaping around on a trampoline – to get closer to God, I suppose – and I can remember seeing that and falling apart. It played around with images that you wouldn't expect and Michael Palin and I later did a lot of jokes for *The Frost Report* that were very heavily based on leaping nuns!'

It would be remiss not to mention 'One-legged Tarzan', which has gone down in the annals of comedy history. It was Peter Cook's first sketch, written at the age of eighteen, performed at Cambridge, and later acted out in *Beyond the Fringe* as 'One Leg Too Few'. In it, Dudley played Mr Spiggott (a name they would use often in future work), a one-legged actor auditioning for the role of Tarzan. Cook, as the producer, tells him, 'You are deficient in the leg division to the tune of one. 'Your right leg I like . . . I have nothing against your right leg. The trouble is, neither do you.'

The Moore–Cook relationship was a disparate coupling evolved out of an attraction of opposites. They were, Dudley claimed, diametrically opposed in everything; indeed, while Peter loved political debates, Dudley preferred to discuss the less intellectual pursuits of women and sex.

Peter Cook, almost three years younger than Dudley, was a sophisticated, urbane, acerbic wit with a mocking, devilish mind and an austere ability to conjure a subject out of thin air, then spin around it an absurd web of the most lunatic logic. Dudley, on the other hand, was gentle, sensitive, outgoing and completely down to earth. He viewed Peter as the driving force behind their partnership. Whereas his own ideas were suburban and innocuous, Peter's became flights of fantasy, outnumbering Dudley's imaginative wanderings 'by sixteen to one'.

> **DUDLEY:** I think I was always mildly intimidated by Peter's mind, the way it worked. He was so imaginative and brilliant. He came out with the most extraordinary ideas and often he conjured them up on the spur of the moment. He never had to give long thought to something. I was gobsmacked sometimes by the things that came out of his mouth!

The phenomenal success of their partnership was unexpected to Jonathan Miller, 'because there was nothing to indicate it was going to happen. And yet when it did happen it seemed quite natural. Once you saw what they were doing together, it seemed inevitable.'

The closing number of every show was 'Goodbye-ee', a silly song that ended in Dudley's trademark high falsetto, and this became their signature tune. When they recorded it some months later, it went straight into the Top 20 on the record charts, where it remained for several weeks.

At last Dudley was receiving the acclamation he had yearned for.

> **DUDLEY:** My parents were both so delighted. Their attitude was wonderful. My dad was thrilled. I'd got them a TV set when I started doing the TV series in 1965. I

> said, 'I'm on TV now, you've got to watch this. You've got to have one in the house.' They didn't have a television. They didn't even have a fridge. They still listened to radio. I remember my mother's greatest compliment to me was when she said, 'I watched you last night and you put me right off to sleep, dear, it was lovely!' Put her to sleep, ha!

Playing jazz in the London clubs, he was surrounded by girls who were drawn to him through his music. A few liaisons lasted longer than the usual flings, one of them being with Shirley Anne Field, who enjoyed Dudley's affections for several months. He even wrote a song for her, 'Field Day for Shirley'. But there was never just one female in his life at a time, and years later, scribbled in the back of one of his diaries, I came across a crammed list of 'Girls To See Again'.

In April 1965, he turned thirty. And for Dudley the usual reflections at this milestone were made all the more intense by a restless urge to return to serious music. His classical side had given way in later school and Oxford years to jazz, but now he felt restless about its neglect. What he really wanted was to write an opera, but he was too undisciplined to get around to it. He had already vaguely mapped out an idea, which was essentially a romantic piece of work that would blend the accessibility of *West Side Story* with the musicianship of *Peter Grimes*.

His practical musical tuition had ended in school, and there lay the root of his frustration. The discipline of daily piano practice had ceased when he entered Oxford, where his studies were concentrated on the theory of music. It was that inability to focus on the technical side of playing and writing music that exacerbated his feelings of inadequacy. He knew in his heart that the potential for something good, if not great, was within him, and yet he seemed incapable of putting it down on paper.

> DUDLEY: I never really had a teacher since I was twenty-two. From a practical point on an instrument I've never had one since I was sixteen and that's a fault, I think. That's basically showing you have no real esteem for yourself. It's not that you feel you're better than anybody but you feel *worse* than anybody. You don't dare show the degree that you have to learn and therefore you don't want to even go to a teacher. In some ways that's good. It helped me when I was doing comedy because I did that on my own but in other ways it's held me back. Certainly in music it's been a very bad thing really to have had that attitude about learning.

He still played jazz with the trio, alternating regularly with John Dankworth at the romantic West End nightclub, the Cool Elephant. It was there, in the early summer of 1965, that he met the girl who would become his first wife.

The beautiful blonde actress, Suzy Kendall, was receiving a lot of attention, although her greatest acclaim would come later with her poignant performances as the poor little rich girl in *Up the Junction* and the schoolgirl with a crush on Sidney Poitier in *To Sir, with Love*.

Unlike most of Britain, Suzy had not seen *Beyond the Fringe* or *Not Only . . . But Also*. 'All I knew about him was his jazz that he played with his trio at the club. The music was incredible and it knocked me out. Of course, within about a week I realised that he was also very much a comedian.'

For Dudley, 1965 was shaping up to be a fruitful year. As well as live jazz performances in the London nightclubs, there were numerous appearances on television (*Juke Box Jury, Late Night Line-Up*, *On the Braden Beat, Sunday Night at the London Palladium, Billy Cotton's Band Show*) and regular radio spots with the trio on *Jazz Club, The Lively Arts* and *Late Night Extra*. There was also an unexpected leading role in *Love Story*, a terse television drama directed by Roman Polanski, and an astonishing and largely improvised mock opera, *Lady Chatterley's Lover*, with Peter Ustinov, in which Dudley took the guise of various composers. Most amazing of all was *Offbeat*, a classical music programme in which he played seventeen assorted characters from the world of music.

The trio recorded *The Other Side of Dudley Moore*, the second jazz album with Chris Karan and Pete McGurk, and Dudley wrote five of the eight tracks, including one for Suzy, the improvised 'Sooz Blooz', which jazz trombonist and broadcaster Michael Pointon considers 'a ten-minute tour de force – a dramatically percussive blues workout full of emotion that even includes a groan characteristic of his piano hero Erroll Garner!' The record became Britain's biggest-selling jazz album of the year. Despite inner yearnings to write serious music, Dudley was still very much engulfed in jazz, and this album was soon followed by another, *Genuine Dud*.

Chris Ingham attributes the appeal of Dudley's jazz to it possessing 'a playfulness and wit on the surface, but always with deep feeling. His powerful, nuanced touch with its baroque specialism makes his crisp licks really sing out. They express a compelling will to swing. And yet some of it is also profoundly moving.'

The success of *Not Only . . . But Also* had now made Dudley and Peter Cook widely sought after for other projects and it was inevitable that films would follow.

Bryan Forbes, who was directing *The Wrong Box*, considered Cook and Moore two of the greatest comedy talents ever to be seen on British television. 'They were absolutely brilliant,' admired Forbes, 'and some of the funniest comedy originated from them. I felt very privileged to work with them. They were great exponents of black humour and I thought they'd be marvellous in the film.' He was right, although holding their own against such a formidable cast (made up of Ralph Richardson, John Mills,

Peter Sellers, Wilfrid Lawson, Tony Hancock, Michael Caine and Forbes's wife Nanette Newman) was not easy.

The comedy centred on a battle between the families of the last two survivors of a tontine, a financial arrangement in which the last surviving member inherits the fortune. While the surviving elderly brothers scheme to kill each other in order to gain the inheritance, Moore and Cook, as their two greedy, villainous nephews, plot against them to grab the inheritance for themselves.

Dudley, for almost the first time in his career, found himself answerable to someone else rather than his own sense of comedy and felt unsettled at having his comedic hands tied.

In spite of his unease, the film was a happy experience for everyone else. 'We were all together a great deal and we had hilarious times,' Nanette Newman recollected. 'There were a lot of laughs, and Dudley was always incredibly funny. Every night we'd go to look at the rushes and end up in fits of laughter.'

John Mills had no scenes with Dudley but often hung around the set watching him work. 'I found it particularly enjoyable to be around him and Peter,' he recalled. 'They always seemed to be laughing, which made it a lot of fun for the rest of us. I can understand Dudley being nervous, but he had no reason to think he was bad, as I later heard he did, because he was nothing of the sort. He was very good.'

Bryan Forbes's own memories were of a hilarious couple of weeks filled with perpetual laughter. 'We used to have marvellous lunches sitting around in the trailer and we laughed ourselves sick. Dudley was always outrageous, with a bizarre, sometimes macabre, sense of humour.'

Although the film was not a box-office success at the time, it has come to be regarded as a comedy classic. Dudley and Peter's first film together may not have been the wild smash hit they both hoped. But they had hardly emerged as losers.

CHAPTER 8

Bedazzled

1965–66

There were still battalions of girls in and out of Dudley's life but it was Suzy Kendall who engaged most of his interest. She had a huge sense of humour and understood his insecurities. Instead of dismissing them as unfounded, she bolstered his self-confidence, encouraging his musical talent with gentle admiration. It was no surprise to their friends when eventually they moved in together.

The popularity of Dudley and Peter Cook had now reached immense proportions. They were courted everywhere, even topping the bill at the Royal Command Performance and throwing in some good-natured, and doubtless not unexpected, jokes at the expense of the Royal Family.

The unprecedented response to *Not Only . . . But Also* resulted in a second series, produced by Dick Clement, who recalled a memorable first meeting with the comedy duo at the BBC's White City studios. 'Peter made me feel deeply stupid, because the speed of his brain was so fast that it overawed me. I felt better later when I heard that Alan Bennett had had the same reaction.

'Peter was incredibly prolific and it gave Dudley an enormous security. They were very easy together and had no real ego problems. It was a very smooth team, and they fed each other extremely well.'

Some of the most inventive and hilarious moments were caught in the filmed sequences which did not always go as planned. One snowy winter's day provided an unexpected gem.

'We were filming an opening segment of Dud and Pete having an out-of-season holiday, and we went to the funfair and asked if we could get the big dipper going. This bloke said he could get it to the top, but with all the ice on the rails he didn't know if it would make the next crest. We all looked at each other and said, "Please let's hope it doesn't!" And as the light started to fade, we got this amazing shot of Dud and Pete getting to the top loop of the big dipper – then it went down and up . . . and then back and forward . . . and back . . . and then it finally got stuck and settled there. It was hysterical!'

> **DUDLEY:** I remember we had a rather muddled sketch about a bumblebee. It wasn't very good but we recorded the song 'L.S. Bumble Bee' as a single. We sang it in a Liverpudlian style and people believed they were listening to a Beatles record. People thought it was John Lennon singing but it was me, for crying out loud! It started to zoom up the charts because everyone thought it was a Beatles record and it did great at first, but when people found out it wasn't the Beatles, it sank without a trace!

Dudley's music had become as satirical as his dialogue, and his Bo Duddley sketch, 'Papa's Got a Brand New Bag', in particular, was notable for its ambiguous lyrics. Occasionally their humour and language went beyond what was considered tasteful on television, resulting in a heavy mailbag for the BBC.

It has been written that the couple finally went so far astray that the BBC pulled the show off the air. In fact they had an open brief to return with a new series. 'The BBC had a laissez-faire attitude at that time,' Dudley recalled, 'and it was left to us whether we would do another or not, and we did eventually come back for a third series.'

Sadly, and with a remarkable lack of foresight, the BBC erased almost all of the tapes. Today, nothing remains of this vintage show except some filmed sequences and a compilation tape salvaged from surviving video.

Stanley Donen, the famed director of *Singin' in the Rain* and *Funny Face,* lived in London and was an ardent fan of *Not Only . . . But Also*. 'Peter and Dudley were the most brilliant artists I'd ever seen,' he extolled. 'They bowled me over. So I got in touch with them and said I'd love to do a movie and could we all think of an idea. It was the first time I'd called any performer to say I liked them so much that I wanted to work with them. Nor can I think of another instance since.'

As it happened, Peter and Dudley had already written a rough script that was a comedy version of the Faust story, with Peter as the Devil and Dudley as the man who sells his soul. Donen loved the concept and they worked on shaping the screenplay. The result was *Bedazzled* and in order to make it on a small budget ($600,000), Cook, Moore and Donen took not a single penny in salary.

It was, Peter Cook would later claim, the only film with which he was ever remotely satisfied. Co-starring Raquel Welch and Eleanor Bron, it was a blithe, bizarre number that turned logic upside down, as Peter was so fond of doing.

Stanley Moon (Dudley) is a cook in a hamburger restaurant and is infatuated with a waitress (Eleanor Bron). Befriended by George Spiggott (Cook, who turns out to be the Devil), he is given seven wishes in exchange for eternal damnation.

It was the first movie that Cook and Moore had carried on their own but Donen saw no nerves. He admired them enormously, which may have helped to allay any trepidation they might have felt. 'The whole point is to have somebody in charge who really appreciates what you're doing, and I adored them both and admired their talents. So there was no question about their being terrified. We all seemed very much of a group.'

> **DUDLEY:** I remember the fair scene where Peter and I were going around on dodgem cars and kept banging into each other and I could not stop laughing! I was sitting next to Gluttony and Peter was next to a French girl. I wasn't supposed to be laughing but I laughed throughout this stupid thing because Gluttony was eating cream buns continuously, stuffing her face and looking bored, and I got the giggles!

There was so much laughter on the film that Donen, too, was in fits of laughter half the time. 'I always say making movies is anything but fun,' he reflected, 'yet there is one exception and that is *Bedazzled*. My main problem was keeping quiet during the takes – I could barely restrain myself from laughing. There was never any tension and we had a lot of fun, but they were both also very serious artists. They didn't take film-making at all lightly.'

If there had been any tension, Dudley would have taken his usual escape route out of it. There was always a piano on the set, and while new camera positions were being set up, Dudley would lose himself in music. Stanley Donen marvelled at the talent of 'a very dedicated musician with a remarkable taste and ear. And out of it came the most marvellous score.'

Dudley's music for *Bedazzled*, which he performed with his trio as well as his close friend, jazz singer Barbara Moore, had

Donen in ecstasy. 'It was agreed from the start that he would do it, and it was wonderful. I loved what he wrote. I expected it to be good, but it turned out to be better even than that. It was full of variety, of all kinds of music.'

Jazz musician Michael Pointon regards the *Bedazzled* score as a remarkable musical conglomeration. 'It had an extraordinary range of musicality from tender sax to a raunchy R&B influence. He used almost every instrument, from trombone with powerful baritone to soaring strings that reflected romance in the air. A couple of the piano-led tracks are reminiscent of Oscar Peterson and another hit just the right mood with bluesy piano and wistful strings. The whole score is a wonderful orchestral mix.'

> **DUDLEY:** I was delighted when I did the score for *Bedazzled*. I remember the first violinist, John Sharp, was a little guy who smoked a cigar and he played so magnificently that he made me cry in the booth! I thought, 'This is coming out of that short little chap with a cigar!' He was just extraordinary! I loved the violin and always wished I was good enough to play it professionally.

Dudley always considered *Bedazzled* one of his favourite films but the public, at first, apparently did not agree. When it was released in 1967, it received a tepid reception that Dudley attributed to the film being so different from anything he and Cook had done since their television series. The general consensus was that they had failed to make the transition from the small screen. Significantly, the film would fare much better in those countries where the series had never been aired. Today it's considered a classic.

For three years, Peter and Dudley had shared a remarkably successful comedy partnership. While making *Bedazzled*, Stanley Donen told Peter that he could become the new Cary Grant.

When filming was completed, Peter decided to pursue that far from inglorious possibility.

And so Dudley, for virtually the first time since *Beyond the Fringe* began in 1960, was entirely on his own.

CHAPTER 9

Cynthia and Other Films 1967–71

Since *Not Only . . . But Also*, Joe McGrath had long wanted to work again with Dudley, and in the spring of 1967 he had the opportunity. Dudley was eager to work with the cheeky Scotsman again. He liked McGrath's sense of humour and his directing style, which allowed his actors considerable freedom.

Together, they conceived *30 Is a Dangerous Age, Cynthia*, about an obscure musician, Rupert Street, trying to carve his niche in life by composing a successful musical before his thirtieth birthday six weeks away. It bore more than a passing resemblance to Dudley's own life, although Dudley, now almost thirty-two, had already seen his landmark birthday come and go without the dream being fulfilled.

The casting of the female lead defeated McGrath for quite a while, even though the answer was staring them in the face. As written in the script, the girlfriend was an artist born in Belper, Derbyshire. Just like Dudley's girlfriend, Suzy Kendall.

'Dudley had actually written the story around us,' Suzy related, 'but he didn't try to get me cast for it. He never even mentioned me. It was Joe McGrath who finally said, "Why can't we use Suzy?" I was very happy that he wanted me to do it, because he was a wonderful and funny man to work for and an old friend of Dudley, which made Dudley feel particularly comfortable.'

Dudley had always used his irrepressible humour and a multitude of different voices to relieve tension. On *Cynthia* he went one step further. 'He got into a habit of farting before each take,' recalled Joe McGrath, 'and it was hysterical. The boy would run across and slate it, and then Dudley would go "Pppff!" I'd see his face turn bright red and I'd say, "Okay, calm down now, calm down and . . . action" – and then he'd blow it! He did that on every take, and in *Cynthia* there were something like six hundred takes! Even if he wasn't in the scene but was on the set, he'd run across and fart before we slated. But it didn't stop him from being professional. There was a great feeling on the set around him, and everybody respected him.'

The role in *Cynthia* was tailor-made to display Dudley's myriad talents. As actor, comedian and musician it was a remarkable show of skill. A high point was his ballad to Suzy à la Noel Coward, which managed within it to mimic Bach, Beethoven, Mozart and Handel. He did it all in *Cynthia*, from playing the piano, violin and mandolin, to singing rock 'n' roll. He even managed a tenor duet with himself, and a bit of soft-shoe shuffle. As one American critic later commented, 'That guy's a British Sammy Davis. There's nothing he can't do.'

The film was a happy one to make for all concerned – particularly for Dudley in working with Suzy. 'He seemed to be very happy at that time and very relaxed,' recalls McGrath. 'He was wonderful to work with, because he gave it one hundred per cent attention and thought about what he was doing. What was marvellous was that he so obviously enjoyed it.'

As well as starring in the film, Dudley was also writing the score. But he was painstakingly slow about it. He was anxious to capture the right music for the mood of the film but, following his usual creative pattern, he didn't produce it until the very last moment. He was still scribbling away when Suzy drove him to the studio where a full symphony orchestra was waiting to record the score. 'He finished it in the car,' she remembered, 'literally minutes before they were due to start recording! But he was always like that, doing everything at the last second. Because he would do so much and reject it. It was never good enough, until finally time ran out and he had to go with whatever he'd done.'

In the greatest thrill of his life, Dudley also conducted the orchestra and was deeply moved by the experience. He was so overwhelmed that, once they had the score in the can, he asked if they could do it just one more time so he could savour the experience again.

> DUDLEY: I thought it was amazing – these people were playing what I'd written down! I just felt overwhelmed! A lot of work went into the scoring of *Cynthia* but I was extraordinarily moved by the orchestra. I remember saying, 'Can we do just one more?' We really *had* it, but I wanted to hear this wonderful sound again! Ha ha! I thought it was great that people were playing things that I'd written. I was very proud of that. Proud and elated.

Dudley was especially thrilled when an American critic later described the score as 'a respectful homage to composers like Elgar and Delius and inventive in its orchestration, creating a sensual feel for mood and atmosphere'.

To Michael Pointon's ears, the score was unusually imaginative. 'It manages to incorporate a multitude of different elements: a scene-setting theme, then reflects Dudley's jazz influences, encompasses dramatic stings, features him singing à la Noel Coward, goes into a comic rhythm and blues routine, and followed by a parody with banjo and tuba of Kurt Weill. All of which leads towards the main romantic motif's dramatic mood with strings. It's incredibly skilful and showcases his vast musical acuity.'

Dudley had agreed to score Clive Donner's *What's New, Pussycat?* but when it came to the crunch, he was still in the midst of composing *Cynthia*. Eventually, Donner brought in Burt Bacharach, who, years later, would score Dudley's Hollywood hit movie *Arthur*.

His reputation as a film composer had gathered momentum, and as soon as he completed *Cynthia*, Anthony Page pressed him to score his film version of John Osborne's *Inadmissible Evidence* in which Nicol Williamson hauntingly played a middle-aged solicitor on the verge of a nervous breakdown.

The score – including a theme tune which Dudley sang himself – was not much appreciated by Osborne, who to Dudley's chagrin deemed it merely 'adequate', but that was sweetened considerably by Anthony Page's vociferous approval.

'I felt he wrote a very effective score,' enthused Page. 'It was very spare, with some sixties pop music – just what was needed for this film. His ability as a composer was brilliant, and I'd always admired that, ever since the first things he'd done for me in theatre at Oxford. He had an incredible love of music, and I could see he was still deeply immersed in that passion.

'There was one occasion when he came to work with me at the studio and I saw him arrive. But he stayed in his car for half an hour and I thought he must be ill, so I went down to him. I found him just sitting there, engrossed in a Beethoven symphony on the radio. He couldn't bring himself to leave the car until it was over.'

In March 1968 Dudley and Suzy flew to New York for the opening of *Cynthia*. At last – approval. The American critics raved about it, some describing it as the best thing they'd ever seen. *Esquire* acclaimed it as 'genius . . . one of the best films ever made with a major talent', but in Britain the film would not be released until later in the year. Dudley's first film alone was a triumph.

Peter Cook and Dudley were soon reunited by British director Ken Annakin in *Monte Carlo or Bust!*, a big-budget action comedy set in the 1920s with a large cast that included Terry-Thomas, Tony Curtis, Susan Hampshire, Gert Frobe, Walter Chiari, Jack Hawkins and Eric Sykes. Dudley and Peter played two competitors in the Monte Carlo Rally who battle obstacles that include snowstorms and precipices and escaped German convicts being chased by lunatic Italian police.

The film was shot in Sweden and Italy and, despite the logistical problems of filming abroad and with such a large cast, Dudley found Ken Annakin to be receptive and easy-going. Like Joe McGrath, Annakin was a director who did not believe in putting actors into straitjackets, which suited Dudley perfectly.

'Some actors really need you to guide them to what you want,' said Annakin, 'but with Dudley it was very much a joint affair and I didn't feel I was forcing anything. He worked very closely with Peter, and they were very happy to be together on the movie. They saw it as a good chance to continue the comedy they were doing so well.'

Despite the upheaval of being on location for so long, it seemed a pleasurable atmosphere around the film, except for Tony Curtis's not unreasonably bad temper when he had to dangle from a cliff by one arm.

Ken Annakin recalled, 'Dudley had a piano in his trailer and he played whenever he had the opportunity. I was very envious that he could just sit there and do it. Sometimes he parodied stuff, but very often he just slipped away into vague compositions that seemed to develop a tune, things he never seemed to repeat.'

When *30 Is a Dangerous Age, Cynthia* was at last released in October 1968, Suzy was away filming on location in Belgrade. Dudley sent a limo to pick up his parents and he escorted them to the London premiere, along with a life-size cut-out of Suzy, which he snuggled close to throughout the whole movie.

The film faced mixed reaction. The American critics had loved it, but less so the British critics who probably expected a film more in line with Dudley's previous slapstick. Joe McGrath blamed the response on the critics' perception of Dudley. 'Here was Cuddly Dudley making his own movie and doing the whole show – writing the music, the script, the acting. And the feeling was, who does he think he is? We had the worst press in the world. Leslie Halliwell wrote, "Dudley Moore, a small star on a small screen who will never make the big one." When Dudley heard that, he got hysterical with laughter!'

By now, Suzy and Dudley – who were, as Dick Clement put it, 'the quintessential sixties couple' – decided to marry very quietly at the Hampstead registry office. They had moved in to a 200-year-old Georgian home on a Hampstead hill where Suzy still lives today. It had an enchanting walled garden where squirrels romped, and part of the foundation had been built around a tree trunk. Underground springs ran through the basement and the four-storey house had the ambience of a small country manor.

'We became homebodies,' described Suzy, and they did, on the whole, prefer to stay home alone or entertain friends at little dinner parties. And play music, of course. Dudley had a piano in the first-floor living room and a Hammond organ in the basement kitchen, so he was able to wander between instruments as the mood took him.

> **DUDLEY:** Life was very gregarious then. We used to go down the King's Road on a Saturday and we *always* had lunch at the 235 – cottage pie with Brussels sprouts and gravy! Afterwards we wandered up and down the King's Road going into the antiques markets. The mid-sixties were

a lot of fun, actually. When we were home we always had friends dropping by. And Suzy would cook my favourite roast lamb and browned leeks with Brussels sprouts and roast potatoes. And jelly. Real jelly!

Sometimes they took drives into the country in Dudley's black Maserati, a flashy number with its own fridge, in which he stashed lemon-flavoured lollies and champagne, but which caused him immense irritation 'because the ice was always melting when the engine was turned off!' If he forgot to turn off the fridge, the battery would be dead the next morning. The windshield wipers didn't work too well either and once, when Dudley was doing a two-week wintry tour of England, he had to keep stopping to use a potato to wipe off the rain.

Sometimes they would take off in Suzy's car, her second yellow E-type Jaguar. Dudley had bought her the first as a present, but the day he gave it to her he parked it overnight in the street from where it was promptly stolen. Immediately – even before notifying the insurance company of the loss – he replaced it with an identical model.

Peter and Dudley's next film venture was in Richard Lester's black comedy *The Bed Sitting Room*, based on a bizarre anti-war play by Spike Milligan and John Antrobus. Set just after the end of the shortest nuclear war in history (two and a half minutes), the film satirised the horror and devastation of nuclear war to emphasise its pacifist message.

The story has a handful of survivors trying to overcome the physical mutation effects of radiation. Among them: Ralph Richardson, pregnant Rita Tushingham and her overzealous parents, Mona Washbourne and Arthur Lowe, who slowly mutate – one into a cupboard and the other into a parrot which is eventually cooked and eaten. Peter and Dudley play two moronic policemen whose main contribution to the scene of disaster consists of a warning to 'Watch out, move along!' which they hurl down through megaphones as they hover in a broken-down Volkswagen suspended beneath a helium balloon.

One unsettling event occurred when Dudley and Peter had to go up in the balloon on a very windy day – something the balloon expert who accompanied them confided he would never normally do in such weather. The moment he spoke, the balloon fell violently to the ground and Peter, who had been kneeling down, suffered a severely damaged cartilage. He had been planning a month's vacation, and he got it – most of it spent in hospital.

Dudley's earlier score for *Bedazzled* had so enchanted Stanley Donen that he asked Dudley to score his newest movie, *Staircase*, with Rex Harrison and Richard Burton as two gay hairdressers. Donen regarded Dudley as a remarkably perceptive composer. 'I knew he would do a wonderful job and sure enough he wrote a most fabulous score which was a perfect fit for the film. I can't stand scores that try to evoke an emotion from the audience that is lacking in the scene. Dudley was able to write a score that didn't plead for an emotional reaction but supported and complemented the sequence. The score for *Staircase* was astonishing in its musicality. I asked him many times after that to score for me again, but by then he was a movie star.'

Dudley's classical side was still very much in the closet. He once said he felt safer in jazz because, unlike in classical music, mistakes could be amended. Some of his closest friends felt that he gravitated towards jazz because he was running away from the greater challenge of classical music.

Violinist friend Robert Mann disagreed. 'What he did in jazz was a very positive commitment. It wasn't to escape. It was purely because he loved it. Certainly he questioned the idea of playing classical music in performance, but only because he knew that he had not put in the physical preparation that was needed. And it wasn't because he was lazy. It was a lack of motivation to really commit himself to a public stance with classical music. The closest he got was in the kidding around in the parodies.'

In the living room of Bentham House, Dudley was at his happiest playing piano to Mann's violin. It was evident to Mann that he was a capable instrumentalist on the piano but hadn't spent the hours that were necessary to give him the physical strength in his fingers, 'so he was much more at home playing in a way that would satisfy a Bach rather than a Brahms. We almost never got together without playing at least one Bach sonata for violin and piano.'

If *Cynthia* had failed to live up to Dudley's hopes, *Monte Carlo or Bust!*, released in July 1969, surpassed them. Showing Cook and Moore in one of their best performances together, it won them at last the critical accolades that had been lacking for their previous film encounters.

Dudley was ebullient and, revitalised, went back into the music studio to record a new jazz album, *The Dudley Moore Trio*, with Chris Karan on drums and Jeff Clyne on bass.

The healthy box-office returns of *Monte Carlo or Bust*! gave Cook and Moore a much-needed ego boost, but that was promptly deflated when *The Bed Sitting Room* opened. The critics had no idea what to make of the social farce, though they certainly made enough of it to know they did not like it.

The previous year, Dudley had seen Woody Allen in *Play It Again, Sam* on Broadway and thought it the funniest play he'd ever seen but, daunted by Allen's brilliance, he turned down producer David Merrick's offer to perform it in London. In the summer of 1969, however, he changed his mind and agreed to stage an English adaptation.

Play It Again, Sam focused on the trials and tribulations of a young film critic struggling to revive his self-respect and sex life after a demoralising divorce. His confidence shattered, he conjures up the spirit of Humphrey Bogart as a sexual role model. But his vain attempts to emulate Bogie's dashing love-making techniques are doomed, and his search for self-identity leads him to the realisation that he is more acceptable to women as himself.

It was ironic that Dudley was playing a man suffering from the pain of a divorce because after only fifteen months of wedlock he was now experiencing acute marital problems himself. He simply wasn't cut out for marriage. It bred in him a feeling of being trapped, closed in, and the demands of being answerable to another person made him feel less in control of his life. His feelings influenced his preparation for the role and gave his performance a deeper sense of pathos.

When the play opened in London at the Globe Theatre in September 1969 it was to inevitable comparisons with Woody Allen. Dudley was undeterred. He liked the role immensely and identified with the hero's deep anxieties, which resembled his own.

Two months after *Play It Again, Sam* opened, Dudley and Peter embarked on a third and final season of *Not Only . . . But Also*. It began broadcasting in the spring of 1970, and their teaming was as fresh and funny as it had ever been, the creative relationship as effective as always. Theirs was a mutual admiration that allowed each to benefit from the other and draw inspiration.

Dudley was curiously flat when the series ended, perhaps because it gave him more time to reflect on what was happening in his personal life.

Robert Mann arrived in London to give a series of concerts and was sorry to see the break-up of two of his favourite people. 'They were very fond of each other, and even through all their break-ups, Dudley was very concerned and anxious about Suzy. It wasn't so much that he was unhappy that it was ending, but more because it was causing pain to everyone concerned. His one positive strength during this romantic unhappiness was the solace he found in his jazz.'

Not Only . . . But Also had become such a major success outside Britain that Peter and Dudley were now being courted by other countries. In January 1971 they flew to Sydney to film two television specials for the Australian Broadcasting Commission, broadcast in Britain under the title *Pete and Dud Down Under*. While there, Dudley embarked on a three-week tour with Chris Karan and Peter Morgan, now the permanent bass player after Pete McGurk tragically committed suicide. The tour was hugely successful, and the trio recorded an album there entitled *Today*.

Somehow, whenever Peter and Dudley came together, creative ideas poured out of them. The spring of 1971 in Sydney was no exception, and out of it flowed their next collaboration.

CHAPTER 10

Behind the Fridge

1971–73

The ideas that Peter and Dudley nurtured led to a new revue which would combine old sketches from the past with a series of new ones. They decided to premiere the revue in Australia and it was booked on a five-month tour to begin in late summer. Dudley titled it *Behind the Fridge*.

> **DUDLEY:** When we were in New York with *Beyond the Fringe*, Alan Bennett and I used to have dinner together at Barbetta's every night before the show. I always had the same meal – gazpacho soup, fettucine and chocolate mousse – every night for about a year! The maitre d' always greeted us with the words, 'Ah, Meester Cook, Meester Moore, Be'ind the Fri'ge. He couldn't get Alan's name right, or the name of the show, and I said to Alan at the time that it sounded like a good title. So that's how *Behind the Fridge* got named!

Shortly before leaving for Australia, Dudley's father became ill and Dudley flew to England and stayed in Dagenham for the next month to be near him. When his father died, he took the loss hard. He played the organ at the funeral but couldn't stop sobbing. He had loved the sweet-natured man with the quiet, hidden disposition and wished he could have known him better.

> DUDLEY: I remember waking up one morning, horrified that there would be this terrible hole where my father had been. I was very unnerved. It was very hard losing my first parent. There was so much I wished we could have said to each other. So much I wish I could have asked him. But being so much like him, finding it hard to express emotions, it all went unsaid.

Work seemed the only salve, and he plunged into shaping the new show with Peter Cook. Though twelve years older than in their *Fringe* days, if anything they had become even more impish and irreverent. The interim years of their partnership had honed their talent and they were now more polished and self-assured than ever before, with an even greater gift, it seemed, for sending audiences into paroxysms of laughter.

There were fifteen scenes in *Behind the Fridge*, three of them being Dudley's piano pieces. A couple of their earlier trademark sketches included 'One-legged Tarzan', and as usual they poked fun at the vicissitudes of life.

'Gospel Truth' was one of the funniest and cleverest sketches they'd ever written. It had Matthew, a reporter researching an in-depth profile of Jesus for the *Bethlehem Star*, interviewing Arthur Shepherd, who claims to have witnessed the birth of Christ. It was inevitable that the sketch would outrage some people, and the theatre was inundated with protests of sacrilege from religious groups.

The Bible-bashers notwithstanding, the entire show was an uproarious success when it opened in October 1971. They played nightly to sold-out audiences and Dudley was ecstatic. But the relationship between the pair was not so enchanting. It was now becoming seriously threatened.

Ever since his Cambridge days, Peter Cook had been a social drinker, but his alcohol intake had grown so out of hand that he was often bombed by the time he walked on stage. As Dudley later told lyricist Leslie Bricusse, a friend since the sixties, 'He comes on so hopelessly drunk and starts ad-libbing on something that's got nothing to do with anything you've ever performed. Imagine being in front of fifteen hundred people and trying to get through it, never knowing what you're going to get.'

Though Dudley and Suzy had split, they continued to pour out their innermost feelings to each other. Dudley wrote to her from Melbourne: 'Getting the show into shape has been something of a headache, especially when Peter is consistently throwing wine, spirits, champagne and Valium down his throat at a rate that shows up on stage. He refuses to believe that drink plus Valium is a pretty irritating combination and makes people doubly pissed.'

In spite of all that, there were marvellous reviews, though the duo managed to get themselves banned from Australian airwaves after using 'filthy' language on a talk show. 'Peter said "pissed", "bum", "tits", all our familiars,' Dudley wrote to Suzy, 'but I guess Australia is further behind the times. I switched the microphone off, but nobody seemed to pick up on that – a case of visual euphemism!'

Early in February 1972, after a wildly successful five-month tour, Dudley and Peter returned to Britain, where the show was to be mounted later in the year under Joe McGrath's direction.

But there was no protracted rest for Dudley. In huge demand, he guested on several variety shows, from Val Doonican to Sheila Hancock, and played dozens of gigs with his trio. There was also a BBC television series with Lulu and he had immense fun working with the perky singer in *Not Only Lulu But Also Dudley Moore*.

His Oxford peer Patrick Garland organised a poetry reading with Diana Rigg, Michael Hordern and Malcolm Muggeridge at which Dudley played the piano, and his rendering of a Scott Joplin rag elicited a subsequent letter of praise from a normally curmudgeonly Muggeridge.

At a party, Dudley met 24-year-old Lynsey de Paul, who'd just had a big hit as a songwriter with 'Sugar Me'. Their romance almost didn't get off the ground, quite literally, since the first time he went to her flat he sat on her couch – as antiquated as the great-aunt from whom she'd inherited it – and promptly fell straight through it to the floor.

It wasn't the only inadvertently slapstick moment. One night he took Lynsey with him to a recording session and arrived to pick her up in a rented Beetle. Somehow it had suffered a shattered windscreen and Dudley punched a tiny hole so he could see to drive. When they got back inside the car he slammed the door – and two seconds later the entire windscreen fell out on top of him.

It was now, after a three-year absence, that Dudley returned to films in Will Sterling's ambitious version of *Alice's Adventures in Wonderland*. It had fifteen-year-old newcomer Fiona Fullerton as Alice, Michael Crawford the White Rabbit, Ralph Richardson the Caterpillar, Flora Robson the Queen of Hearts, Peter Sellers the March Hare and Robert Helpmann the Mad Hatter. Spike Milligan and Michael Jayston rounded out the stellar cast.

Dudley, in an endearing performance perfectly suited to his childlike demeanour, played the Dormouse. He had to wear a heavy disguise, and during the Mad Hatter's tea party his two false front teeth accidentally fell into the teapot. But when the film was eventually released, it was a box-office disappointment in which the vast talents and special effects were largely wasted. Neither Dudley's delightful performance nor John Barry's brilliant score was able to save the production.

By then, Suzy and Dudley had agreed to formally end their

marriage. 'In hindsight,' Suzy told me, 'we should never have got married. We were just so happy the way we were before.'

The night before his divorce, Dudley closeted himself for hours in the flat of his friends Lysie Kihl and George Hastings, improvising emotional music that revolved around Suzy and himself. They were both unhappy that their lives had not managed to converge successfully, for they still bore the deepest affection for each other and always would.

At least their friendship, unlike the marriage, would never die.

When *Behind the Fridge* opened in London at the Cambridge Theatre in November 1972, it was with great expectations. The previews had been tremendous, and the show was booked for a solid six months. But the opening night was a near catastrophe and portended troubled times ahead.

A backstage snafu caused a delay in the curtain going up. But it was not a technical hitch that was preventing the show from opening on time. It was Dudley's partner. Peter Cook was hopelessly drunk.

Joe McGrath had to dress Peter and walk him around his dressing room to try to sober him up. And that, McGrath is convinced, was the night that everything changed between Peter Cook and Dudley Moore. Until then, Peter had been very much the leader of the two, the man who usually had the last word in the writing and what they would do. That night the balance shifted completely.

'Dudley was very angry,' recalled McGrath. 'He told me, "I've had it. I'm getting out of this. It's driving me up the fucking wall. It's totally out of control, and I've got to make my own future." And that's when he began to take over and become very strong.

'Peter was a zombie on stage, and Dudley had to carry him through the entire first ten minutes of it. There wasn't even an understudy. How do you understudy a two-man show?'

The London critics weren't as wild about *Behind the Fridge* as their Australian counterparts, although *The Times* called it 'original and intelligent fun and fans will need no encouragement to see the pair in action'.

Alexander Cohen, who had known the duo since *Beyond the Fringe*, wanted to take the show to Broadway. At first Dudley refused; he was concerned Peter's drinking would deteriorate further and that it would be 'hell on wheels'. But eventually he capitulated to Peter's pleas and Alex Cohen's generous offer to pay them $7,000 a week each plus a percentage of the box office, and in the late summer of 1973 the couple found themselves headed for America's East Coast.

> **DUDLEY:** I was very anxious about it. I told Peter on the plane going over that we had to make the show work. We'd won a Tony for *Fringe*, and we owed it to ourselves to equal that success. But by the time we landed in New York, Peter was already drunk again. I had to fill in both our entry forms at Immigration while he sat crying silently in a corner. He used to cry quite a lot. He was not a very happy character. He had a lot of angst but he didn't talk about it. Just like I didn't talk about mine to him. I think we both gravitated towards being isolated. His was an anxiety that was inexpressible.

Normally the more dominant of the two, Peter may have been upset over his own incapability at that moment. Whatever the case, the tears continued in the bustling customs hall.

It did not bode well for the months in America that lay ahead. Nor for the future of their partnership.

CHAPTER 11

Tuesday
1973–76

Behind the Fridge needed to be reworked for American audiences – not least its name – and they decided on the new title of *Good Evening*.

They launched into rehearsals, and it was now that producer Alexander Cohen caught a whiff of bumpy times ahead. 'We worked intensively,' he told me, 'and Dudley was always good at that. But Peter was constantly either changing rehearsals or turning up late for them.'

Good Evening premiered in October 1973 in Boston – where Peter fell off the stage into the orchestra pit during a blackout – and opened in New York two weeks later. Dudley was full of trepidation, but critics proclaimed the show 'the surprise hit of the year'.

By now, Peter's erratic behaviour had resurfaced, causing considerable concern, particularly to Cohen. 'He'd lost his ability to control himself and he was pretty bad,' Cohen recalled. 'There was one day when he didn't show up at all for the matinee. Finally we went to his apartment, broke in, and found Peter passed out on the bed. We did everything to him – threw water over him by the glass, revived him, literally slapped him awake and dragged him in the car to the theatre.'

In the meantime, the theatre announced that Peter had been delayed in a traffic accident, and Dudley went on stage and entertained the audience for forty-five minutes. The show finally went on almost an hour late. 'It was unheard of in the theatre,' says Cohen. 'It was irresponsible and unprofessional – which is about the worst thing I can say about a human being.'

Some time earlier, Dudley and Peter had created two characters who revelled in salacious conversation, and their underground act went down riotously when they performed some of it in the New York clubs. For a lark, they decided to hire a recording studio and make some private tapes of their improvised chatter. The results were the infamous Derek and Clive, who would become in time as notorious as their renowned idiots, Dud and Pete. In fact, Derek and Clive were really punk versions of Dud and Pete who loved to talk dirty. Real dirty.

They recorded their conversations with wild abandon and strictly for their own fun, going beyond the boundaries of their usual work. They had intended to record just one item, but what they ended up with was a mass of material that dealt with the unspeakable.

The sketches relied entirely on the use of vulgar language, and the choice of subject matter made them completely unsuitable for general distribution. Sex, religion, masturbation – nothing escaped their lewd attentions. One track, 'The Worst Job I Ever Had', was Peter describing in graphic terms how he'd had to remove lobsters from Jayne Mansfield's rectum.

Dudley justified the tapes by pointing out that entire classes of people in Britain talked like Derek and Clive, whose sole means of communication was in obscene language. He had always had a ribald sense of humour and claimed to have been 'talking dirty' since the age of thirteen. He found it fun, and was always baffled when this more outrageous side of his humour was greeted with puritanical shock.

Ten years earlier, while in New York with *Beyond the Fringe*, Dudley had enjoyed a brief but passionate fling with American sex kitten Tuesday Weld, who'd been introduced to him by producer Henry Jaglom, a protégé of Orson Welles. A former child star, with a pouting, pubescent sex appeal, the thirty-year-old actress resembled Brigitte Bardot. Now she and Dudley resurrected their relationship.

One of the most talked-about personalities in Hollywood, in earlier days she had been the archetypal show-business brat, which led to her being dubbed Tuesday Wild. She did little to eradicate the reputation, which was epitomised by her appearing on a national talk show barefoot, unkempt, and clad in an old nightgown.

> **DUDLEY:** I never could understand Tuesday or many of the things she did. I thought it was slightly weird that she ate with her fingers. Incomprehensible actually. There's a reason why cutlery was invented. Tuesday has always been a mystery. But nothing surprises me about human nature.

Robert Mann recollected the night that Dudley turned up at his flat near Central Park with Tuesday in tow. 'She came in, said "Hi", and walked straight into our kitchen without saying another word. Then she opened the fridge and found a rather exotic jar of chutney, which she took out, found herself a spoon, and then sat down on the sofa eating the entire jar of chutney.'

Tuesday was capable of being both endearingly childlike and sexily sophisticated. It was her other side that Dudley wanted to change – the erratic behaviour that manifested itself in awful tantrums and an aggressive humour.

Dudley was now playing jazz whenever and wherever he could. Taking advantage of the success of *Good Evening*, he found himself in much demand by the Manhattan clubs, among them Michael's Pub where Woody Allen often played clarinet, and he was always being persuaded to give impromptu performances after the curtain came down at night on the show.

Good Evening was an unmitigated triumph. The wildly impudent revue won a Grammy for Best Spoken Word, and Dudley and Peter won a special Tony award for their 'unique contribution to the theatre of comedy'. It was such a hit that it was booked for a national tour starting the following year, though Dudley was trepidatious about Peter's problem with alcohol.

Peter Bellwood knew Cook well and had shared a flat with him in London. 'When he was sober Peter was a very sweet and gentle man underneath his acerbic character, but when he was drunk he could be quite vicious.'

Alexander Cohen concurred. 'There was a good Peter Cook and a bad Peter Cook. When he was sober, he was a very good, intellectual and wildly witty man who was vastly entertaining. When he was drunk, he was a nasty anti-Semite, violent about minorities. Not a nice guy to be around at all when he was drinking.'

Despite Dudley's reluctance to go on tour, once again Peter cajoled him into agreement and in February 1975 the show opened in Washington.

Dudley saw his fortieth birthday come and go without the trauma that had been attached to his thirtieth but he was becoming restless. He was ready to move on to some greater challenge than *Good Evening*. 'Frankly,' he wrote to his mother from Philadelphia, 'I wish the show were over. I have performed it enough times now to satisfy my wildest enthusiasm.'

Tuesday's increasingly erratic behaviour now led to Dudley deciding to break up with her. But his life was suddenly disrupted by her announcement that she was pregnant. Dudley had never felt himself to be parental material 'and I was afraid at the thought of being tied to anyone for twenty-odd years'.

Nevertheless, his sense of honour ran deep and he asked Tuesday to marry him. But once Tuesday had been given something, she didn't want it. No sooner had she agreed to marry him than she changed her mind; she went back and forth, too, about keeping the baby. It drove Dudley delirious, but eventually they made it to Las Vegas where they tied the knot in a small wedding chapel in September 1975.

By then, *Good Evening/Behind the Fridge* had run for four years across three continents – a record for a two-man show, and especially remarkable given the deteriorating relationship between the pair. By the time *Good Evening* reached Los Angeles in July 1976, Dudley knew he'd come to a crossroads. Tuesday Weld had decided to resurrect her career in Los Angeles and, now that he was married to her, Dudley made the decision to remain there, too, to forge a new career in America.

He hired ICM agent Lou Pitt, who needed no introduction to his work. From *Beyond the Fringe* to *Good Evening*, Pitt had long admired Dudley's talents. He did not share Dudley's beliefs that Hollywood was not ready for 'a club-footed dwarf with a Dagenham accent'. To him, the measure for all success was talent, and Dudley had a surfeit of that. He was infected by his new client's fierce determination to become a success in America.

'He was absolutely ready to explode,' Pitt recalled of their first meeting. 'He'd made a commitment to settle down and advance his career here and he had a solid desire to work in American films. He was very frustrated. He'd come from such a rich performing background but had yet to translate it to an American film audience.'

Off stage, Dudley's personal life had become quite turbulent. Tuesday was unpredictable and argumentative, and there were endless volatile rows, but he could not turn to his work for relief because he was having even larger problems there with Peter's drinking.

'I always thought Tuesday was a remarkable actress, but she wasn't a homebody,' reflected Dudley's close friend Peter Bellwood. 'There was one time when she'd made a nice dinner and she gathered up the plates afterwards, continuing to talk, and without so much as batting an eyelid she put all the dirty plates with the forks and knives on them in the fridge! It was all so completely unconscious that it was delightfully loony. This sort of stuff was going on all the time.'

When his son, Patrick, was born in 1976, Dudley was jubilant. Tuesday's mother, Jo, recalled them drinking a toast and then Dudley went into the garage and played the piano for over an hour. It was, she said, the most triumphant and glorious music she had ever heard.

> **DUDLEY:** We lived in a rented house in Bel Air and the garage made a perfect studio. I had no idea of what I was going to do but I was content to play the piano there for about a year. At one point when I began to get a little itchy I went around and saw producers but they didn't know what to do with this small, middle-aged guy from Dagenham. I suppose I was waiting for them to say, 'Oh my God, you're the fellow we've been looking for!' but of course it never happened.

By now, the private *Derek and Clive* tapes that Dudley and Peter had recorded a few years earlier had somehow multiplied like rabbits and burrowed their way through the showbiz world with wild abandon. They had become so popular underground that Island Records offered to issue them on an album and the first of a trio was released under the title *Derek and Clive (Live)*. They were, Dudley admitted, 'the most obscene things you've ever heard in your life'.

It was a wonder the albums ever made it past the rigid censorship controls of the time. It comprised such vulgar and sexually oriented jokes that the cover had to carry a warning: 'This record contains language of an explicit nature that may be offensive and should not be played in the presence of minors.' Considering the comic reputation of the duo, everyone probably thought the warning was some sort of joke. Until they played the record.

People were amazed that Dudley, who wrote such emotional music for his jazz albums, could have such a ribald outlook. But, as he pointed out defensively, without implying any other comparison, Mozart, too, had a very scatological sense of humour. 'He was always talking about farting and cunts and asses.'

The album was an outstanding success, selling over 50,000 copies within a few weeks of its release. Four thousand copies were exported to America, and the record became the duo's biggest-selling album. It would be followed by two more – *Derek and Clive Come Again* and *Derek and Clive Ad Nauseam* – and they remain three of the most notoriously raunchy comedy albums ever released. 'We went just about as far as we could go with pure filth,' Dudley admitted gleefully.

But while Dudley was holding forth on the unspeakables, life in the Moore household was loaded with marital rumpuses, not least because Dudley insisted on being able to go off with other women. He had never believed in, nor understood, the concept of monogamy and was constantly moving out of the house and staying in hotels. As Suzy Kendall had observed, he simply wasn't marital material. He found marriage altogether too confining and he felt trapped.

At least for a while, he would be able to escape domestic strife with a packed work schedule waiting for him in Europe.

CHAPTER 12

Turning Points
1976–77

In June 1976 Dudley flew to London to begin work on a new film with Peter Cook, *The Hound of the Baskervilles*. It was a comic version of the classic Sherlock Holmes tale, and something he very much wanted to do. The ideas were his, and they both thought it could be 'the funniest film ever'.

It was a busy time for Dudley, crammed with recording sessions and musical appearances on radio and television. There were meetings with Chris Karan and Peter Morgan to set up engagements for the trio, a party for Nanette Newman, and a speech at the Royal College of Music as a favour to his former Oxford tutor, Bernard Rose.

A Guinness commercial took him to Amsterdam for a few days, several cabaret engagements at Burke's club with the trio kept him musically busy and at Ronnie Scott's jazz club he was ecstatic to join Dizzy Gillespie for an improvised interlude.

During rehearsals for *Baskervilles* Dudley visited his mother for his Sunday roast lamb lunches. By now, years of therapy had brought him to understand that, despite all the angst he'd suffered during childhood, his mother had always done what she had thought best for him. He felt a strong allegiance to her now and enjoyed his visits. With life becoming fairly hectic for him these days, the Dagenham home was one of the few places he was able to relax and feel cosseted.

Years later, when I was writing his biography, Dudley uncovered a photo of that house and a mass of early family photos, including many from his teenage and young adult years, which had been lying, forgotten, for decades.

> DUDLEY: There's my mum on her wedding day with her brother and mother, that must have been in the twenties . . . This is a photo of Dad's orphanage, he was adopted and was in the Colony of Mercy for Epileptics, an orphanage in Scotland; my mother told me he got beaten every night on his bare feet for no reason . . . there's me with my parents and my sister Barbara – she was cute – outside our house in Dagenham . . . that was me with my first prize for everything at eleven in form 1b . . . I love this photo of me as a cub scout . . . Gosh, I don't believe it! Here's the magazine of the County School, Dagenham. December 1950, page thirteen, Stratford Music Festival, first prize! . . . Here are my cigarette cards, I collected them like mad . . . and that's a photo of me with a black eye, for crying out loud – the infamous school photograph and I had this HUGE black eye! . . . That's me as a sheikh in a play at Oxford in '58 or '59 . . . and this photo is when I first got drunk at Oxford and fell in the canal! . . . And that's a picture of the Magdalen Tower at Oxford, which I love so much that I ordered hundreds of Christmas cards with its picture on the front . . . a lot of this stuff goes back to my boyhood, for crying out loud. I can't believe I kept it all! I don't even remember seeing most of it.

Late in June 1977, filming began on *The Hound of the Baskervilles*, under the direction of Andy Warhol protege Paul Morrissey. Peter Cook later described it as 'a mess with some funny moments'.

Dudley agreed the film was a debacle, attributing the failure to its director. 'Paul Morrissey frustrated us at every turn, and we should have dumped the entire idea.' But he and Peter had chosen the director, expecting him to be easy to work with. He turned out to be the reverse and they disagreed entirely with Morrissey on the subject of comedy.

The film presented Peter Cook as a comic version of Sherlock Holmes, complete with hairnet and dressing gown. Dudley was cast in multiple roles, first as a moronic Dr Watson, then as Mr Spiggott, a hopping one-legged lunatic, and finally as Sherlock Holmes's mother. On paper it seemed funny enough, but on celluloid it fell flat.

When filming ended in July, Dudley returned to Los Angeles, where Tuesday had found them a beach house in Marina del Rey, a tiny town nestled between Beverly Hills and Santa Monica. He stayed long enough to buy the house and to see a psychoanalyst. But he insisted Tuesday retain the Bel Air house they were renting. By then he had come to accept his need for isolation. He felt a security in its familiarity, a familiarity borne out of his early hospital sojourns as a child. From then on, he always ensured that the woman in his life had another home to go to whenever he had that urge for solitude. If she didn't own one, he bought one for her.

Dudley was now racking up his frequent-flyer miles, jetting back and forth across the Atlantic almost weekly. In London, he and Peter Cook appeared in an ABC documentary *To the Queen! A Salute to Elizabeth II*, performing some outrageous skits on the lifestyle of the Royal Family.

By then, Paul Morrissey had edited *The Hound of the Baskervilles*, which Dudley scored on a shoestring budget, but both he and Peter thought it so awful that they edited another version of their own – the one that would ultimately be released. Their version, said Peter, was 'marginally better, but there's still no making it any good'.

The film flopped miserably when it came out in England; in America it would not be released for two more years.

Which, as it happened, was lucky for Dudley, who was on the threshold of taking his first major steps in Hollywood.

Part Three

CHAPTER 13

Hollywood
1977–78

The latter part of 1977 was a busy time for Dudley.

In England there were jazz bookings at the Cambridge Arts Festival and discussions for a new Australian tour with the trio. He and Peter were offered £20,000 to film several commercials for the London Electricity Board, and they began negotiating for a third *Derek and Clive* album.

The extraordinary success of *Derek and Clive* had reached American ears, and they were becoming cult figures across the Atlantic. Their notoriety led to an appearance on American television, where they hosted a segment of NBC's irreverent late-night comedy show *Saturday Night Live* with Chevy Chase.

Lou Pitt, Dudley's new agent, was beginning to see a lot of interest in his client. 'He had a tremendous cultish following and I kept getting calls from people who had the *Derek and Clive* recordings. It was only a question of someone being in a position to take advantage of that.'

Somebody was. That someone was Chevy Chase.

A huge fan of Dudley and Peter, he was about to make his first movie, *Foul Play*. 'I may be shooting myself in the foot,' he told Lou Pitt, 'but I just have to have Dudley play a part.'

Dudley was flattered and pleased when Pitt relayed the conversation, but after reading the script he turned down the offer. To him, the sexual pervert in *Foul Play* was just another sex-starved twit and the kind of caricature part he was anxious now to move away from. He was tired of playing undersized, oversexed idiots.

Colin Higgins, who had scripted *Harold and Maude* and *Silver Streak*, was making his directorial debut with *Foul Play*. Keen to secure Dudley for the film, he suggested threading two roles together into one. Faced with Higgins's relentless pursuit and a greater character opportunity than first presented, Dudley gave in. In November 1977 he flew to San Francisco for ten days of filming. His fee was $27,500. There had been many turning points in his career up till now, but this film would be the one to set him firmly on the road to stardom in America.

Foul Play was a comedy thriller in which wisecracking, affable police lieutenant Chevy Chase falls for librarian Goldie Hawn, who becomes unwittingly involved in a plot to assassinate the Pope and is chased by various nefarious creatures of the underworld. Enter Dudley as a chubby, sex-obsessed and sex-starved maniacal orchestra conductor who rescues Goldie from her pursuers in a singles bar and offers her safe refuge in his apartment – a haunt crammed with sex toys. His subsequent romantic failures with Goldie become the film's running gag.

The film climaxes with Dudley conducting a glitzy performance of *The Mikado* in the presence of the Pope. Chase arrives in time to foil the dastardly assassination attempt and is romantically reunited backstage with Goldie, while our hapless conductor, anxious to avoid another unlucky encounter with her, disguises himself in sunglasses to finish the concert.

It was a small part, but it was just the kind of role that Dudley had always carried off with comic brilliance.

He worked well with Colin Higgins, who would later direct the comedy hits *9 to 5* and *The Best Little Whorehouse in Texas* before his untimely death at the age of forty-seven.

Dudley only had three scenes, but he milked them for all he was worth. 'There was one take in the police station,' Chevy Chase laughed, 'where we must have done it forty times because I just kept laughing my guts out every time Dudley walked by. I remember looking at the rushes and saying, "God, is he funny!" Goldie was in hysterics all the time.'

Goldie Hawn, a bubbly girl with an Academy Award already behind her, found Dudley immensely entertaining. 'He was one of the funniest people I've ever worked with,' she giggled at the memory. 'We did one scene that became a tour de force for him. We must have shot it twenty-five different times, and he was just as funny every time. I remember howling with laughter and thinking, "How can he make it seem so fresh every time?" Maybe the first or even the second time, but twenty-five? He was hilarious!'

Dudley admired Chevy Chase, a creative young comedian who was a regular part of the innovative *Saturday Night Live* team. Most of Chevy's work on that show was entirely improvised, whereas Dudley's improvising had usually taken place within the framework of a scripted outline.

Chevy was such a fan of Dudley and Peter's early English films that he could almost quote scenes verbatim. 'Probably one of the funniest movies I had ever seen,' Chase told me, 'was *Bedazzled*. It's a classic. It was absolutely brilliant. And, much as I admired Peter Cook, the talent that Dudley had was so extraordinary, it went even beyond that.'

Chevy, whose own humour, like Dudley's, came from tremendous rage as a child, was glad to have Dudley's support during his first film. 'Acting is a way of hiding oneself. It's a form of denial of who we really are. Extroversion in comedians like Dudley is really a symptom of introversion. We're basically very shy, have a very low self-esteem, and we're like children who need a quick fix, or else we wouldn't be performing.'

At that time, Chevy admits of himself, he was 'full of crap and full of myself', yet he was almost reverential of Dudley and learned a great deal from the seasoned comedian.

'Comedy's about making people laugh,' Chevy expressed, 'and at the end of the day, it's all about getting the laugh without going so far over the top as to be unbelievable. It took me a long time to reach that point. Dudley combined both and helped to show me how to do it. He was so good in *Foul Play*, so wildly weird and funny, that it affected me for years. My problem then was that I simply didn't know how to act. I'd done *Saturday Night Live*, sure, but I didn't do what Dudley did. By watching his performance, I learned so much. I learned more from him than he'll ever know.'

Dudley enjoyed the film but was unhappy with his performance. He considered it over the top and predictable – just as he had expected it to be when he'd read the script. But with its July 1978 release, his performance almost upstaged both the film's two stars. Observed Bryan Forbes, 'It was Dudley at his best. He was incredibly funny and absolutely brilliant.' Critics were generous with their praise, and *Newsweek*'s David Ansen declared, 'Comic laurels go to the pint-sized Dudley Moore as a closet swinger eternally caught in *kinkiness interruptus* by endangered Goldie; it's a crude running gag which Moore milks for more than it's worth.' The film became a major box-office hit and grossed more than $70 million.

While *Foul Play* continued to garner accolades for him, Dudley took his trio – Chris Karan and Peter Morgan – on tour in Australia and New Zealand. In Sydney, during a concert at Sydney Town Hall, they also recorded a new album – *The Dudley Moore Trio Live* (also released as *Dudley Down Under ... Live)*. It included 'Song for Suzy', and Dudley threw in a jazzed-up version of *Scheherazade* and a Chopin pastiche. 'It was a bit like performing in an aircraft hangar,' recalled Chris Karan, 'but we had a lot of fun. We had a terrific momentum going, because we were playing every night, and I think being together for all that time came out in the music.'

Chris had been with Dudley since 1961 and the formative days of Peter Cook's Establishment club in London. Now he sensed time was running out for the trio. 'Dudley was getting more and more involved in Hollywood, and I could tell that's where he wanted to be and that his career was going to be there. I had a feeling we weren't going to do very much after the tour was over.'

He was right. It would be another fourteen years before the trio would perform together again.

Dudley had been absorbed for years in psychotherapy, to the occasional amusement of his British friends. Bryan Forbes was visiting California with his wife, Nanette Newman. 'How much is it costing you to go to analysis every morning?' he asked Dudley. 'A hundred and fifty dollars an hour,' was the answer. 'Why don't you pay me instead?' Forbes suggested. 'Nanette and I would be happy to talk to you, and we'll even cut the price!'

Years later, Dudley ruminated with me about his long foray into psychoanalysis which had begun in the early sixties in London.

> **DUDLEY:** I suppose it was my club foot that led me to therapy. I don't really know any more. I had a great obsession about my height for a while. That's gone. I'm still not too happy about my foot but in a way I don't know that it matters any more. I've talked about it a lot. Probably to my detriment and it may have somehow subliminally put people off. You know – 'This guy is always talking about his fucking foot!' They probably felt, 'Well, who cares?' in the end!

In Los Angeles, Dudley's treatment had evolved into group therapy, where he sat in a circle with others and chatted endlessly about his inner problems. When he felt weighed down by the gravity of the situation he threw out the odd joke and filled the room with laughter. He spoke so openly there that other group members began turning to him for guidance. He liked helping them and when asked if he'd like to co-lead a group studying substance abuse, he agreed.

As one of his therapists told me, Dudley missed his true calling. 'He came to the therapeutic world with an inherent ability to be a therapist. It was natural for him to want to reach out and help other people. The insight he had into humanity, his perception and sensitivity about people, and the understanding that he had for the entire psychotherapeutic process was highly unusual.'

While Dudley was pouring his heart out each week, he attracted the attention of legendary director Blake Edwards, another group member. Edwards, married to Julie Andrews, had made the classics *Days of Wine and Roses* and *Breakfast at Tiffany's* in the early sixties before moving to Europe for six years where he resuscitated Peter Sellers's ailing career with a series of *Pink Panther* films.

After one particularly illuminating group session, Blake drew Dudley aside and asked how he'd feel about making a movie with him. Dudley was surprised but elated. 'I guess my posturing during therapy had seemed like auditioning after all!' Dudley's vulnerability, his openness, his availability to suggestion all seemed ideal qualities for the role Blake envisaged.

Like Chevy Chase, the director had long been an admirer of Dudley's work. Years earlier, after seeing him in *Bedazzled* he had tried to obtain the rights to turn it into a musical with Dudley. He particularly loved the sequence with the nuns on the trampoline and thought it would be terrific to capture that on stage. It never happened.

The role he offered Dudley now was as *The Ferret*, which Blake hoped would spawn an entire series, as *The Pink Panther* had done. He saw Dudley as the inept son of a superspy who assumes *The Ferret* code name with hilarious results. Blake knew comparisons with Inspector Clouseau from his *Pink Panthers* would be inevitable, but he saw *The Ferret* more as a suspense comedy rather than burlesque slapstick like the *Panthers*.

Dudley loved the concept and signed a contract with Blake to make five *Ferret* films, the first of which he would also write. He was excited about the fun and silliness that he anticipated with Blake and couldn't wait to get started.

In the meantime, he reunited with Peter Cook to record a new and final album, *Derek and Clive Ad Nauseam*, to be distributed with a vomit bag for those who might find its contents too extreme. They also taped a video version of the session, which would eventually be released as *Derek and Clive Get the Horn*.

The album, which Dudley never felt to be as good as the others, was even more vulgar than the earlier ones and contained more than a hundred uses of the word 'fuck'. One of the sketches has Clive telling Derek that he had masturbated over a picture of the Pope; in another he expresses the wish to be a murderer like Myra Hindley so he can have visits from Lord Longford, who turns him on.

It was their third and last album. And, although they continued to see each other and discuss potential ideas, it would be virtually the last time the two would work together. To Dudley, the film version was a documentary about two people who wanted to see the back of each other.

DUDLEY: When we made the film in 1977 it was basically the story of two people breaking up and that is obvious from the tapes. It was about two people who were tired of working together. We were very aggressive with each other. Everyone thought we'd taken something, but we hadn't, we just got very belligerent with each other. Peter's rage was bitter and seemed directed at me a bit. I don't know why. I didn't actually confront him though. I just let it pass. Like I always did.

The long collaboration was essentially over. Dudley had already struck out on his own, and now that he was living in America, he felt committed to a different professional life. Peter had perhaps first sensed the break-up during the run of *Behind the Fridge*, seven years earlier, in Australia. There, after one of his drunken soliloquies on stage, he had turned to Dudley and said, 'I suppose you won't want to go on working with me now.' Dudley didn't, but he remained with him nevertheless.

According to Alex Cohen, their Broadway producer, Peter felt abandoned, but Cohen insists it was not Dudley's fault. 'He gave and gave and gave until there was nothing left to give. You could hardly call that abandonment, but I think that's how Peter viewed it.'

Cook had often said the relationship he shared with Dudley was the best of his career. Their friend, Peter Bellwood, had known Cook for many years and understood him better than most. 'He was very affected by Dudley leaving, and had the capacity to feel deeply rejected and abandoned. It had been a collaboration where you just looked up to heaven and hoped it would last. When that best collaborator decided to leave, it became hard to deal with on a rational level.'

A few days away from the start of filming his new movie, *10,* Blake Edward's star, George Segal, walked off the film. Blake immediately sent the script over to Lou Pitt. He was offering the part to Dudley.

Pitt read it and thought it was sensational. It was provocative, with a lot of different levels to it, and he could see it was a great opportunity. He called Dudley late at night in London where he was visiting his mother and told him he loved the script and thought he should do it.

Lou's call was followed by another from Blake. Surprised and tickled by his interest in him, Dudley read the script as he flew back to Los Angeles a few days later while Lou Pitt sweated for his decision. Pitt was convinced this would be a breakthrough movie for Dudley and was anxious for his response.

He need not have worried – Dudley loved the script. 'I'll do it!' he told Lou when he landed in Los Angeles, and he jumped as high as his short frame would take him.

Which, as it would turn out, was nowhere near as high as the stardom that was waiting for him just around the corner.

CHAPTER 14

A Perfect 10

1978–79

In those heady final days of 1978, Dudley had the same feeling he'd enjoyed twenty years earlier when he had just left Oxford and was plunging forward to make a career for himself. There was an excitement in the air, a sense of starting over again in a new world.

Word of this intriguing import was already circulating around town. The Hollywood Women's Press Club presented him with their Golden Apple award for Male Discovery of the Year, given to the most exciting new male personality on the Hollywood scene. It was obvious he was no newcomer, but the audience present at the awards gave him a standing ovation when Bette Davis announced him the winner over another new arrival whose time was yet to come – Richard Gere.

These early American years were exciting and full. There was an optimistic buzz in the air and Dudley was feeling happy and hopeful. He was now settled in the terracotta Marina del Rey beach house Tuesday had found, where Rudy Vallee had once lived, and it would remain his home through four marriages until he sold it in 1999 when he moved to New Jersey. The only discordant note was that his stormy marriage to Tuesday collapsed just before he began filming *10* and she moved to New York, taking their son, Patrick, with her.

It was ironic that Dudley had won the role in *10* through George Segal's last-minute departure for this paralleled what had happened when Blake had made his first *Pink Panther* film. Peter Ustinov had been set to play Inspector Clouseau but backed out suddenly, leaving Blake to recast the movie. His choice was Peter Sellers, and the result was a successful chain of *Pink Panther* movies and the renaissance of Sellers's career.

Dudley's role in *10* – that of a 42-year-old man suffering from a midlife crisis – was perfect casting and was changed only slightly to allow him to step into the shoes vacated by George Segal. Instead of a Beverly Hills dentist, Blake made the key role of George Webber into that of an award-winning songwriter, allowing Dudley to display his prowess at the piano.

A victim of middle-age restlessness, George becomes smitten by a gorgeous blonde, Bo Derek, whom he spots in a car en route to her wedding. Pursuing her to the church, he later returns to discover her identity then leaves his girlfriend, Julie Andrews, to follow this goddess to Mexico where she is honeymooning with her new husband. He believes that if he can acquire this fantasy girl – an eleven on his rating scale and therefore, to him, the perfect woman – he will also find total happiness. Ultimately he realises he has confused beauty with perfection and returns to his girlfriend.

Dudley was thrilled about embarking on *10*. It was his first starring role in an American-based, American-financed film, and it came at a time when he really wanted to play that kind of part. His fee was $100,000, which seemed a fortune. In terms of what the film went on to make it was a pittance.

Filming began in November 1978 in Los Angeles, before moving to locations in Mexico and Hawaii.

In *10*, Dudley was able to play a role that took him far away from the caricature parts of his past. Previously he had always played characters with funny accents or different faces. He had clung to these as protective covers, afraid to discard them and be stripped bare. Now he felt ready to project his own qualities into a part. George Webber was basically a straight role, made funny by the situations he got into. Dudley's portrayal, sensitive and vulnerable, was of a man trying desperately hard to be sophisticated but being constantly tripped up by his distracted clumsiness.

Blake Edwards knew he'd made the right choice. In Dudley, he saw some of the same attributes that had attracted him to Peter Sellers – an extraordinary physical comedy coupled with an uncanny instinct for comic timing. Yet Dudley had something more, if it could only be captured – a deep sensitivity that was not only endearing but would also bring a touching realism to the role. 'I kept sitting in those therapy groups listening to Dudley,' Blake told me, 'and there were so many things in his personality that coincided with the character in *10*. It was amazing.'

Julie Andrews, who also became a close friend, had the fondest memories of working with Dudley. 'At first he was a little shy but eventually we got to be great chums. We had our Englishness in common, and certain kinds of vaudeville jokes and shtick. He was adorable. We laughed a great deal and had an enormous amount of fun. I adored his irreverence. The delight of working with him was tremendous, and it was lovely to watch his instincts at work.'

DUDLEY: I know Julie had reservations at first about working with me because she's so tall and I'm so short. Blake asked me to wear five-and-a-half-inch heels and I said they'd look like medieval torture boots. But I got these boots anyway and Blake fell down laughing when he saw me. It was just too ridiculous! We had those boots gold-plated on a platform!

Dudley radically changed his appearance for the role. His fine hair was permed, he wore one-inch lifts in his shoes to make him look a little taller and he had also gone on a crash diet and lost over a stone.

> **DUDLEY:** I was always trying different diets. This one was a breakfast diet and meant that for breakfast I ate a plate of trout, usually two, with Brussels sprouts, broccoli, green beans, snow peas and cabbage, which I liberally sprinkled with powdered seaweed concentrate. After that, I had a fruit dessert of papaya, figs and nuts. With that lot inside me I didn't eat again for the rest of the day. And I didn't even think about eating until I was in bed at night, when I would fall asleep dreaming of the following morning's meal!

Over the previous two years, group therapy had brought Dudley to the point where he now felt at ease with himself. After years of feeling inadequate because of his height and his club foot, he was now recognising that he was acceptable as he was. His height, his foot, his leg – these still made him uncomfortable, but now he was able to live with his discomfort without feeling inferior because of them.

He applied all of his feelings to the role, and allowed his vulnerability to expose itself. He had spent so many years trying to hide it that he felt a kind of relief and a calmness in allowing his real self to come forward for the first time to meld with the characterisation.

The role of the perfect ten was played by 22-year-old Bo Derek, a stunningly beautiful actress married to film actor John Derek, a leading man during the 1950s. She had made only two previous films, but was remarkably self-assured in spite of her lack of experience.

10 was a huge step for her, made less intimidating by the

atmosphere on the set and her co-star's relaxing attitude. 'He was marvellous to work with and wonderfully talented,' she reflected. 'He had the quality of being lovably funny and sexy at the same time. I think he was a little self-conscious, but he was very sweet and made it very easy. He knew this was all pretty extraordinary for me and was very sensitive to that.'

Bo and Dudley were, in Blake Edwards's opinion, a perfect couple. 'We couldn't have done any better. She was such an unusually beautiful-looking woman, and when you put that together with the qualities that comprise Dudley, it was a magic pairing.'

Even more magic was the combination of star and director. They were a brilliant team, Dudley and the director who had steered Audrey Hepburn and Jack Lemmon to Oscar nominations for *Breakfast at Tiffany's* and *Days of Wine and Roses* respectively. Dudley relished the time he spent with Blake, who he felt was the best director he'd ever worked with. Blake seldom discussed scenes with him and allowed him to do his own thing, even to colloquialising the script a little, and Dudley felt a freedom he had never felt before. If this was what it was like to make Hollywood movies, then Dudley wanted more.

'There's nothing about Dudley that I don't like,' Blake offered appreciatively, 'and I can't say that about many people – particularly people I've worked with. He's just an amazing human being.'

For Julie Andrews, making *10* was one of the best experiences she had ever known on a film set. Not only was she being directed by her husband, but she was working with someone who was immense fun and who wanted nothing more than to have a wonderful time while he worked.

'Blake and Dudley were terrific together,' she laughingly told me. 'They were two naughty boys – deliciously funny and outrageously ribald. Whenever Dudley did something particularly funny, Blake would break up and practically be on his knees. It was just a marvellous experience and lucky all round. Dudley was one of those rare, wonderful choices, and Blake has that phenomenal instinct that sees the possibility.'

> **DUDLEY:** Blake was terrific. He was the best director I'd ever worked with because he left me alone and we were able to print the first or second take and move on. We didn't have to do twenty-seven takes to get it right. Luckily he didn't offer any direction, didn't offer any solution to any scene. He left it to me. I wanted to do the part sort of straight and he agreed. I think he'd planned it another way, then with me there it came out a different way.

Back in England, Peter Cook was feeling quite bereft, and periodically rang Dudley's mother and Suzy Kendall as a way of feeling closer to his erstwhile comedy partner. Although he knew their partnership was really over, he still harboured hopes of future projects together – especially another series of *Not Only . . . But Also*.

'I do think that when we manage to do another series,' he wrote to Dudley teasingly, 'your mother should become a regular along with Dud and Pete. I don't want to press you when things are obviously going so well for you in the States. I like to think that when you become "hot" and "enormous", it will make it easier for us to do a decent movie together with our choice of director.'

Peter was feeling especially happy just then. 'I think it's probably to do with seven months' sobriety (with four major lapses) that has brought about this change,' he wrote. 'For the last month I have no longer resented not drinking, something I never thought would happen.' Peter believed *Derek and Clive Ad Nauseam* to be their best album so far and loved what he had seen of the film they had shot at the same time. 'It works really well visually,' he told Dudley. 'Some of the stuff in the control room is hilarious. Never have two comedians slagged each other off so comprehensively!'

By the first week of January 1979, as filming on *10* continued in Hawaii, the word was spreading in Hollywood that Dudley's performance was turning out to be exceptional. Tony Adams, Blake's producer, called Lou Pitt and told him that Dudley would become a sex symbol from the film. 'Are you crazy?' replied Lou, and decided Tony was nuts.

Tony Adams wasn't the only person to be raving about Dudley's work. Orion, the production company who was financing the film, had seen some of the rushes, and Mike Medavoy, one of its executives, called Lou Pitt to tell him of his excitement about Dudley. 'That internal enthusiasm is always a trigger,' explained Pitt, 'and I knew something big was going to happen for Dudley from *10*.'

In the latter part of filming, Dudley had to shoot some of his more intimate scenes. One of them had him running across the hot sand in a baggy sweatsuit that covered up his gammy leg. The result was astonishingly Chaplinesque.

> **DUDLEY:** It wasn't intentional. I've never wanted to look like Charlie Chaplin. I don't mean that nastily but I've never wanted to follow somebody else's character. There was a lot of mime in that section of the film but I do whatever I can with a sort of technical approach and not with any feeling of following anyone. I wore the baggy pants because I can't wear bathing shorts on film. Cosmetically, my club foot is not the Venus de Milo!

Bo found Dudley's antics hilarious – to his occasional irritation. He especially objected to her giggling while they were rolling around in the surf together. 'You can't giggle,' he admonished her. 'You're supposed to be serious.' She still couldn't stop.

Apart from the giggling, he found her easy and comfortable to work with. He was particularly charmed by her husband, John Derek, who almost daily left photographs outside Dudley's hotel room that he had shot on the set, some of which he first elegantly framed.

There were, however, some moments where Dudley felt very ill at ease. They came when he and Bo were naked in bed as they romanced to a recording of Ravel's *Bolero*. It was an embarrassing interlude for Hollywood's newest British import.

'I think he was rather shy,' Bo Derek recalled, 'and a little nervous, although he really didn't show it. I purposely tried to make it as casual as possible, so as not to make him more nervous than I think he was. I felt we were both kind of nervous, and whenever we finished something we would look at Blake for reassurance.'

> **DUDLEY:** I was very embarrassed to do the nude scenes. Normally there are about ten people around the camera helping out, but when we came to do the nude scene, about *fifty* of them came out of the woodwork! And immediately I stripped off, the lighting cameraman fell into peals of laughter! I couldn't believe it! I was very relieved when we finished it but the awful thing was that the next day Blake decided to shoot it all over again in dimmer light! So I had to go through it again! Though that time the cameraman didn't laugh . . . I guess because he'd already seen all I had to offer!

When the scenes in Mexico had been completed, they packed up to fly back to Los Angeles to resume shooting in the studio. Dudley was given a parting gift of a naked inflatable doll that he gleefully cuddled, entertaining cast and crew as he simulated a sexual encounter.

> **DUDLEY:** I didn't know how to get rid of this flaming blow-up doll, so I put it in the top of my suitcase and covered it. The problem was that as I was carrying my cases into this Mexican airport they said we'd have to show our bags because of the danger of fruit flies entering the US! All I could think was, 'Oh my God, I've got this naked rubber doll right in the top of my bag!' I was shitting myself! I think I expected them to arrest me. I don't know how I got around it but luckily they didn't look. Oh Gawd, I tell you, it was really a hairy moment!

Back in Los Angeles, Dudley had a piano on the set which he played between takes. Bo Derek was deeply moved when she first encountered the musical side of her co-star. 'Hank Mancini had written a lovely theme tune for the film. It was gorgeous and everyone loved it. Then one day, while the crew was setting up lights, the place started getting quieter and quieter, and then I heard Dudley playing this theme tune. And all of a sudden it took on a whole new magic that it hadn't had before. To watch him play was just incredible, and it was another side of him that I don't think anyone had ever seen.'

Playing the piano in between filming gave Dudley tremendous enjoyment. He played for himself, and it didn't matter if there was one person around or fifty hammering away; as long as he could play, he was happy. 'It was a sheer delight to watch him,' said Julie Andrews, who cherished those moments as a bonus to her day. Before filming was over, Dudley went into a studio and recorded cassettes of some of his music, which he gave away as parting gifts.

Dudley came away from *10* having thoroughly enjoyed the best film experience of his career. He was becoming attuned to his feelings and expressing what he really felt inside. For the first time he had felt comfortable to let those inner feelings emerge on screen, thanks partly to the security Blake had imbued in him and partly also to the cumulative results of his years of therapy. He had projected his real personality onto the character he played, and it had worked.

He was now feeling the happiest he'd ever felt about himself. Previously he had not been saying, doing, or being what he wanted. Now he felt himself creeping towards that objective. He had to some extent come to terms with the inner demons that had been battling away inside him for forty-odd years. 'The discovery of myself was the single most important development that had ever occurred in my life.'

Socially, he was everywhere. There were parties a couple of nights a week, premieres, screenings, and interviews with journalists who were clamouring at his publicist's door. Dudley's diary these days was so crammed that when one day appeared empty of engagements, I saw he had written across the page with an exhilarated scrawl, 'FREE!!'

Simultaneously with his new-found success, Dudley found himself in wild demand as a single man. Women were pouring out of the woodwork as they had during the sixties in London. He had become, in his mid-forties, God's gift to women. He was surrounded by them and had no qualms about enjoying it. In a pre-AIDS era, he believed adamantly in having as many female friends as possible and earnestly proclaimed his belief in 'the meaningful one-night stand'; he couldn't understand why people took a pejorative view of such behaviour. He was, he admitted gleefully, girl crazy. The only difference between him and the sex maniac he had played in *Foul Play* was that no one could remotely describe Dudley as sex-starved.

Not surprisingly, his comment about meaningful one-night stands found its way into the British and American press, with the inevitable distortions. Irritated with the way his remarks were being so publicly misinterpreted, he wrote to one magazine:

> Please don't perpetuate a misquotation that makes it seem as if I am suddenly running riot with heartless callous encounters with women. Firstly, you make it sound as if I'm making up for lost time after years of deprivation. Secondly, don't perpetuate a quote that trivializes a notion that was meant affectionately. I said, 'I am all in favour of meaningful one-night stands or one-week stands or one-year stands.' You give a callous tone to a remark that was affectionate and humorous.

But like many of the letters he wrote to critics when he felt unfairly attacked in the press, it was never sent. He was an inveterate letter-writer, writing constantly to friends who were scattered all over the world. He was especially proud of his fans and so much did they mean to him that he always answered his own fan mail.

By now his stormy four-year marriage to Tuesday Weld was all but over and they were hammering out a divorce settlement. During their time together they had endured over twenty break-ups, culminating in their final year-long separation, though Dudley flew constantly to New York to spend time with his son. Constant arguing and fighting had made life stimulating, but their character differences could not be resolved.

Marriage may not have worked out for him, yet Dudley had an intense desire for a close relationship. Still, he was also afraid of commitment and preferred to live alone, recognising that he functioned better that way.

And then he met 29-year-old blonde singer Susan Anton. They had met at an awards show in Los Angeles and the attraction for both had been instant and electric.

When they got together on their first date, they both thought they'd made a huge mistake. At five foot ten, Susan towered over him. Dudley had forgotten how tall she was, and Susan had forgotten how short he was. Awkwardly, they walked through the hotel where Susan was performing to get a bowl of soup, with Dudley's left shoe squeaking uncontrollably. 'Here we were,' Susan recalled laughingly, 'this tall woman and this short man and his squeaky shoe going into the coffee shop for a bowl of wonton soup in the middle of the night in Las Vegas. What chance did this relationship have?'

But the more they talked, the more they began to feel comfortable with each other. Susan found Dudley's receptiveness refreshing. He had a gift for understanding people and accepting them for the way they were, and she felt a rare sense of being truly understood.

The man who'd been enjoying his widespread popularity with the opposite sex now found himself wanting only to be with this one woman. Suddenly the need for one-night stands was being replaced with a desire for monogamy.

Foul Play had just been released in England, and although Ada Moore had not yet seen it, she was basking in the praise her son was receiving. 'A boy at the post office said you were very good,' she wrote to him, 'he is the post-mistress's son, quite a charmer . . . and in the *Sunday Mirror*, a paper I do not usually buy, the comment was very favourable. "Riotously funny scenes," they said, "and well worth a visit".'

Dudley was now being written about in the British newspapers as an emergent Hollywood star who was receiving invitations to the most exclusive parties and being lauded in the gossip columns. But, they asked, whatever had happened to the once-stinging satirist who wasn't afraid to knock the system or ridicule the holiest of establishment figures? Had he gone stereotypically Hollywood?

Dudley hadn't gone anything. He had never been a satirist. The label had stuck from *Beyond the Fringe*, but the satire had come from the other three performers. Dudley himself had always been too afraid of reprisal to knock or ridicule the system. As for going Hollywood, all he was doing was enjoying the fruits of his labour. If, by English standards, relishing the sunshine, living on the beach and mixing in celebrity circles meant that he had 'gone Hollywood', that was tough luck.

His lifestyle was fairly modest and certainly no more luxurious than it had been in Britain. He had never been materialistic, had never felt a need to surround himself with possessions, aside from an impressive wine collection and occasional antiques that gave him aesthetic pleasure. True, he had his 1963 Bentley, but he had imported that from England mainly as an asset to sell if he ran out of money.

With filming on Blake Edwards's *The Ferret* scheduled to start in late summer in Europe and Brazil, Dudley flew to London briefly in June. He saw his family and made a guest appearance on *The Muppet Show*, in which he played the piano and had a row with Animal. Afterwards he was presented with a silver Kermit that registered him as 'guest No. 79'.

While there he saw *Derek and Clive Get the Horn*, the film he and Peter Cook had made of their last *Derek and Clive* record. He liked it a lot more than the record but before any sort of release could be contemplated it would need to be viewed by the British Board of Film Censors for a rating. It was highly unlikely that they would find in it much to approve.

Some time earlier, a prankster had somehow substituted the covers on multiple copies of the first album with ones that announced the recording as a reading of *Black Beauty*. That was particularly unfortunate for one seven-year-old girl who found herself introduced at an early age to the scatological smut of Derek and Clive. It was unfortunate, too, for the distributors, who were royally sued by the child's father.

Returning to Los Angeles, Dudley was feeling more settled than ever – a sense that was reinforced by the arrival from England of more than seventy pieces of luggage, including paintings, furniture, his electric piano and his Hammond organ. The rest of his books and records were also on their way across the Atlantic, and with their arrival Dudley's move from England would become permanent.

By Hollywood standards, his airy beach house was modest. It had three floors and three bedrooms and the front door opened on to a beige and white living room that was dominated by a black Yamaha grand piano. One end of the living room was a dining area with a French table that seated twelve people. The other end had sofas that looked out on the beach.

Dudley was glad that he had chosen to put down roots in America. He found himself at ease around Americans and in tune with their line of thinking and their openness. Americans were comfortable being ambitious and derived pleasure from being successful and he felt his own career would flourish in the midst of that attitude.

As *10*'s release date grew closer, there was a growing sense of anticipation. Heavyweight publicist Paul Bloch had been assigned to shape Dudley into an international movie star. 'The word of mouth is incredible,' he wrote to Dudley. 'A lot of very important people are very excited about your role in it!'

Dudley himself was remarkably cool about the excitement. After all, he'd been performing for twenty-one years now, and the vacillations in his success over the years had inured him to the potential of great acclaim. Still, recognising that he was on the brink of a new career direction, he was feeling less anxious about his future and more relaxed about what life might bring.

But there were still career setbacks. Just a few weeks before the start of shooting, Blake Edwards had cancelled *The Ferret* because of budget difficulties. Dudley was deeply disappointed. He'd really wanted to do it and had looked forward to the series.

His disappointment didn't dampen his new-found popularity, which saw him in great social demand. He especially enjoyed

Sunday afternoon parties at Julie Andrews and Blake Edwards's house where the *10* gang gathered for dinner and watched movies and other friends stopped by, among them Michael and Pat York and Michael and Shakira Caine.

One evening, while dining with friends, he met 'a shy artist wearing crazy tennis shoes'. His name was David Hockney. Another afternoon he went to brunch at Jane Seymour's house. For a while Dudley had dated Jane and often told Ruth Forman, his new secretary whom he'd also briefly dated, that he was 'just popping round to Jane's house' and would see her later.

In October 1979, *10* was released with a huge publicity campaign. Orion may have been hoping for a reasonable success with the film, but no one was prepared for the overwhelming, runaway hit that it became. Critics were mesmerised by the fantasy of *10* and by Dudley's magical performance. 'Mr Moore is superbly comic,' declared the *New York Times*. 'With this film he at last becomes an American film star.' *Time* magazine noted, 'This film could provide him the chance, finally, to find the large audience he deserves.'

It did. The public embraced it instantly. Lou Pitt was amazed. He had thought the film good, but had not envisaged such a phenomenal success. The night it opened, he visited several cinemas and was astonished to see the lengthy queues of people lined up around the block. Audiences loved the film. They flocked to see it not once but several times, and became so involved in the story that they talked back to the screen. One man became so angry with Dudley for not consummating his relationship with Bo Derek that he jumped out of his third-row seat and shouted to the screen, 'Are you fucking crazy, George? Do it, for Chrissakes!'

10 became the surprise hit of the season and signalled megastardom for Bo and Dudley. Bo's serene face smiled from magazine covers on every newsstand. Her cornrow hairstyle from *10* was soon in demand in hair salons across the nation, and John Derek enhanced his wife's appeal by merchandising a million-selling poster of his blonde goddess. At twenty-three, Bo had become Hollywood's new sex princess.

Blake Edwards was ecstatic with the reaction. In order to make the film with Dudley, he had been forced to accept a substantially lesser fee for himself than when George Segal had been his star. 'Orion said my deal was too rich to allow for Dudley, because he was an unknown factor. So I agreed to take a percentage of the gross instead. Thanks to Dudley, I got very rich indeed!'

As well as having a flair for physical comedy that evoked memories of Chaplin, Dudley had proved also to be a convincingly romantic leading man. Hollywood found itself with a new male sex symbol. Tony Adams had been right after all when he'd made that early prediction to Lou Pitt.

Julie Andrews had always agreed with Tony. 'I wasn't surprised about the reaction to Dudley, because I knew he was very sexy. I was thrilled at the success of the film and for what it did for him, and I think it gave him great confidence.'

Dudley himself was amazed at the reaction. He thought the film was funny and warm, but he was astounded at the gigantic hit it became and that people were returning to see it three or four times.

The reception to *10* was overwhelming and his performance was brilliant. Enter me with my BBC television crew for the first of dozens of interviews, this one for *Film 79*. From my apartment window overlooking Sunset Boulevard, I could look out and see a billboard with the cut-out figure of Dudley swinging from Bo Derek's cleavage. Women's rights groups protested but the billboard remained in place.

Stardom was not new to Dudley. He'd enjoyed years of success in Britain before his move to America. He'd been there, done that, and regarded with some bemusement his new embrace by America as a bit of a lark.

DUDLEY: It's nice to be known here. It's very pleasant to feel that I may be recognised by my dangling image! In fact, I have to say I'm basically very proud and happy to be dangling so prominently in Los Angeles! Seriously, it felt very natural to do this film and so I was very ready to play this sort of role. Also, in the last two years I've changed to a certain extent . . . or rather I've not changed, I've fallen back on who I am. I've become much more myself. The fact that I've accepted myself for who and what I am is the greatest change in me. I think I always knew who I was, but the difference is I now allow myself to be who I am. I own up to it.

By pure coincidence, some time earlier Dudley had written a treatment for a screenplay on exactly the same subject.

DUDLEY: The motivation for my screenplay treatment was the passage of time, which is something that was intrinsic in *10*. It was the fear of going through my entire life not following my instincts and my feelings, and who cares what anybody else says. It was the fear of missing out on that. Coming to the end of my life and feeling I'm about to drop off and I haven't really done what I wanted to do. That must be the most awful feeling in the world and I don't want that to happen to me.

Dudley poured out his feelings towards work, America, his new home, always with a twinkle in his eye. But the moment we began talking about his music, he abandoned his jocular tone and became serious. And when he sat at the piano and played for me, the first of many such occasions, I was captivated by the exquisite music that streamed out of his mind without any previous thought. He painted pictures with music and it was breathtaking.

DUDLEY: I do a lot of improvising. It's probably the most uninhibited way for me to perform because I follow a feeling. It's delicious for me. I've had my jazz trio since 1959 and recorded on and off over the years. I'm hoping very much that I'll be able to play over here. I guess I'm sort of inhibited in a sense because music means so much to me that I'm almost afraid to expose it. But with what's happening with *10*, I might feel more comfortable about doing it. I've started playing on talk shows so I'm gradually introducing myself musically to people here.

That television interview almost became my last. Dudley's ability to improvise jazz was remarkable and at the end of our interview I asked if he would improvise a theme for *Film 79*. I thought back in London they might consider it a unique way to close the programme. I was so enthralled by the music he was playing that I failed to notice we'd used up almost an entire roll of film on his impromptu performance. Later I was admonished by my producer, who reminded me of the high cost of film and warned of dire results if I was ever again so reckless with the programme's budget.

Overnight, it seemed, Dudley had become a massive success. *10* catapulted him into an American heaven more adulatory and offering richer rewards than he had ever experienced in Britain. It was a far cry from his earlier attempts to interest producers in 'this small, middle-aged guy from Dagenham'. Now they were clamouring at his agent's door.

CHAPTER 15

Susan's Sex Symbol
1979–80

At forty-four, Dudley had suddenly become America's newest, and most unlikely, sex symbol. Feminists were angry and vociferous at his image being suspended so prominently above the streets of Los Angeles, but Dudley just chuckled with amusement over the political debates raised by the ads and settled into a cosy acceptance of his new image. There was, he thought, something rather droll about becoming a sex symbol at his age.

His new persona came as no surprise to his friend Peter Bellwood. 'He'd always seemed much of a sex symbol to me. I never thought of him leading a monastic existence. After all, he was always surrounded by birds.'

As for Blake Edwards, he had already witnessed Dudley's sex appeal in countless group-therapy meetings. 'We had some terribly attractive ladies there, and I saw how they went after Dudley and how they felt about him.'

Back in London, his former co-*Fringer* Alan Bennett, also, was not surprised. 'I thought it was all rather a lark! When someone you know very well becomes a sex symbol, it's a bit of a joke. My only surprise was that they hadn't got on to him sooner!'

10 had opened Hollywood's portals for Dudley and given him a new-found confidence at a time when he had been questioning his future. Now he was basking in glory and trying to catch his breath. Some, coming fresh to such a reception, might struggle to keep everything in perspective, but Dudley took it in his stride. He had, after all, lived with some form of success ever since his *Fringe* days in 1960. What was new now was the sheer scale of it, so much greater than anything he had experienced back home. And this time he wasn't lurking in the shadow of Peter Cook; the acclaim was for him alone.

'I think,' Dudley told me then, 'you get to a point in your life where you say, not in a blasé way, "There's no reason why I shouldn't be successful at what I do." If you assume you're going to be successful, then you generally are.'

Few artists had come to America as a virtual unknown and scored as heavily as Dudley. Most of the British actors working in Hollywood, like Michael Caine and Roger Moore, had been known previously to audiences through their international films, but not Dudley. Hollywood was starting to pay attention and to consider him bankable – the only thing that really counts in the film industry.

Meanwhile, Orion's Mike Medavoy, who had seen Dudley's potential long before *10* was completed, sent Lou Pitt a script that Orion had acquired from Paramount. He was certain Dudley would be perfect for the film. Its title was *Arthur*.

In the winter of 1979, *Variety* announced that Lou Pitt had negotiated colossal earnings for Dudley's next two movies. For *Wholly Moses!*, a biblical spoof, it was claimed he would earn ten times the salary of *10* and more than thirty times the salary he'd been paid for *Foul Play*, so crashing through the million-dollar barrier. For the second movie, *Arthur*, it was reported he would be paid substantially more than $2 million. Actually, it wasn't until after the release of *Arthur* (for which his fee was $400,000) that Dudley moved into the millionaire bracket.

Wholly Moses! cast Dudley and Laraine Newman in dual roles, with Dom DeLuise, James Coco, Madeline Kahn, John Houseman and Richard Pryor lending support. The story was not dissimilar to the previous year's *Life of Brian* from the *Monty Python* team about a man whose life parallels that of Jesus.

Harvey (Dudley) is a language professor, vacationing in the Holy Land. Inadvertently, he and another traveller (Laraine Newman) discover some ancient scrolls bearing the legend of Herschel, an overlooked hero whose life parallels that of Moses. The scrolls reveal that Herschel (Dudley) had been floating down the Nile in a cradle on that same fateful morning as Moses, but with a helpful shove from the latter he had sailed on past the bulrushes, leaving Moses to be the one to be discovered and groomed for greatness. Years later, Herschel is standing on a mountain and hears God talking to him. What he doesn't realise is that Moses is standing on the other side of the mountain. Herschel believes he alone is being addressed, and that it is he who is being ordained to set free his people from captivity in Egypt. With the help of his wife, Zelda (Laraine Newman), he sets about achieving this end, always one step behind Moses.

Dudley had the same misgivings about *Wholly Moses!* (which he considered absurd) that he had originally felt over *Foul Play*. In the latter he had ignored his instincts and allowed himself to be talked into the role and ultimately it had led to great acclaim.

Filming took place in Death Valley, the arid desert beyond Los Angeles. In the sweltering heat, there were, inevitably, moments of jollity, mainly between Dudley and director Gary Weis and between Dudley and Laraine, who shared a similar humour and background. Both had been among the first of a new breed of performers to write their own comedy material. Laraine had been one of the original cast members on *Saturday Night Live,* and had met Dudley briefly when he and Peter Cook had appeared on the show two years earlier.

She found him adorable and sexy. 'I was very attracted to him, and we dated for about a second. We had a common language, and we laughed our guts out. Dudley and Jimmy Coco were very funny together, too, and when Jimmy wasn't around, Dudley and I often went off and played stupid word games that kept us in stitches. We spent a lot of time waiting and laughing.'

Ultimately, everything bad that could happen to a film happened to *Wholly Moses!* It was a creative disaster. When the film was released the following June, it was to abysmal reviews, although Dudley emerged reasonably unscathed. 'Its only redeeming feature,' wrote Gene Siskel in the *Chicago Tribune*, 'is the comic pacing of Dudley Moore,' while *Variety* claimed, 'a couple of okay slapstick moments remind us how funny Moore can be'.

Dudley had spent so many of his early years dreaming of fame, fortune and beautiful women. Now he had them all. And he was finding that American fame brought with it a different reaction from the public. In Britain, people treated celebrities with dignity: they looked, but tended not to stare and rarely approached. Now people were stopping him wherever he went. His supermarket trips, in the past fairly swift, became longer as people congregated around him while he pushed his shopping trolley down the aisles; he seldom escaped from the dry-cleaners now without signing a few autographs; and in restaurants dinner was constantly interrupted by visits from other diners wanting to shake his hand.

The pint-sized comedian was up there with the Hollywood elite. He was invited to Hollywood A-list parties and exclusive screenings. Cary Grant was his neighbour at one of these gatherings, Gene Kelly at another. He found it all very exhilarating, and this was reflected in his letters home.

His former music master and friend, Peter Cork, recalls that he and Dudley years earlier had seen a film starring Leslie Caron.

'When he got to Hollywood, he had a date with her, and he wrote and told me about it. It was extraordinary. He also said in his letter how Alice Faye had come up and spoken with him. I think he was very astonished by everything that was happening.'

Occasionally, Dudley left messages on my answering machine. He spoke to it in a stream of consciousness as if having a conversation with a live voice, often punctuated with bursts of laughter. He had no concept of time and I once clocked a message at ten minutes long.

> **DUDLEY (phone message):** I meant to tell you when I saw you but I forgot – I thought you might be interested to know for the story you're doing that I have a strong desire to sing, which I used to do a lot as a kid in class from the time I was six till I was twenty-two. Then I dropped it and I miss it a lot. I used to sing in the choir at church, too. Maybe that's something I could start doing again. I'm not sure how but I feel very strongly about resurrecting it. I miss it a great deal. Anyway, this is something I wanted to tell you in case you want to use it in the story you're writing. Unless you've already written it of course . . . in which case I'm too late! Ha ha!

Early in 1980 Dudley flew to Europe to promote *10* to the European press. It was a whirlwind tour that took him to Paris, Stockholm (where he ate the only mooseburger of his life), Brussels and finally London. There, he was put up royally in Claridge's and once he'd finished with the European press he spent the next few days distributing presents to his mother and sister Barbara and her family, and catching up with Suzy Kendall, Peter Cook and his trio members Peter Morgan and Chris Karan.

A week later he flew back to Los Angeles, and less than three hours after the plane touched down he was sitting among a gaggle of Hollywood stars at the Golden Globe Awards, far from the Dagenham home he had just left. His jet lag did not for a moment spoil his pleasure at being considered one of the Hollywood in-crowd. Nor was he too disappointed when his Golden Globe nomination for *10* failed to convert into a win – the nomination itself had been enough to thrill him.

By this time, *10* had already made $50 million in America on a $5 million budget. Dudley had been paid a flat $100,000, but from now on he would always also receive a percentage of the profits from his films. It was all a little bewildering, as he admitted to me at the time.

> **DUDLEY:** I don't know what I'll do with all this money. You can say it's very silly and in many ways it is. But there you go. That's the system here. I don't know what I'll do with it all. It'll make me more mobile but I'm pretty mobile anyway. I don't know if I'll buy another house somewhere, though I'm very happy in this one. I'm very content with the piano and the books and the dogs and some food to eat. I don't really need very much.

It was now that Dudley read the script that had him cackling with laughter as he turned the pages. The script was *Arthur*. His agent, Lou Pitt, recalled Dudley being in raptures over it. 'He called me when he reached page seven and said, "This is fantastic!" He called me on page fourteen and said, "I love it!" and he called at page sixty and said, "I've just got to do this! Who do I have to sleep with?"'

At the end of April 1980 Ada Moore received a letter from Dudley. He told her he expected to start *Arthur* a few weeks later in New York and was searching for an apartment there, large enough for his son and his nanny to stay with him during the filming. 'Patrick can come and visit me on the set and see me at work, and I'm looking forward to really getting to know him during that period.'

Arthur, he told her, was the funniest script he'd ever read, and he couldn't wait to start filming. 'John Gielgud has been cast and I'm very pleased about that,' he added, 'but we're still looking for a lead girl. They've looked already at about 200 and nobody seems to fit the bill completely.'

As it happened, Liza Minnelli had originally been offered the role, but had twice turned it down because she felt she wouldn't spark with the other two actors who had been touted for the lead. Now the producers approached her again, without much hope that she would change her mind. But she did change it, and instantly. There was no way she could resist working with Dudley, whose humour she had long appreciated.

Before the cameras began rolling on *Arthur*, Dudley flew to Cannes where he was royally feted by the press, then on to London and his mother's traditional roast lamb lunch in Dagenham. He had inherited from her a careful attitude towards money. He was not a big spender, had invested wisely, and was now fairly wealthy. He worried about Ada Moore living alone, and wanted her to enjoy some luxuries. Since his father's death, he had been sending her a few hundred pounds every week but she refused to spend it, saying she didn't need luxuries and, besides, if she had any, someone would probably try to steal them. She may have been anxious that his success would not last, that one day she might again have to provide for her son. 'No, I'm not spending that, dear – you might need that for a rainy day,' she told Dudley every time he suggested she buy something. Much later, Dudley would discover she had saved over £8,000 for his son, Patrick.

DUDLEY: She was absolutely delighted that I had got to a point where I could support myself. And you can understand it because my dad did a mail-order electricity

> course in Scotland, and he'd had a real hard time dragging himself to a point where he could have a job. He got a job finally with Stratford Railway and all he did was electrify coaches. He was with those people for fifty years. They gave him a watch when he retired which I've still got. So you can understand why my mother was relieved that I was able to make money myself.

In the first week of June 1980, filming began on *Arthur*.

CHAPTER 16

Arthur

1980

What makes a movie so unforgettable that it stands out from thousands of others and becomes the one with which an actor is most associated for the rest of his life? For Dudley, such a movie was *Arthur*. It was the film that would define him and forever inscribe him in the annals of film history.

A fabulously spoiled and rich drunk, Arthur Bach was a happy, fun-loving millionaire with a cackling laugh that will not rest; a man with no desire to grow up, who liked to play with toy trains and surround himself with childish amusements. His wastrel activities are aided by his grudging butler Hobson (John Gielgud), whose affection is tempered with caustic contempt. But Arthur faces an awful dilemma: either marry the local dreary deb down the road (Jill Eikenberry) or have his $750 million fortune cut off. He agrees to do the right thing (marry), but then falls in love with a shoplifter, Linda (Liza Minnelli). Even Peter Pan has integrity, so Arthur reluctantly returns to his fiancée. But he has not counted on the intervention of Hobson, who unknown to Arthur is dying and wants to see his employer happy in love before he departs from this world. Ultimately, Arthur renounces his inheritance and prepares to march off, penniless, into the sunset with Linda but, as befits any perfect fairy tale, the matriarch of his family finally relents and grants him his inheritance.

> **DUDLEY:** The dialogue is what made me want to do Arthur. I thought it was wonderful. But it almost ran into a snag. I had a meeting in the Polo Lounge with Steve Gordon, the writer-director, and he said, 'Can you do it in American?' I said there was no way I could do it in an American accent because it would encroach upon my performance. Luckily, thank goodness, he left it at that and never mentioned it again.

Dudley was in raptures over the role. He was drawn to Arthur's desire to enjoy himself to the fullest. And to laugh constantly. 'Sometimes I just think funny things,' Arthur tells a bewildered hooker after bursting into laughter for no apparent reason. To Dudley, Arthur was a nice, rather lonely man even though he was outrageously smashed a lot of the time. Dudley played him for real. He did not really think of Arthur as an alcoholic; more as a person with a tremendous penchant for enjoying life, who did things to excess and wanted everyone else to have a good time too.

Dudley had always been fascinated by stage drunks. Once, during a performance with Vic Lewis's orchestra in 1959, he had staggered on stage pretending to be drunk and managed to maintain the act the entire time he was playing.

Leslie Bricusse, who had known Dudley since the sixties in London, recalled a night early in their friendship when he first saw Dudley's alcoholic emerge. Bricusse had been dining with the actor Laurence Harvey at the Guinea restaurant off Berkeley Square, while across the room Bryan Forbes and his wife Nanette Newman were dining with Princess Margaret. 'Dudley came in and joined us, and as we were leaving we stopped at the Forbes's table. Dudley could do a marvellous drunk, and he turned to Princess Margaret and said, "Goo' eve'ing, Yer Royal Highnessh. I shu'pose a blow job is out of the queshtion?" It was hysterical!'

Dudley was delighted at the prospect of working with Liza Minnelli. Liza, the daughter of Judy Garland, had grown up around great American comics from Oscar Levant to Milton Berle. She had always been funny, but nobody had really known it. Certainly not Steve Gordon. At the first run-through of the script, he turned to her in surprise. 'You're really funny!' he praised. 'No shit!' retorted Dudley, who had always loved Liza's humour.

> **DUDLEY:** Liza was terrific. She's a wonderful comedienne and she learned a lot of it from her mother. She was wonderful to work with. She always is and always will be. I remember following her and Peter Sellers home once in London. They were in the back of a cab. I met her when she was engaged to Sellers. I was still driving my mini then. And I followed them to Peter's flat in Park Lane or somewhere in Mayfair. So I already knew her a bit when we came to do *Arthur*.

Liza adored Dudley. Seldom had she met anyone who made her feel so understood. 'He had this incredible gift for making one feel important as a person – important for what's inside. He responded to the person I was underneath in a way that no one else had done. He made me feel very special, and I loved him for that.'

They were an excellent team. Dudley was at his comic peak and, with him, Liza was funny too. 'We went together so well,' she affirmed. 'We had the same kind of humoristic vision and travelled the same way in our heads. We'd almost feel guilty about it, because all someone had to do was say, "Nice morning, eh?" and we'd look at each other and for some reason we'd get hysterical! We could barely get through anything without breaking up laughing!'

The opportunity to work with John Gielgud gave Dudley

particular pleasure. There was tremendous respect and humour between the two, and Liza could see they derived enormous enjoyment from being together in spite of their different personalities. Whereas Gielgud was quite reserved and introverted, Dudley was all over the place, playing the piano and enjoying what he was doing.

> **DUDLEY:** I tried to be Rabelaisian with him as much as possible, trying to gee him up and get him going. I knew he didn't want to be called Sir John. He wanted to be called Johnny. But nobody could bring themselves to call him Johnny because he sounded so swish. So there I was trying to be hearty as hell with him!

Liza Minnelli also grew very attached to Gielgud. 'He hated to be called Sir John by anyone he liked or had known a long time. So I called him Uncle Johnny all the time, and he got a great laugh out of that. He was very funny,' she recalled fondly, 'and had a huge sense of humour, but he was never quite sure he was being funny. His lines were very raunchy, and to hear them spoken in that brilliant accent was magic. I just cracked up when he said to Arthur, "Perhaps you'd like me to come in there and wash your dick for you, you little shit?" It was wonderful, but he kept turning to me and Dudley and asking, "Was that funny?" He was never sure.'

A shy, quiet, self-effacing man, Gielgud enjoyed one of the best film experiences of his entire career. It was particularly ironic since he, like Liza, had initially twice turned down the script. 'I thought it was rather smutty and a vulgar little film so I refused it,' he admitted to me. 'But each time they asked me, they put up my salary twice, and in the end I decided to do it.'

Although their acting backgrounds were entirely different, the veteran actor responded ebulliently to Dudley's energy and humour and was impressed with his spontaneity. 'He was awfully clever because he improvised quite a lot,' Gielgud remembered. 'We used to rehearse all the time, but each time we did it, Dudley would throw in other little jokes and gags. I loved his humour and his sense of invention, of being able to go into a scene and decorate it with little touches of his own. He kept very correctly to the script most of the time, but one always thought he might suddenly come out with something unexpected. He was wonderful and very funny as Arthur, but I wasn't surprised by that, because I'd always admired him ever since *Beyond the Fringe*.'

Working on *Arthur* was like being part of a close, happy family for five months. Sometimes, when filming ended early, Dudley and Liza went off for supper together. They spent hours talking and laughing, and formed a tight bond that endured for years.

Occasionally Susan Anton joined him in New York and John Gielgud was always amused to see them together. 'She was a very nice girl and very, very tall, which used to make me laugh. I remember watching them walk off the set together. He'd have his arm around her waist while she towered way above him and they'd stroll off into the moonlight. It was charming and funny.'

During the hot New York summer, Dudley spent a lot of time with violinist Robert Mann, who lived just off Central Park. Mann was renowned for his musical evenings when the cream of the classical music world congregated in his living room to give impromptu concerts. Dudley loved being part of those salons, although he was nervous at playing the piano in such elite company.

One evening Mann was playing chamber music with violinist Itzhak Perlman and members of a string quartet. He suggested to Perlman that he and Dudley play together. 'What can he play? He just plays jokes on the piano,' answered Perlman, familiar with Dudley's notorious parodies. Mann thought about it for a second then suggested Chausson's *Concerto in D Major* for violin, piano and string quartet.

The piece was a particularly long and tricky one, and pianists had been known to omit some of the notes even when recording it. Dudley, who had never seen the music before, studied it for five minutes then said he'd try it. 'I could see Perlman smirking like mad,' grinned Mann, 'while the others looked on very sceptically.'

What Robert Mann knew, but the others did not, was that Dudley had an extraordinary ability to sight-read. He had always been astounded by this exceptional facet of his friend's talent and to his immense delight Dudley read and played almost every note in the concerto. 'I had a wonderful time enjoying the open mouths of all the musicians! Itzhak was dumbfounded – he couldn't believe anyone could read like that! They all burst into applause when he'd finished.'

Meanwhile Liza Minnelli was beginning to sense an edge to Dudley. 'I could see the artistic melancholy of the musician in his eyes. It's a horrendous strain to be funny for eight hours every day then wait for the next scene and then come back and be funny again. In between takes there was nothing to do, and I could see the musician in him was suffering.'

She arranged for a piano to be installed in Dudley's dressing room at the Astoria studio. 'It was wonderful to hear his music,' she savoured. 'I would hear these beautiful, melancholy and incredibly tender interpretations of songs coming through the walls. Sometimes he'd play pieces he'd written, and other times I'd hear him play something absolutely silly. In a funny way I could judge when to go in and out of his dressing room by what he was playing.'

As *Arthur* continued filming in a hot and very muggy New York, often Dudley played the piano while Liza sat beside him belting out song after song in her unmistakable voice. 'There's a point in any film where you can't remember the beginning and you can't see the end. We were just at that point, and Dudley's music helped get us through those frustrating times.'

In the film, Arthur has Hobson to rely on for his food. In real life Dudley relied on himself. 'He had a stove in his dressing room,' laughed John Gielgud, 'and he used to cook lunch for himself every day. I don't know if that was because he didn't trust the studio catering!'

It was more likely because it was the only way he could be sure of getting his favourite fish every day, and cooked the way he liked it. It was not unusual to see Dudley walking around with a couple of frozen trout that he would place on a radiator to thaw and then cook slowly.

Gielgud was sorry when the filming of *Arthur* came to an end. 'I loved working with Dudley enormously. Both he and Liza were very sweet to me, and enormously professional and proficient. They were both so charming to me, because they must have seen what a good part I had and it was really their film. They were a delightful pair, and I felt very much at ease with them.'

His only disappointment was that he hadn't spent more time with Dudley. 'It was a great pity we didn't do anything together off the set,' he said wistfully, 'but then we were all working so hard. I can't say how much I loved being around him.'

Soon after filming ended on *Arthur,* Blake Edwards, who had become Dudley's close friend since their brilliant collaboration on *10*, came up with a suggestion that he take over the role of Inspector Clouseau in *The Romance of the Pink Panther*. After a parting of their ways, Blake had given the rights to Peter Sellers to make the film on his own, but when Sellers died of a heart attack in 1980, Blake decided to go ahead with the movie himself.

Dudley was keen to work again with Blake but had strong reservations about stepping into Sellers's shoes. He had decided by now that he didn't want to go on playing the kind of bumbling characters with which he'd been identified earlier, and Clouseau epitomised those roles. Accents, apart from regional British ones, had never been his forte, although in all likelihood Blake would have tailored the role to suit Dudley. More than that was the greater concern that he would be criticised for taking over from Sellers, and he was sure the inevitable comparisons would not work in his favour.

Wholly Moses!, which had opened to such unfavourable reviews in America just a few weeks after Dudley began filming *Arthur*, was about to be released in Britain, and in October 1980 Dudley flew to London to promote the film.

While there, he visited Magdalen College where his Oxford music tutor, Bernard Rose, was conducting the choir in the chapel. Dr Rose persuaded Dudley to go into the organ loft, where he played some of Bach's most intricate organ music. His former master was astounded. 'Even though he hadn't played those pieces for about twenty years, Dudley played them awfully well. And having done that, he then went down to the antechapel, where there was a grand piano, and played the fool. It was amazing! He extemporised brilliantly.'

Today the reminder of Dudley's Oxford sojourn is emblazoned with his name taped onto an organ stop in Magdalen Chapel.

In London, Dudley reunited with Peter Cook to film three television commercials as Pete and Dud for Barclays Bank. Fifteen years on, the memorable characters they had introduced in *Not Only . . . But Also* were still much beloved in the British public's minds.

The film they had made of their last *Derek and Clive* session, titled *Derek and Clive Get the Horn*, had now been presented to the British Board of Film Censors. In November 1980, censor James Ferman wrote to the film company, informing them of the difficulty facing the board. As he observed:

> The point of this comic exercise is to be as offensive as possible and to break every taboo the performers can think of, however outrageous the results. Cutting would

> be pointless although we believe that the sequence about Jesus Christ and the sexuality of the lower half of his body is probably blasphemous in the legal sense of the term. The offensive references to the Pope and the Holocaust are not, in our view, illegal, though they will certainly prove deeply offensive to some people . . . There is no member of the Board who feels this particular film should be granted a certificate for general distribution and we do not think that many local authorities would be happy to see this sort of thing playing in their own public cinemas.

It was, really, no less than anyone had expected, and it would be another eleven years before the film would become widely available to the public. Meanwhile, some copies were already floating around Los Angeles, and Dudley was happy to screen it for any of his friends who asked to see it. The first screening was hosted by Peter Cook's close friend, Brenda Vaccaro, and she threw one of her famous parties to mark the occasion. 'It was a triumphant success! Everyone came out for it – even members of the *Monty Python* troupe who were in town. Peter was staying with me then, and he was extremely proud of the film because it was an example of their exquisite brilliance at doing comedy together.'

As 1980 drew to a close, Dudley sent his mother a Christmas card. 'I wish,' he wrote wistfully, 'I could tell you more easily how I love you but an awkward gesture will have to do. I know you can understand.' He never knew what to call her – Mum, Mother or Mater – and in this card, which she kept until her death, he called her the lot.

In January 1981 Peter Cook landed the role of butler in an NBC comedy series, *The Two of Us*. He was excited about the Hollywood sitcom. Brenda Vaccaro noted his elation was compounded by the fact that he had been off alcohol for twenty-two months.

'Peter had been a bit sad that his career wasn't taking off, and he felt a strong competitive strain with Dudley. He very much wanted to work here and be successful, even though he always said he didn't, and now he was getting his shot at it. He was in the best shape ever and Dudley was so happy and proud to see him in such great condition, ready to go to work and prospering. He was there with him all the way and he couldn't have been a more supportive friend.'

For several years Robert Mann had been urging Dudley to perform classical music in public, but Dudley had always refused the challenge, convinced he was not of the calibre for concert performance. Mann disagreed. He believed Dudley had the artistry. What he needed was more practice. 'He always improvised for fun but he never worked on passages.'

Mann's persistence paid off. Dudley capitulated at last to his friend's 'wet-noodling me to death', and practised in earnest with the violinist for an upcoming concert. Nevertheless, he remembered 'going backwards into the whole thing kicking and screaming'. He didn't feel comfortable and finally he broke down and cried, 'I'm just not good enough, can't you understand!'

Robert Mann believed otherwise and pushed Dudley mercilessly until suddenly it really did feel right after all.

Dudley had been in America for five years but had never performed at a public concert. His music meant so much to him that he had been afraid to expose it to judgement. True, he had ventured tentatively forward by playing jazz piano during talk-show appearances, but that was as far as it had gone.

Now he was ready to meet the challenge.

CHAPTER 17

Musical Rhapsodies

1981

Dudley had for a long time been keen to resume music professionally, but had lacked the confidence to try. While he was well known in Britain for his virtuosity at the piano, in America they were oblivious to this side of his talent.

He had met cellist Lynn Harrell at one of Robert Mann's musical evenings during the New York run of *Good Evening* in the 1970s and, like Mann, Harrell had been encouraging Dudley to perform in public. In the spring of 1981 he was in Los Angeles, performing for the Los Angeles Philharmonic's chamber music society, and he persuaded Dudley to join him in one of their concerts.

It was Dudley's unannounced classical debut in America, and his mastery at the piano as he accompanied Harrell and flautist James Walker in Weber's *Trio in G Minor* took the audience by complete surprise.

Dudley anticipated some snotty remarks and he got them from one local critic, who rated him a '6', but he was pleased with his first public American effort. So was Ernest Fleischman, the director of the Los Angeles Philharmonic.

Fleischman offered Dudley the opportunity to make his orchestral debut in the Philharmonic's upcoming sixtieth anniversary summer season at the outdoor Hollywood Bowl. He suggested a Gershwin evening, a tradition popular with local audiences. The fee would be $6,000 for each of two concerts – far less than the hundreds of thousands of dollars Dudley was now earning as an actor, but more rewarding in personal terms. Thrilled but nervous, Dudley accepted and embarked on a feverish daily practice regime on the Yamaha grand in his living room.

His passion for jazz, however, remained very high. He still owed his long-time friends Cleo Laine and John Dankworth a favour after he'd had to bow out of appearing with them at the London Palladium during the filming of *10*. He reunited with them now in a Hollywood studio and recorded a jazz album, *Smilin' Through*. Dankworth produced, while Cleo sang and Dudley played with a trio consisting of Ella Fitzgerald's second husband, Ray Brown, on bass and Nick Ceroli on drums.

One of the tracks, dating from his Oxford days, was 'Strictly for the Birds', on which Dudley also sang. His early Erroll Garner style re-emerged on this album, and it is interesting to note that Garner, like Dudley, had also been a small man (Garner gained a reputation for sitting on telephone books so that he was almost standing when he played).

Dudley had fun with Laine and Dankworth. They were good-hearted, patient and encouraging and in between the playing there was a great deal of clowning around. Although Dudley's musical taste was shifting back towards his classical roots, he still felt a tremendous jazz influence, especially now as he played alongside Cleo and Ray Brown, one of the great jazz bass players, a former member of Oscar Peterson's trio.

DUDLEY: Ray Brown was a wonderful bass player and I loved working with him and Nick Ceroli who made up

> my trio when we recorded the album. I love Erroll Garner and might play a bit like him, but I know my limitations in the sense that if I was talking to a Garnerphile there are certain things I can't do. I can't play beyond a certain speed, I get too excited and too tense. It was great to work with Cleo and John again. Cleo was very good-hearted and patient, so was John, and very encouraging so it was a really nice experience. And funny! There was a lot of clowning around!

It was a successful reunion and a triumphant return to jazz. As famed jazz critic Leonard Feather wrote in the *Los Angeles Times*: 'That Mr Moore has kept up his piano chops is engagingly illustrated here.'

With Dudley flying to different cities where Susan Anton was performing, Ruth, his secretary, often drove him to the airport in the black Jeep she'd been able to buy after Dudley had gifted her with the down payment for her birthday. Many times she suggested renting a limo, 'but he was just as happy having me take him in my Jeep or in his BMW. At the airport he'd go scurrying off, carrying his own bag, and I often watched him and thought, "Doesn't he realise how rich and famous he is?" He could easily have hired a limo and had someone carry his bag for him.'

Days away from *Arthur*'s release, Leslie Bricusse attended a screening in New York. 'I was sitting between Dudley and Liza and they were nervous as kittens. They didn't know for one second whether it was at all funny, while I sat there pissing myself for two hours. I told them it was one of the funniest movies I'd ever seen, but they just didn't know. Comedy is a very difficult thing to define, and neither of them thought it worked.'

Despite the extraordinary success it went on to enjoy, when *Arthur* opened it was to mixed reviews. In the opinion of the *New Yorker*, 'considering that Arthur is a very thin comic construct,

Moore does an amazing amount with the role'. Vincent Canby praised Dudley in the *New York Times*, regarding him 'if possible, more uninhibitedly comic than he was in *10*. His Arthur is an over-age waif and a consistently endearing show-off. His timing is magical!'

Dudley's performance in *Arthur* was so authentic that for the rest of his life he would have to thwart rumours about his own drinking. He always enjoyed a fine wine, but never drank to excess and he was not an alcoholic as the tabloids often proclaimed.

If the critical response was ambivalent, the public reception was in no doubt. From the moment *Arthur* hit the screens, it became a runaway success. Audiences had been starved of this kind of updated screwball comedy, and it became the surprise hit of the summer of 1981. In time it would join that exclusive club of movies to gross more than $100 million.

> **DUDLEY**: Arthur was a character that I loved immensely. In fact I expressed to Liza when we were doing *Arthur 2* that I would just like to play this character for the rest of my life. I said, 'It's ridiculous, it's pathetic but it's true – I would like to play a character who is like this for the rest of my life.' It fascinated me no end for some reason. I was very taken with him.

A week after the opening of *Arthur*, Dudley stepped on stage at the Hollywood Bowl to make his American orchestral debut with the Los Angeles Philharmonic. With Michael Tilson Thomas conducting, Dudley played *Rhapsody in Blue*, and was greeted with tumultuous applause and infinite surprise by the 20,000 people present, most of whom had no idea that Dudley was a musician. At the end of the concert, he rounded things off with a taste of jazz in a set of Gershwin tunes, Moore-style.

Susan Anton described the night as 'a total triumph – especially what he did with Ray Brown and Nick Ceroli. That's when he really comes to life, in the jazz.'

Dudley wrote to his mother a few days later, having already telephoned her with an account of the concert. She was proud of his success as an actor, but it was his classical music achievements that gave her the greatest pride and pleasure.

His performing fervour had now taken a hold. He was, at last, taking heed of Artur Schnabel's reference to 'playing with love and patience'. Dudley had always had the love but only now possessed the patience to break things down slowly and go over each piece, practising in a way he had never done before.

The transformation of Dudley Moore was complete. He had become an international movie star who, as the tabloids were fond of saying, had the unlikely distinction of being worth almost more per inch than any other star in Hollywood. It wasn't bad for a kid from Dagenham whose greatest wish as a youth was to have enough money to buy a bike. Now he could have the most expensive bike in the world if he wanted.

Back home, Ada Moore, now eighty-one, was feeling particularly nostalgic. She pulled out photos of herself as a young girl and studied old photo albums with Dudley. 'I don't know why you say you were unhappy as a child,' she told him. 'Look at this picture of you.' And she showed him one where he was smiling happily.

In October 1981, after suffering a series of strokes, Ada Francis Moore died. As a major Hollywood movie star, Dudley had all the acclamation he had always longed for, but he had now lost the woman who had done more than any other to shape his life, with all its ambition, fears and years of inner loneliness.

CHAPTER 18

Six Weeks

1981–82

Dudley's mother had been the most important influence in his life. The inheritance that Ada Moore bequeathed to her son came not with her death but during her lifetime. Unintentionally she left him with a multitude of emotions from which he would never be entirely free. His proclivity for isolation, fear of rejection and abandonment, a perpetual need for love – all stemmed from the turmoil of his childhood when he had thought himself to have been unloved. But his years of therapy, an understanding of his parents' true feelings towards him and the tremendous public acclamation he enjoyed had, if not eradicated them, at least helped to assuage the demons.

After his mother's funeral Dudley remained in London long enough to record for ITV a variety show, *An Audience with Dudley Moore*, with guests Lulu, Shirley Bassey, Tom Conti and Peter Cook. Then he returned to Los Angeles to shoot *Six Weeks*, the first dramatic film of his 22-year career as a performer.

Six Weeks was a moving story about the last weeks in the life of a dying girl, and Dudley had been looking forward to it immensely. It was the only time, other than *Arthur*, that he had called his agent after reading the script and told him he absolutely had to make the movie. Other people had also been keen to do the film. Nick Nolte and Audrey Hepburn were to have starred in it at one point and just before the script came to Dudley, Sylvester Stallone had been set to play the lead.

Tony Bill, a hot young director who had won considerable acclaim with his first feature, *My Bodyguard*, and who co-produced *The Sting* and *Taxi Driver*, was hired to direct the $9 million film. He was delighted by Dudley's passion for the project and excited at the idea of showing a serious side of the actor that audiences hadn't seen before.

In *Six Weeks*, Dudley played a married Congressional candidate, Patrick Dalton, who befriends thirteen-year-old ballet student Nicky Dreyfus (Katherine Healy), and subsequently her rich cosmetics tycoon mother Charlotte (Mary Tyler Moore). When he learns Nicky is dying of leukaemia yet is bent on helping to get him elected, he allows her to work on his campaign. Gradually they all fall in love. Patrick leaves his family and Nicky 'marries' him to her mother. When he discovers that in order to campaign for him she has sacrificed her greatest hope – to dance Clara in *The Nutcracker* at the Lincoln Center – he arranges for it to happen after all. That night, after achieving her dream, Nicky dies.

In a way, Dudley considered the theme similar to that of *Arthur*. Arthur had wanted to have a tremendous amount of fun every second, and *Six Weeks* also was about grabbing hold of life, enjoying the moment and realising one's dream. Despite its tragic conclusion, it was uplifting and filled with joy and humour. Dudley adored the story, and it would elicit some of his best and most natural work as an actor. He was drawn to its theme about the urgency of living and saw in its enthusiasm for life a message of optimism.

Mary Tyler Moore was America's sweetheart. She had risen

through television sitcoms, first with Dick Van Dyke and then with her own shows. Since her highly praised dramatic performance in Robert Redford's *Ordinary People*, she had read mediocre scripts for two years before being offered *Six Weeks*.

Mary was instantly drawn to her co-star with the same surname who also happened to share the same birthday as her father. 'He was hysterically funny. Off camera he was wondrously entertaining and bright. On camera he was a wonderfully talented dramatic actor. I wasn't surprised, but I was very impressed.'

Tony Bill was enthused by his two Moores. He was just the kind of director with whom Dudley liked to work. Bill believed in allowing his actors to get on with the job without interference, and yet he encouraged a collaborative effort and Dudley enjoyed the team spirit that existed on the film.

Any film set that Dudley worked on was guaranteed to be full of fun and laughter. But one thing he tended not to do was perform practical jokes. He felt it took massive advantage of people, and it reminded him of adverse things that had been done to him when he was a boy. There was one exception: Handi-Gas. Dudley had recently discovered this small rubber accordion fart machine, and he unleashed the new toy on his unsuspecting colleagues with irrepressible glee. Tony Bill collected so many takes of Dudley at play that he assembled an entire outtake reel in which the fart machine was the main star.

Dudley and Handi-Gas were inseparable. One night Dudley and Susan Anton went to the cinema to watch *Ordinary People* and sat in front of two old ladies who clearly had been expecting to see the comic Mary Tyler Moore of her TV sitcoms. 'She's not at all like Mary Richards!' one of the women yelled at the screen, whereupon, Susan recalled, 'Dudley let out the biggest fart you've ever heard! Those poor little women were so disgusted they got out of their seats and left the cinema!'

The tiny gadget was so popular that Dudley had the

manufacturers ship them to him by the carton, and he passed out dozens to the entire company. Mary Tyler Moore had some made in silver that she gave as farewell gifts to the cast and crew.

I became an unwitting target when I took my BBC television crew onto the set to interview Dudley and Mary for *Film 81*. The three of us were walking together across the stage when I suddenly heard a loud fart from Dudley next to me. Startled, I pretended not to hear. Then another fart even louder than the one before. Embarrassed, I tried to keep walking without pause. Until another fart – the loudest I had ever heard in my life, and I turned to look at Dudley. Both he and Mary had the widest grins on their faces. Mine was bright red – until Dudley held out his hand and showed me Handi-Gas sitting innocently in his palm.

Throughout the filming Dudley kept an electric piano in his trailer dressing room, and during breaks he practised for his next concert in New York a few months later. Filming every day meant he was having to get up at three every morning in order to practise.

With Peter Cook's television series, *The Two of Us,* scheduled to air, Dudley ensured he wouldn't miss it. He jotted a reminder in his diary and underlined it twice in thick ink. But when he watched the show he was disappointed that it failed to make full use of Cook's talents. The series was greeted with a less than rave reaction, which gave the British critics cause once more to examine Cook's career since his break-up with Dudley.

Late on New Year's Eve, Dudley flew with Susan to New York to prepare for his New York classical debut two days away, practising with Robert Mann on New Year's Day at his Manhattan apartment. It was reminiscent of all the times they had played there over the years. Those evenings, Dudley felt, had been 'glorious battlefields strewn with dismembered notes', although Mann's recollection was of many remarkable musical achievements. Then it had been for fun. Now it was for real.

If Dudley was nervous, he showed no sign of it the next night when he walked onto the stage of the Metropolitan Museum's Grace Rainey Rogers Auditorium. His New York debut was in front of the toughest musical audience in America but he was determined not to feel intimidated. This was, after all, what he most enjoyed doing – playing music. 'Just remember you enjoy it,' he reassured himself as he took his seat at the huge Bösendorfer grand piano. With him were Robert Mann on violin, Stanley Drucker on clarinet and Joel Krosnick on cello.

They played Bach, Mozart, Bartok and Delius, and at the end of the evening the audience let Dudley know he had not embarrassed himself. Their long applause acclaimed a highly proficient pianist. The *New York Times* wrote the next day, 'He neither advanced the cause of music nor caused himself one moment of disgrace,' and the tough *Washington Post* conceded, 'He played well if not exuberantly.'

Susan Anton was thrilled and proud. She saw in Dudley an elation that he had taken on the task and accomplished it. 'Dudley always lived in fear of other people's opinions, and I think that always dictated too much to him. He didn't allow himself to fully enjoy anything, because he was always waiting for the arrows through the heart. Especially with his music. It's through his music that you really see and feel Dudley's soul. It comes right out of his fingertips onto the keyboard.'

Dudley had now achieved a goal that he had never believed he could reach. Early in his twenties he had thought he would always be too nervous and technically inadequate ever to become a concert musician. Now he knew he'd been wrong.

Music these days was uppermost in his mind and back in Los Angeles the following night he embarked on composing the score for *Six Weeks*, a task which would take him through much of the summer of 1982. Not counting *The Hound of the Baskervilles*, which he had mainly improvised in 1977, he had not scored a film since *Staircase*, thirteen years earlier.

Writing the *Six Weeks* music did not come easily; it evoked emotional memories of his childhood and the mother he had so recently lost. It was at the piano that he felt most in touch with his emotions. He was deeply moved by what he was composing and felt for one of the rare times in his life that he was doing a good job, though getting it out was a combination of 'absolute bliss and absolute hell'. The music he wrote could never be a complete release for his emotions, Dudley said, it could never fully illuminate his huge darkroom of memories. But it must have helped. The score he ultimately produced was haunting and exquisite and quite simply the best musical work he would ever create.

Six Weeks director Tony Bill believed Dudley rose to extraordinary heights and excelled himself. 'But I think he burned himself out on it. He put so much into it that he never wrote another score and I don't think he ever felt that passionately again about anything else.'

When the Academy Award nominations were announced in February 1982, Dudley was stunned to find himself nominated for his work in *Arthur*. Sir John Gielgud was nominated, for Best Supporting Actor, as was Burt Bacharach's score for the film. Liza Minnelli, to Dudley's great disappointment, was not.

But Liza was not too dispirited. 'I knew I did a good job and in a funny kind of way that was enough. I also knew it was Dudley's time. It hurt my feelings, but it was fine because I knew I'd done such good work. And I was so proud of Dudley and John.'

Dudley had always found himself responding to specific emotions in a film script, as he did with his music. He was attracted to joy, tenderness, compassion and humour, and saw sadness and humour as interlaced. He had learned that comedy was simply another side of drama and whenever he had been faced with great pain his tendency had usually been to laugh. He was drawn towards characters who wanted to enjoy themselves no matter what the circumstances against them, and to those who seemed to be breaking out of their mould – perhaps because he himself had spent a lifetime trying to break free of the restraints and expectations that society had put on him through class and physical appearance.

His next movie encompassed all that he found most appealing.

Early in 1982, Dudley began work on *Lovesick,* written and directed by Marshall Brickman, who had been Woody Allen's collaborator on several films. Dudley played a psychiatrist who fantasises over a patient (Elizabeth McGovern) and experiences ghostly visits from Sigmund Freud (Alec Guinness). The cast was rounded out by John Huston as his former teacher.

In Marshall Brickman's eyes, Dudley was a romantic leading man in the vein of Marcello Mastroianni, Jean-Paul Belmondo and Cary Grant, a performing animal who loved to give people pleasure through laughter or music. 'Very different from Woody Allen, who always anguished when he had to perform.'

Dudley had been particularly excited at the prospect of working with Sir Alec Guinness. Ever since he'd seen his classic first film, *Great Expectations*, he had admired the venerable actor. He had even fantasised about him 'as the brother I'd never had'. But to his disappointment Guinness spent most of his time in between scenes alone in his trailer.

Lovesick was a typical Dudley Moore set, full of humour and music. Brickman, who likened directing a movie to a bad baseball game – 'with a lot of waiting around and then a bit of action and then more waiting' – admired Dudley's attitude. 'He understood how everybody's best work occurs in an atmosphere of ease and fun, and he always went about creating that mood on the set.'

It was his humour – sometimes very scatological – that took young Elizabeth McGovern by surprise. 'His Handi-Gas gadget was impossible, and people on the set loved it that here was this hottest movie star in America who could be so crude! It just warmed us all up.'

Brickman, whose job it was to ensure order in the chaos, was equally amused by Dudley's running gag. 'In the middle of intense emotional love scenes there'd be this sound of breaking wind and we'd have to stop the camera. He'd apologise profusely, then do it again. And each time he said, "I'm sorry, I promise I won't do it this time." And it just got funnier and funnier. It was his way of being an irrepressible imp and loosening everybody. He couldn't help himself. He was five years old.'

In March 1982 Dudley attended the Academy Awards as a Best Actor nominee for *Arthur* and performed on stage with Liza Minnelli. He had been somewhat embarrassed to be nominated with such distinguished veterans as Henry Fonda, Burt Lancaster, Warren Beatty and Paul Newman, all of whom had been previously nominated, and he was relieved to lose to Henry Fonda, who had given a poignant performance with daughter Jane in *On Golden Pond*.

> **DUDLEY:** Thank God I lost to Henry Fonda. It was the first time he'd won. And he died shortly after that. I'd have felt terrible if I'd won, though nobody believed me, of course. Maybe they feel so very strongly about winning Oscars that they can't believe someone wouldn't want it. I don't know. Fonda was this great screen legend. If it had been a newcomer maybe I'd have been disappointed. But Fonda! It would have taken away enormously from any joy.

Dudley did take an Oscar home that night, but it wasn't his own. John Gielgud had asked him, in the event of his winning Best Supporting Actor, to accept on his behalf, and carrying out this task gave Dudley immense pleasure. He was thrilled that Gielgud's performance had been recognised by his peers.

Dudley was now one of the most popular Englishmen in the world. If in his heart he was short, in Hollywood he stood tall. The earlier wave of British expatriates known as the Hollywood Raj generation of actors such as Ronald Colman, Douglas Fairbanks and Basil Rathbone had now been replaced with a newer, younger British colony that included Michael Caine, Joan and Jackie Collins, Jacqueline Bisset, Leslie Bricusse, Jane Seymour, Malcolm McDowell and Michael York. Dudley was friendly with them all.

Most Sundays, Leslie Bricusse and Michael Caine alternated in throwing open-house lunch for any Brits in town. Dudley was a welcome visitor and Bricusse noticed that the women flocked around him. 'He was a phenomenal personality with a blasting humour and totally adorable and irresistible. He always played the piano, of course – usually jazz – and everyone loved that. It's what made Dudley tall.' Bricusse captured these occasions on tape, and somewhere is a recording of Dudley playing piano duets with André Previn, each improvising his impressions of various jazz players, Dudley as Erroll Garner and Previn as Oscar Peterson.

Dudley was now happily ensconced in his Marina home. He'd been living there for several years and felt comfortably settled. It was his house, he told me in the summer of 1982, that was a key reason for his living in California.

DUDLEY: I've invested a lot of money in my house so I'm not going to move. It's almost as simple as that. If I went back to England and I was in a house that I'd done up, I bet I'd stay. If I suddenly went out the door and found myself in Hampstead High Street I'd probably be fine. Because it doesn't actually matter where I am as long as it's some sort of centre of activity in the acting area or musical area, culturally some sort of centre. I like the weather here and I like being on the beach. The main thing is that I have friends here but then wherever I live I accumulate friends. It's not the town that attracts me, though I don't know that I'd live in too many other places apart from New York, London

> and maybe Sydney, which I love. It's a very comfortable life here. And I enjoy my house. But also it's a place for me to work. That's the other enjoyable side of being here. There's a lot of work around and I like to be in a place where I can work. I may elect not to but I know it's there if I want to.

What he next wanted to do was *Romantic Comedy*, an adaptation of Bernard Slade's Broadway play, which teamed him with Mary Steenburgen as the writing partner of his boorish playwright who doesn't realise he's in love with her or that she loves him. Their timing is a mess: when he's married, she's not, and when he's not married, she is (an allusion to a Hemingway quote about his own emotions towards Marlene Dietrich).

Director Arthur Hiller brought with him considerable acclaim for his earlier films *Love Story, The Out-of-Towners* and *Silver Streak* (written by Colin Higgins, who had directed *Foul Play)*. They were an impressive trio of talent and Dudley enjoyed filming the comedy, which was more verbally than visually witty – something that always appealed to him.

Dudley and Mary, then married to Malcolm McDowell, established an instant rapport that evolved into a deep friendship; Mary's propensity for collapsing into uncontrollable giggles encouraged Dudley's playful nature. She found him riotously funny, admitting it 'was like unleashed hysteria to be around him'.

Dudley revelled in making Mary laugh and ruin takes. When she had to film one particular close-up and look romantically at Dudley, who was standing behind the camera, she recalled him staring downwards, 'and stupidly I looked down to see what he was staring at; he had unzipped his pants and had one of those erasers with a brush on the end poking out erect from his trousers. Of course, I completely collapsed!'

At the same time as filming *Romantic Comedy*, Dudley was also preparing to record the *Six Weeks* score. As soon as he finished shooting a scene, he would dash outside the soundstage where a car was waiting to whisk him across to a dubbing theatre on the other side of the MGM studio.

When it came time to record the score, he played the piano and shared conducting chores. He even managed to add new bars of music and write the instrumental parts on the spot. Music editor Else Blangsted, who became a lifelong friend from then on, recalled the orchestra being so moved by his score that, in an unprecedented act, they presented Dudley with four dozen red roses on the final day.

When Peter Cook's series *The Two of Us* was cancelled, Peter felt obliged publicly to deny charges of failure in his own career in the wake of Dudley's superstardom. 'My career is not a flop,' he told reporters, 'and I'm not jealous of Dudley. I never wanted to be a big star. Perhaps if I had been born with a club foot and a height problem I might have been as desperate as Dudley to become a star in order to prove myself. That's all he ever wanted. I don't have the same need to prove myself.'

Dudley, as usual, shrugged off Cook's remarks and professed not to be affected by them. Cook always claimed never to have meant any of his disparaging comments to be anything other than jest, but he must have been remarkably insensitive not to have recognised the hurt he was doling out.

At Christmas, *Six Weeks* was released. And it resulted in the most painful setback that Dudley had suffered since moving to America.

During public previews earlier in the year, *Six Weeks* had received an amazing reaction, notching up the second-highest audience response since *Jaws*. Universal were so excited about the reaction that they decided to make the film their Christmas movie. It was an appalling mistake.

Dudley's publicist, Paul Bloch, knew the timing spelled disaster. 'You can't bring out a film at Christmas about a young girl dying.

People want to rejoice during that season, not cry, and they rejected the film entirely – which was sad, because it was a very poignant movie and Dudley's music was phenomenal.'

Dudley had put more of himself into this role than in any previous film. It was the richest acting experience he had ever achieved, and he gave some of his best work as an actor. When the film failed to ignite the box office, it left him feeling angry and confused by the adverse reaction. And he was devastated that his evocative score into which he'd poured his heart and soul was overlooked.

Jazz broadcaster and trombonist Michael Pointon found the score deeply moving. 'You can sense the pensively troubled and heartfelt approach taken by Dudley, again echoing his affinity with Oscar Peterson's sensitive touch. With its moving, angst-filled undercurrents it evolves virtually into the form of an elegy. This mature score shows how much Dudley's talent had developed in a comparatively few years; it indicates that even if he'd never been a performer his special talents might have taken him more in this direction.'

When *Lovesick* opened early in 1983, the critics were infinitely kinder than they had been with *Six Weeks*, but it was another film that would end up taking a nosedive at the box office.

'Forget *Six Weeks*,' urged the *New York Times*. 'Dudley Moore, incomparable in *10* and *Arthur*, is back doing what he does best.' And he really was. He was funny and sensitive simultaneously. *Time* magazine, while noting that some of the script wandered into 'contrived predictability', declared, 'Moore gives a subtle, warm, finely tuned performance and Elizabeth McGovern shows enormous promise. The two of them form an odd combination but it works.' This review gave so much pleasure to Dudley at a time when he was desperate for reaffirmation that he scribbled in his diary, '*Time* liked *Lovesick*!!'

In spite of a lack of widespread appeal for his latest movies,

Dudley emerged third in a national popularity poll of actors, behind Burt Reynolds and Clint Eastwood. Whereas those two men were seen as strong and macho, in Dudley people saw a vulnerability and sensitivity that was immensely endearing. Just as he had redefined the term 'sex symbol', so he had established new parameters for the role of the traditional hero.

Dudley was forty-seven, yet age had not tarnished his endearingly boyish looks, and the press continued to compare him to lovable, huggable animals like teddy bears and puppies.

Success had not changed his unassuming manner. He still drove himself to work in his orange BMW or the white Bentley with its baby-blue leather seats. At home he answered his own phone, made many of his own appointments, and cooked his own meals.

Several months earlier, while he was still riding high on the success of *Arthur*, Lou Pitt had secured for Dudley a hefty fee of $2.5 million for a comedy remake of Preston Sturges's classic 1948 thriller *Unfaithfully Yours*. It was a hundred times more than he had received for *Foul Play*, his first American film, and was solid validation that, despite the failure of *Six Weeks*, he was still regarded as a fully fledged, multimillion-dollar Hollywood star.

CHAPTER 19

Stardom and Doubts

1983–85

In January 1983 Dudley began filming *Unfaithfully Yours*, now transformed into a comedy in which an obsessed orchestra conductor (Dudley) mistakenly believes his young wife (Nastassja Kinski) is having an affair with his violinist friend (Armand Assante) and plots to kill her.

Howard Zieff, director of the hugely successful *Private Benjamin*, had several years earlier persuaded 20th Century Fox, who owned the rights to the original classic movie, to let him make this new version. He had originally wanted Peter Sellers to assume the role of the jealous conductor and had planned to use Sellers's talent for disguise by making him Italian. When Sellers died, Zieff looked elsewhere.

Who else to consider, but the actor who so often seemed to be following in Sellers's footsteps? It was interesting that Dudley should be considered for so many roles that Sellers had either declined or been unable to accept, especially since he lacked two of Sellers's main attributes – he was not particularly good at accents unless they were British, and nor were disguises a particular forte. What he had in common with Sellers, though, was an extraordinary talent for physical humour. Few contemporary comedy actors were able to use their entire body as effectively as Dudley.

Peter Bellwood had observed the breadth of Dudley's comedy since the early days of *Beyond The Fringe*. In his view, Dudley's name belonged alongside those of cinema's legendary comedy icons. 'He's the greatest physical comedian who ever came down the pike, probably since Chaplin or Keaton, and at his optimum he's as brilliant as those guys.'

Meeting 22-year-old Nastassja Kinski for the first time, Dudley was struck by her likeness to the young Ingrid Bergman. She was a beautiful girl with a vulnerable, doe-like quality. Roman Polanski's *Tess* had made her a hot star, but she was very self-critical with a huge lack of confidence that brought out Dudley's nurturing side.

Nastassja was greatly intimidated at playing comedy for the first time, but Dudley helped her to relax and enjoy what she was doing. 'He was like the sun coming up. From the very first day, which was very hard for me, he taught me to breathe in the situation and feed from him. He was so helpful and generous.

'I'd never seen anybody so flexible and light in what they did. The great art is to float above the work, and Dudley could do that. He could change in an instant. He'd walk off and play the most wonderful piece of music, and then we'd do a take and he'd be back and ready. And he could do ten different things in a scene while most actors needed to prepare for one.'

Dudley liked Howard Zieff, whom he described as a teddy bear. He was a director who told his actors what he wanted and then left them to come up with it, although there were occasional arguments over what that might be. There was one brief moment when tempers flared and Dudley lost his cool. During one scene, Zieff asked Dudley for more. 'What do you mean, more!' shouted

Dudley. 'What more do you want? If you wanted more, why didn't you get someone else!'

Mostly, though, his sense of humour was always evident. When an uninvited and unwelcome studio executive turned up on the set and sat down to watch the action, Dudley turned to him and said, 'I'm sorry, you're in my eyeline. Please would you move?' The second time he moved, Dudley told him, 'You're still in my eyeline.' Zieff remembered Dudley moving the executive all the way around the set until finally he gave up and left and everyone broke into laughter.

Not since *30 Is a Dangerous Age, Cynthia* had Dudley been able to incorporate so many of his musical talents within one movie. He played the piano and violin, and conducted the orchestra in Beethoven and Tchaikovsky.

> **DUDLEY**: I had wonderful fun with that. The orchestra was great and I got to conduct them in some pretty complex pieces. We did the last movement of Beethoven's *Fifth Symphony* and the first and last movement of the Tchaikovsky *Violin Concerto* so there was quite an amount of conducting, which I enjoyed no end. I also played the piano and had a violin duet with Armand Assante, which we did as if we were fighting a duel. But I was disappointed that we had to play to recorded music instead of using the real sound because I love the violin.

For the last six months, Dudley had been working continuously. During that time he had experienced two heartbreaks: the death of his mother and the downfall of *Six Weeks*, a project dear to his heart. He had worked hard for so long; now it was time to have some fun for a while. He was, after all, one of the Hollywood elite and in huge demand socially. There were parties and dinners with Glenn and Cynthia Ford, Peter Bogdanovich, Wayne Rogers and Leslie Bricusse; a dinner for John Huston; an auction by Jane Fonda; a reception for David Hockney; dinner for visiting Vice-President George Bush; birthday parties for Mary Steenburgen, Tina Sinatra and Susan George; more dinners with Peter Bellwood, Francis Megahy, Parker Stevenson and Kirstie Alley, and Michael and Pat York; and an invitation to Liza Minnelli's concert in Universal's new amphitheatre.

Dudley needed to recharge his batteries, and for that he turned to his music. He appeared on a glittering television tribute to comedy legend Bob Hope and, according to the *New York Daily News*, his appearance as concert pianist was 'the one class act in the whole three hours'.

> **DUDLEY:** I liked Bob Hope and he seemed quite fond of me. He turned up as a surprise guest on the *This Is Your Life* that they did of me and I thought it was very nice of him to have done that. He was a very sweet man. It's funny . . . that whole post-*Arthur* period was packed with activities. I was doing a lot of things and was very sociable. I went to a lot of parties and I had a lot of friends.

With an engagement set for New York's prestigious Carnegie Hall, Dudley applied himself assiduously to six hours of daily practice at home. Despite his love for acting and comedy, it was to music that he turned for greatest fulfilment. It was, for him, the more visceral art, the one through which he became emotionally charged. Given a choice, emotionally he would choose music; financially he would choose acting, although within a decade it would be his music to which he would turn to fill both needs.

As his former music tutor, Peter Cork, had observed, 'What is incredible is how he does brilliantly with one career and then opens up in another. But in the end it always comes back to the one thing that was always the most overwhelming – his music.'

For the Carnegie Hall concert, Dudley chose to perform Beethoven's *Triple Concerto* with violinist Robert Mann and cellist Nathaniel Rosen. Pinchas Zukerman, who would later marry Dudley's ex-wife Tuesday Weld, conducted the St Paul's Chamber Orchestra.

'He did himself and the music proud,' said the *New York Post* the next day, and he played 'with an arresting style'. *Time* magazine considered his performance 'sensitive and well paced', and the *New York Times* critic declared that Dudley 'came away with considerable honour', adding 'clearly he is no amateur fumbler at the keyboard'.

He performed the *Triple Concerto* again at the annual Aspen Music Festival in Denver. He was, his publicist Paul Bloch described, 'brilliant, exciting and humorous'. The night was wildly triumphant. Never before had Dudley received so many standing ovations. 'I don't think this can possibly be duplicated in the years ahead,' Paul told Lou Pitt as they drove back from the concert. 'There'll be more concerts, but nothing can possibly be as successful as this.'

In August 1983, Patrick arrived to spend the summer with his father. Now that he had turned seven, Dudley was enjoying the youngster's blossoming personality. He was an artistic boy who loved to paint, and Dudley's most cherished gifts were the paintings his son gave him. The walls of Patrick's room at the Marina beach house were covered with his colourful efforts. He had also inherited his father's musicality. Just as Dudley had done around the age of six, Patrick was now clambering on to his father's piano stool and tinkering with the keyboard, fascinated with the black and white keys and the sounds that emanated from them, and Dudley was looking forward to the time when they would be able to play duets together.

After a six-month break, it was time to return to work. *Best Defense* teamed him with Eddie Murphy (though they never appeared on screen together) and Kate Capshaw as Dudley's wife. Murphy played an American tank commander demonstrating a new tank, at the heart of which is a sophisticated navigational gyroscope. When it goes awry, the tank goes berserk, demolishes an Arab village and ends up in the heart of the Iraqi war zone. Dudley was the gyroscope's inept designer who had appropriated a rival designer's plans.

Kate found Dudley hugely entertaining. He made going to work every day fun in a way she had seldom known before. As for Eddie Murphy, who had met Dudley some time earlier at a screening for *Derek and Clive Get the Horn*, he was already hooked. He was an ardent fan of *Derek and Clive*, whose scatological vulgar humour was right up his street.

Dudley had never quite got over the disappointment of *Six Weeks*, so he was cheered when the release of *Unfaithfully Yours* received an enthusiastic response. Richard Schickel in *Time* magazine declared the film better than the original and 'the range and control of [Dudley's] facial expressions are a joyous astonishment'. The film, he recommended, was 'smart, well paced, nice-looking and reminds you of Hollywood's good old days without making you mourn for them'.

Early in 1984 Dudley joined other Hollywood Brits to raise money for the British Olympic Team at the upcoming Olympic Games in Los Angeles. While Julie Andrews, Tom Jones and Anthony Newley sang, Dudley performed at the piano with Cleo Laine and John Dankworth. Leslie Bricusse, who organised the gala with Michael Caine and Sir Gordon White, the British entrepreneur who flew the British flag from his home near the Caine mansion, was in fits of laughter over the 'Dying Swan' routine that Dudley resurrected with Dankworth. 'As he played the piece, Dudley kept changing keys and playing lower and lower and moving his body at the same time until he came off the piano stool on to the floor. He ended up lying on the floor under the piano with his hands above his head, still playing! It was brilliant!'

Blake Edwards had long wanted to work again with Dudley after *10* and at last they were reunited with *Micki and Maude*, a comedy about a married television presenter whose cellist mistress, Maude (Amy Irving), becomes pregnant at the same time as his lawyer wife, Micki (Ann Reinking). Feeling bound to both, Dudley marries his mistress and gets away with bigamy until Micki and Maude meet in the hospital as each is about to enter the delivery room. Banned from seeing either of his babies, the end of the film sees him continuing a secret relationship with each woman, unknown to the other. Somehow it didn't seem inappropriate for Dudley to end up with two women by his side. He was, after all, now perceived as one of the screen's most romantic lovers.

With *Micki and Maude*, Dudley was in top form and Blake loved him in the role. 'The combination with Ann and Amy was just terrific. It worked so well, and we all got along wonderfully. We had the best time on that film.'

Ann Reinking agreed. 'Laughter makes you feel good, and a man who makes women feel good is going to be very popular with them. I think Amy and I just sat and laughed for three months! It loosened us up so much that we did things I don't think we thought we could do.'

Dudley flourished in Blake's free and vivacious presence. Their sense of humour was compatible, and Blake, not to be outdone, brought his own share of laughter to the set. In a scene where Dudley had to open a closet to get his coat, a man in a gorilla costume jumped out at him and wrestled him to the bed as if trying to make love to him. Producer Tony Adams found it hilarious. 'Dudley was absolutely shocked; he thought someone was trying to rape him! Blake had set the whole thing up with the prop man. The whole film was a constant state of Blake doing something to poor Dudley! And of course they both had their little fart machines with them.'

It was a comedy very much in the style of a French farce, with lots of doors slamming, people running in and out of rooms, and Dudley constantly trying to escape discovery by one or the other of his wives. Ultimately, though audiences were generally unreceptive towards *Micki and Maude*, the critics regarded the film favourably. When it was released in England, lain Johnstone, reviewing for *The Times*, declared it 'very funny thanks to a splendid comic performance by Dudley Moore. The film belongs to Dudley, [who] surmounts the random inconsistencies of the plot . . . blending emotion and humour with the touch of a Cary Grant.' Hollywood clearly agreed and awarded him a Golden Globe.

Adding to the pleasurable reviews, Dudley was delighted to catch up with his long-time friend, jazz singer Barbara Moore, who was visiting Los Angeles for two weeks. She stayed in the elite Hollywood hotel, the Chateau Marmont on Sunset Boulevard, and Dudley sent a limo to pick her up one morning and bring her out to his house in the Marina.

'I spent a lovely day with my little treasure,' she recalled. 'We sat at the piano and had a giggle and talked and sang and played music. Later that day we took a delightful walk along the beach by the Marina, and every elderly person and child we passed along that stretch stopped to greet him, they were so pleased to see him. I found it very moving to see my old friend so beloved like that.'

Barbara didn't see him again before she left. When she checked out of the hotel, she went to the reception desk to pay her bill.

'There's no need for that,' the manager told her. 'It's already been taken care of by a friend.' He refused to tell her the name, but Barbara knew 'damn well who it was. That's the only time in my long life that a man ever gave me anything. It was precious. He had no need to do something like that, but that was Dudley. I loved the largesse and warmth of his heart. You could toast your hands on him.'

Dudley enjoyed playing the piano in places where he could see his friends, dine well, and play when the mood took him, so it seemed a natural move when his *Six Weeks* director Tony Bill suggested they partner together in a restaurant in Venice, California, close to his home. Other investors included Liza Minnelli and Tina Sinatra, and in August 1984 their establishment, 72 Market Street, opened amid the Hollywood fanfare that accompanies a special occasion. The oyster bar and grill became an instant attraction for the local showbiz crowd. The celebrity circle flocked to the restaurant, partly in search of good cuisine and also in the hope of seeing Dudley play the gleaming black grand piano in the main dining room. They weren't disappointed.

Dudley's romance with Susan Anton, so powerful and obsessive in its early days, was now entering its final stages. Their relationship continued to linger on pleasantly, as Dudley put it, but he was now once again publicly avowing his disbelief in monogamy 'unless it happens to fall on one like a Russian satellite out of the sky'.

Towards the end of the summer of 1984, a bizarre incident took place. A hand washed up on the beach just yards away from Dudley's house. Knowing his propensity for anxiety, I expected to find him concerned and worried when I visited him. But he professed to be relatively unmoved by the discovery.

DUDLEY: I'm not worried about violence here. There used to be kids screaming at three in the morning on the beach here but the police cleaned that up. Mind you, there was a murder out here a while ago. So there is violence around but there's also the natural violence which we're supposed to be encountering very soon in the next thirty seconds or thirty years and I think, 'What the shit is going to happen?' I don't know. Maybe it's perfect for my psyche to be in a situation where I may be obliterated at any moment!

> But I don't feel the urge to move. I'd feel exhausted at the prospect of finding a place and trying to make it my nest again. I'd rather sort of sit in the front line here and be washed out to sea. It does worry me that the house is so close to the water's edge.
>
> I was thinking last night, what if an earthquake happened and all my windows blew out? I'd be open to the world. What would I do if people came in? Say, 'Hi, how are you?' Invite them in to tea? I don't know. Seriously, it is a frightening thing. What would happen, what *will* happen if an earthquake hits? I'm having a geology report drawn up. Not that I can do anything. I just want to know what the hell I'm in for. Will I end up in the sea? Will I be underground? What's going to happen? It's troubling.

Leaving behind his geological trepidation, late in the year he flew to London to begin filming *Santa Claus – The Movie*. It was his first production in England since *The Hound of the Baskervilles* in 1977, and he was paid $4 million, the highest fee he'd ever received. *Superman* producers Ilya and Alex Salkind had lured him into the $50 million extravaganza, directed by Jeannot Szwarc, who had made *Jaws* 2.

Dudley's role was that of Patch, chief assistant to Santa Claus (David Huddleston), who is manipulated into joining an unscrupulous toy baron (John Lithgow) in a plot to overthrow Mr Claus. The role had been written especially for Dudley and its childlike elements of eagerness and innocence greatly appealed to him. He had always wanted to make a special-effects movie and loved the idea of speeding through the sky in a flying car.

On the first day of filming, he walked into the studio and found a Selfridges bag hanging inside a wardrobe door. The 'S' had been covered up to read 'Elfridges'. For the next couple of months he became surrounded by a smaller world, with a new language that encompassed words from 'elfishness' to 'elf-efficiency'.

Dudley had long wanted to make a fantasy film, and one that his young son would enjoy, but he found it immensely uncomfortable to be cast in the midst of hundreds of other men of his own size, although many were smaller. The first time he saw them all together, he broke out in a cold sweat ('I thought it was fucking ridiculous!'), and after every take he reverted to Derek and Clive-like obscenities in rebellion against the innocent niceness he had just portrayed as Elf Patch.

The Salkinds had advertised the film in the trade papers as the most expensive movie ever made, and were hoping to launch a series of *Santa Claus* movies, but it was not to be. Dudley found the filming quite boring, alleviated only by a harmonious relationship with John Lithgow.

Lithgow, who had grown up around the theatre and won a Tony for his first Broadway play, had long been a dedicated fan of Dudley. 'As a teenager,' he recounted, 'Dudley was one of my great heroes, because I'd seen *Beyond the Fringe* on Broadway. I knew every single sketch and we discussed them endlessly.'

It was through their *Fringe* discussions that John saw Dudley's angst over his floundering relationship with Peter Cook. 'He had such a complex relationship with Peter, and they were at that sad moment where Peter was so jealous and bitter about Dudley's success that the friendship was basically evaporating. I think Dudley was hurt and confused.

'It sounded as if he had done an awful lot to try to help Peter, but to no avail. Dudley felt very guilty about his own success – and how could he not? Peter's life was such a shambles, and at that point Dudley's life was still wonderful. He was basking in the glory of being a movie star, although I did slightly feel he was beginning to worry because *10* and *Arthur* were behind him.'

One night Dudley took John to Langan's Brasserie, where

he was instantly pronounced *persona non grata* by owner Peter Langan, who had never forgiven him for not investing in his new restaurant. 'I want to let you know,' Dudley complained later to Michael Caine, Langan's partner, 'that another person was just thrown out of your restaurant.'

'Oh God!' replied Caine. 'You wouldn't believe what great business Mirabelle round the corner is doing because of all the people Peter's throwing out of our place!'

After he returned to Los Angeles, I visited Dudley at his beachside home to interview him about John Gielgud for an authorised biography that Sheridan Morley was writing. Dudley was happy to reminisce about the man for whom he had the utmost admiration, and he hoped there'd be another opportunity to work with him in the future. We were sitting on the settee in his living room when our interview was suddenly interrupted by a strange noise.

> **DUDLEY:** Hang on a minute, what was that sound? Is that someone whimpering? It's coming from under this couch! Oh lor, one of the dogs must have got stuck underneath it. I'll bet it's Minka, the samoid. But she's so big, I can't imagine how she got there and now she can't get out! We'll have to lift up the couch. I hope you're strong enough. You take one end and I'll take the other. Cor blimey, if it isn't one thing, it's always another around here! The dogs have the brains of a lentil pea!

Since *10*, Dudley had come to believe he was at his best when projecting facets of himself in a role. He wanted more than anything to show the tender side of his personality rather than the more manic, farcical side. Yet the films in which he expressed that had not been so successful. It was ironic, since with *Six Weeks* and *Lovesick* he had done some of his best work as an actor. In those he had moved away from the physical humour that identified him so closely with Peter Sellers and towards a realm of charm more reminiscent of Cary Grant. Even *Unfaithfully Yours* and *Micki and Maude*, in which he had reverted to elements of his former caricature behaviour, had not fared too well.

During the early eighties everything Dudley touched had turned to gold. He had reached a peak he had never known before, both as actor and musician. But the overwhelming success he had found with *10* and *Arthur* had not been sustained, and the earlier roller-coaster pattern of success and failure was repeating itself.

He felt hurt by the critics' vituperative attacks on his more serious films, and was disappointed that his fans, whom he adored, would not allow him to be someone other than an amiable drunk or a crazed sex maniac. Disillusioned, he told Lou Pitt he was taking a year off from making films. Aside from his mental fatigue, he was, after eleven films in eight years, physically exhausted. He needed a break.

Dudley's relationship with Susan Anton was now over and for the first time in years he was alone. He contemplated his approaching fiftieth birthday with some ambivalence. He still looked much younger than his age and retained an inherent boyishness about his nature. Forty hadn't been bad at all but fifty sounded serious. He found himself reflecting on his various accomplishments and what might now lie ahead.

In April 1985, Dudley turned fifty.

Part Four

CHAPTER 20

Reflections
1985

The months leading up to Dudley's fiftieth birthday had been a period for reassessment. He considered spending more time with his music. Maybe he would do some concerts, he pondered, maybe not. He felt a strong urge to re-evaluate and perhaps to reorganise his life. He knew that anxiety about middle age was normal. But now that it was upon him, fifty didn't seem such a depressing age after all.

His last few films had hardly set the box office on fire and, though the potential success of a film had never been his reason for working, it was disappointing that they had not been greeted with more enthusiasm. In Britain, the press criticised him for making mediocre films that had the sole merit of swelling his personal fortune. Dudley dismissed the accusations and defended his choice of work. None of the scripts had been vacuous or meaningless. Some had been highly intelligent, and most had been very funny. Money had never been his motivation for work; he judged a film by the script, and if he liked it and believed he would have fun making it, then he chose to do it. It was easy for some to say that he had picked the wrong ones, but he had no regrets about those he had chosen, except for *Wholly Moses!* He had felt them to be good at the time, and still felt that way.

It was apparent that the public wanted to see Dudley in his more extreme characterisations. In *10* and *Arthur* he had given them a persona that they loved, and they wanted more of that vulnerable lovability wrapped inside an outrageous exterior. But since *Arthur* he had moved away from slapstick and was now finding himself trapped by two of his greatest personal assets – his sensitivity and his charm – and audiences hoping for another *Arthur* found it hard to accept him in such different roles.

As he had always done when he needed emotional solace, Dudley turned to what he felt most at home with – his music. By day he practised classical works; by night he played jazz at 72 Market Street. People turned up just to hear him play. The bar was jammed with standing room only. The sole disadvantage was that people remained at their tables after dinner to continue listening, which meant less turnover for the restaurant.

Ray Brown, Dudley's occasional bass player, joined him there once. He found the clatter of cutlery too noisy for his taste, 'but I learned later that's the way Dudley liked it. He didn't want to feel everybody was listening to him.'

Dudley's jazz was a particular favourite with the legendary Oscar Peterson. Dudley considered him an extraordinary pianist, but it frustrated him that he was unable to emulate Peterson's velocity and the ease with which he attacked the piano.

'Dudley was a very warm player,' appraised Peterson, who first met him in 1973, when paying homage to his talents in *This Is Your Life*. 'He's a very honest player and gives it the full range of emotions. Jazz is instant composition, so you have to really speak your mind musically at a given moment. And, unlike many jazz pianists, Dudley becomes very involved in what he does.'

One of Dudley's improvised jazz sessions caught the attention of the *Los Angeles Times*' eminent jazz critic Leonard Feather, who noted, 'His hands have never lost their touch.'

He was still immensely popular with women, and they gravitated towards him just as they had in his earlier jazz-playing days in London clubs. It made no difference that he was short, had a club foot, and walked with a limp; to women the world over he was adorable, and it was no surprise when a new American poll voted him one of the world's most eligible bachelors.

Dudley's aversion to monogamy was back in full bloom. He was popular and he continued to take full advantage of his immense sex appeal. He felt as youthful as ever and, though age might have etched his laugh lines a little deeper and given his face an extra maturity, he didn't look much different from when he had arrived in America ten years earlier with Peter Cook.

Yet his life was about to take another turn, for he had just met the woman who would eventually become his third wife.

CHAPTER 21

Brogan

1985–86

Actress Brogan Lane was twenty-nine years old, warm and gregarious with a magnetic exuberance for life. Dudley had met her briefly when she'd been an extra on *Six Weeks* but when he encountered her again a month after turning fifty, he fell head over heels.

'She was a breath of fresh air,' Peter Bellwood reminisced of the beautiful, leggy brunette. 'Dudley always had very glamorous girlfriends, and Brogan was no exception. But she didn't live the glamorous life like some of them, and she was completely down to earth, which is a lovely quality in a person.'

For the time at least, Dudley had eyes only for Brogan and they adopted a life of easy comfort filled with friends and barbecues and picnics. In this relatively new atmosphere of calm and peace, Dudley spent more time at the piano. His impatient, rushing nature had slowed, and he was anxious to master music in a way he had not done in the past. Instead of dashing through a piece and allowing his impatience to limit his achievement, he spent hours breaking down sections of a concerto, practising rigorously until, having mastered one piece, he could continue to the next. At last he was taking the time to do what he should have done thirty years earlier.

Visiting Dudley during this period, I found him in one of his reflective moods and together we went through more drawers full of memorabilia that he'd hoarded over the years, much of which he hadn't looked at for decades.

> **DUDLEY:** Here's a photo of Peter, Jonathan and Alan and me outside the theatre in NY where we did *Fringe* . . . and cor blimey, this is a fax from Peter – 'Dearest Dud, Thinking of you, I love you' – and he's drawn a squiggly face under that . . . Here's a letter from Barry Humphries – he walked out of *Play It Again, Sam* and he wrote to me his apology and explanation . . . Here's another fax from Peter – 'Dearest Dud, I miss you, love, me' . . . these are some clippings, I don't usually read reviews but I must have looked at some I suppose because I remember writing letters to critics who'd been particularly nasty about me . . . This photo is from *Unfaithfully Yours*; I had my hair permed and it grew alfalfa sprouts! . . . That's me with Miss Piggy, I like that picture . . . Ah, I wondered what happened to this – here's the *Derek and Clive* video; we could watch it later if you want. We recorded three albums and the third one is quite impossible. My mother liked anything I did but she said she wouldn't have Derek and Clive in the house!

When at last Dudley made his first public appearance in months, it was at a Los Angeles gala for the Princess Grace Foundation. He was warmly applauded for his pianistic virtuosity and it was, Prince Albert wrote to him after returning to Monaco, 'a wonderful musical moment'.

Accompanied by Brogan, in November Dudley flew to London

for the royal charity premiere of *Santa Claus* in the presence of the Prince and Princess of Wales. Inadvertently, Brogan upstaged Dudley through her unawareness of British royal protocol. While Dudley was in the men's room, she took their tickets and sat in a seat at the front of the circle next to Diana, where Dudley should have sat. 'I'm sure we're in the wrong seats,' Prince Charles told her, not wanting actually to say that protocol required a man to sit between two women. 'No, we're not,' Brogan assured him, blithely unaware of any faux pas, and pulled out the tickets. 'Look, here are our seat numbers.' Still Charles insisted, 'I'm sure we're in the wrong seats.' Brogan looked at him closely, then suggested brightly, 'Well, let's see *your* tickets, then!' Charles gave up and sat down.

Back home, the night before *Santa Claus* opened in Los Angeles, Brogan threw a huge party for all Dudley's friends. The film had not been the masterpiece Dudley had hoped for and she wanted to create a cushion for the antipathy she anticipated he'd face in the press reviews the next day.

'What I loved about Brogan,' reflected Peter Bellwood, 'was that she was always pushing him to stay in touch with his friends and his past. She cared so much about him and was always setting up social things where he would get together with his friends.'

American comedienne Joan Rivers had taken her unique brand of acerbic humour to Britain, where the BBC had given her a talk show with Peter Cook as her sardonic sidekick. She asked Dudley if he would appear on the show, and in January 1986 he was reunited publicly with Peter.

The pair's relationship was now a shadow of what it had been. As partners, they were immortalised in the annals of British comedy; as friends, Peter's drinking and public jealousy towards Dudley had distanced them. Hurt by the continual bombardment of Peter's seemingly relentless caustic fire, Dudley had stopped calling him during his visits to London.

Even before *Beyond the Fringe*, it was Peter Cook who had been the handsome and brilliant golden boy, the one who felt he would end up as the film star. By all accounts, he was the one who craved the stardom. 'Peter always longed for that type of show-business success,' avowed Jonathan Miller. 'He wanted to be a movie star, and envied Dudley that particular success. God knows why – it seems to me to be a deplorable condition. He was very envious of someone he knew very well who was no longer working with him and who had made it in the terms that he felt "making it" should occur. Alan Bennett and I were always rather puzzled by both of them in that respect.'

Peter's girlfriend, Lin Chong, who later became his wife, saw how it distressed Peter when Dudley came into town without phoning. 'Peter didn't realise how much he could hurt a person. It was just his sarcastic manner of speaking, and he assumed Dudley would know that he loved him, and would forgive anything he said. It didn't cross his mind that he could hurt Dudley. But he misjudged his sensitivity.'

After their brief reunion on the Joan Rivers show, unknown to Peter, Lin went to see Dudley and told him Peter had mellowed. It was a turning point and their friendship seemed to grow again.

Life settled into a domestic pattern for Dudley during the early months of 1986, and with Brogan by his side he enjoyed mixing with the Hollywood elite. They joined Jackie Collins and her husband, Oscar, at their Beverly Hills nightclub, Tramp's, and had dinner with Bob Dylan at Chasen's. Joan Rivers invited them to a dinner party at her Bel Air mansion, and Brogan was fascinated by the regality with which the comedienne conducted the proceedings, particularly the beeper that Joan kept by her side to summon the butlers for each new course.

Jonathan Miller had added a new talent to his versatile repertoire and become an opera director of considerable distinction. His version of Gilbert and Sullivan's *The Mikado* at the English National Opera had recently been a huge success with Eric Idle as Ko-Ko, the Lord High Executioner. Peter Hemmings, English director of the Los Angeles Civic Opera and an old friend and fellow Cambridge scholar, asked him to direct it as part of the next UK/LA Arts Festival two years ahead.

Hemmings suggested casting Dudley in the role of Ko-Ko – a proposal that was received with some ambivalence. 'Dudley was an obvious choice to me. I'd always felt Ko-Ko must be the archetypal sexy little man, and that's what Dudley had always been in his films. But Jonathan was somewhat doubtful at the time, and so was Dudley. I think he'd got to the point where he was a bit afraid of public stage performance. So I took Jonathan down to Dudley's restaurant and we all sat together and talked. Gradually, as the place filled up, the two of them started playing to an audience, with bits of old *Fringe* skits creeping in. I knew by then I had them hooked.'

Jonathan's *Mikado* was not a traditional one; he had updated the setting by fifty years and abandoned the usual japonaiserie, the fad that had inspired Gilbert's libretto. Instead of Japan in the late 1800s, the action now centred on the 1930s art deco lobby of an Anglo-American hotel in Florence. The result was somewhat reminiscent of Noel Coward.

Dudley was intrigued by the idea of turning *The Mikado* into a kind of English romp, and he also liked the prospect of singing 'in a mildly serious way'. It would give him the chance to pretend he was a choirboy again, reliving one of the few periods of his youth he passionately missed. During his Oxford days he had often played piano in the orchestra pit during Gilbert and Sullivan operas, but he had never performed in one on stage. He relished the prospect of spending several weeks in the company of Jonathan Miller, whom he considered one of the most extraordinary men he had ever known, and he expressed his glee to me at that time.

DUDLEY: I had done something on his television programme *The Body in Question* where he asked me what happened in my mind when I was reading a piece of music and I was rather embarrassed to find that I couldn't tell him, but thankful to know that was the right answer! That one doesn't really know how it's done; it just happens, it seems, the transference of notes into the mind and onto the keyboard.

So I'm looking forward to doing *The Mikado* with Jonathan. It'll be nice. I like the idea of doing it because he's directing it and I've always enjoyed him. He's a nice man, one of the nicest men around. He's such a sweet man, fun and intelligent. So it's a great opportunity to have an excuse to work with him. And though I've never done a Gilbert and Sullivan opera before, it seems like a piece of mischief that might be amusing.

Dudley's life with Brogan was opening him up to the outdoor world for the first time in his adult years. She was constantly persuading him to venture into activities previously unexplored – even skiing, though that necessitated having boots specially made for his club foot. 'It devastated him to have his foot exposed, but he did it, and we went on the bunny slopes. He was so proud of himself.'

One of their more adventurous excursions was white-water rafting. Dudley was reluctant, but Brogan begged him to try it. He planned the trip with his usual methodical care and invited a few friends to join them. He sent limousines to pick everyone up and one weekend in July, Peter and Sarah Bellwood, Lou and Berta Pitt, and Kirstie Alley and Parker Stevenson found themselves screaming down a river in northern California. It was hair-raising, even though they were rafting down the easiest part of the river.

Despite Dudley's initial reluctance and extreme nervousness, he soon became the captain of the group and sat in the front of the boat, wearing a huge grin and screaming bloody murder. People on passing rafts recognised him. 'Hey, Arthur!' they shouted. At one point his raft became embroiled in a water fight with another one, and they were soon hurling buckets of water at each other.

Peter Bellwood was amused to see his old chum having so much fun. 'Dudley got into this with bells on, and in his over-enthusiasm to saturate the other boat, he not only threw the entire bucket of water over them – including the bucket – but also managed to fling himself into their raft! Whereupon they took him captive and rode away! So we lost Dudley and our bailing bucket, and we had to enter into negotiations with this other raft in order to get him back – which took quite some time!'

Back on dry land, Frank Sinatra, a passionate admirer, asked Dudley to perform with him on stage in the gay musical *La Cage aux Folles*. Dudley liked Sinatra and thought the chemistry between them could be interesting, but his instinct told him he wasn't right for the role of Albin, the ageing drag queen. He didn't like the show, nor did he consider himself ancient enough to play the part. Flattered by Sinatra's request, he was tempted to ignore his instinct and do it anyway, but finally he declined the offer.

He was also suggested for Alec Guinness's landmark role in *Kind Hearts and Coronets* and a reprise of Peter Sellers's *Ladykillers*. He turned them both down but was flattered when Eric Sykes approached him with a proposition.

DUDLEY: We had lunch together round the corner from his office and he told me about the film he wanted me to do. It was called *The Plank* but I felt it wasn't right. It was an English comedy and there was a lot of mime in it. Eric tried to persuade me that I'd be a good mime but I didn't agree. I

> would have loved to have worked with him and I liked him a lot. He was on our show in the sixties and we had a blast. I thought he was very pleasant and a very funny guy.

Dudley had also been asked to do a musical version of *Arthur* on Broadway. He turned that down, too. He couldn't imagine *Arthur* as a musical. Drunken songs, he wondered – how on earth could that work? Besides, he didn't really enjoy musicals.

That was unfortunate for Blake Edwards, who a few years later harboured hopes of Dudley playing the lead opposite Julie Andrews in the Broadway version of his film *Victor, Victoria*. 'He's so musical and I thought he would have been brilliant, but he just didn't want to do it,' regretted Blake. 'I think it was a mistake on his part, but when you think about Broadway, you have to think of a year and a half out of your life. Dudley's music and concerts were important and it would have meant giving that up, but I always thought it was too bad, because it would have been really extraordinary.'

During his long sabbatical from films, Dudley returned to writing. Not music, but words. *Musical Bumps* was a book full of musical anecdotes, interlaced with his own often humorous nostalgia. 'I received my first musical bump at a very tender age when I was summarily informed that I was too small to carry the cross at the head of the church choir,' he wrote. 'Ricocheting about the musical world has enabled me to have a taste of everything from choral singing to cabaret, from madrigals to movie compositions, and from locations as varied as a bar in Greenwich Village and Carnegie Hall.'

He had also written a postscript for a new book, *The Complete Beyond the Fringe*, which incorporated all the scripts from the stage show. 'I don't think I ever had such grand excitement,' Dudley wrote. 'It was everything I had ever wanted, to be on stage in a revue.'

It was now that Brogan tried to reunite the four Fringers. She was three-quarters successful.

> **DUDLEY:** She had arranged for us all to meet at Villa Bianca in Hampstead, which was Peter's local restaurant. Alan, Jonathan and I were there and we were waiting for Peter. Then he rang from Shepperton Studios saying he'd been held up there by filming and couldn't make it. So we sort of dissipated into the night air. I thought it would be great if when we were all sixty we could get together for a new *Fringe*. Peter liked the idea and found it intriguing. But I think it would have been a one-minute joke and wouldn't have worked.

After a year's absence, and living in rented quarters, Dudley and Brogan moved back into the Marina home. With her masterful eye, Brogan had entirely redesigned the house and now that it was complete, Dudley happily gave me a tour.

The Mediterranean-style terracotta house was now decorated in pale beach tones with curving white walls and pine floors, and Brogan's influence showed throughout the three storeys. An antique Coca-Cola dispenser stood next to a rocking horse, and teddy bears filled the master bedroom, its tall French windows overlooking Venice Beach, the local bird sanctuary and a public toilet. On the first landing, Brogan had hung a poster-size blow-up of Dudley's first composition, 'Anxiety', written when he was twelve.

In the vast living room overlooking the beach stood the grandfather clock that reminded Dudley of England, though he had bought it in California. Next to it was his childhood upright piano that Brogan had tracked down and shipped over. Hanging above it was his favourite painting – an English winter scene with children playing in the snow, bought one year down the King's

Road with Suzy Kendall. Two gleaming grand pianos stood back to back, their lids covered with dozens of framed photographs and miniature glass animals. The bookshelves were filled to overflowing with classic literature and a vast collection of sheet music. The bottom shelves housed his numerous LPs while a set of encyclopedias rested on a shelf above a log fire. And in the basement Dudley had installed a cold-storage vault for his wines, capable of holding a couple of hundred bottles.

Over the years, he had acquired a considerable knowledge of wines, though he never regarded himself as a connoisseur. He was perfectly happy to imbibe ordinary plonk, but it was the great wines that interested him and he was willing to invest a fair amount of money to procure the best and rarest vintages – sometimes spending hundreds of pounds on a bottle. He still had a large collection of several dozen cases back in Britain that were being stored by wine broker Richard Kihl, Lysie's brother, and Dudley wrote to him expressing interest in building a collection of outstanding red Bordeaux. 'By the way,' he added, 'my girlfriend and I had a superb 1899 Lafite in New York recently and we will always remember it.' No wonder. It had cost over a thousand dollars – a great deal of money to pay for a red wine, Dudley conceded, but he'd had the most wonderful time drinking it.

Brogan loved exploring those red wines with him. 'We had one bottle that was dated 1891 and we were both wide-eyed, imagining what people looked like back then, what they wore, and how they behaved.'

In February 1987 Dudley was playing jazz at his restaurant when, to his surprise, Bo Derek walked in and joined him on the piano stool. Then Eamonn Andrews emerged from a side door and announced to Dudley the familiar words, 'This is your life!' It was déjà vu for Dudley, who had already heard those words once before, in December 1972. He was now one of a small elite group to be handed their life twice.

Ushered over to ABC's television studios in Hollywood by *Arthur* chauffeur Ted Ross, he was reunited in front of a live audience with his sister Barbara, who had flown in from England, and Peter Cork, his former music tutor. Brogan was there and so were Joan Rivers, Jackie Collins, Tony Bill and Robin Williams. Peter Cook appeared via satellite. Cleo Laine, John Dankworth, Sammy Cahn and Henry Mancini paid tribute to Dudley's jazz acuity, while Robert Mann, Itzhak Perlman and members of the Los Angeles Philharmonic appeared as testimonial to his classical talents.

Dudley took over the piano, with Ray Brown on bass and John Dankworth on sax, and Chevy Chase joined him for a few jazzy moments. The show culminated with Bob Hope dubbing him 'Sir Dudley of Dagenham', for which Hope commanded him to kneel, observing with a wry laugh worthy of Peter Cook, 'It doesn't make a hell of a lot of difference, does it!' Shown in Britain the following month, the programme was transmitted as a rare two-parter.

The televised review of Dudley's life coincided with the end of his own ruminations. He had embarked on his two-year-long sabbatical with the intentions of reassessing his life and revitalising his creativity, but nothing much had emerged beyond a long rest, a great deal of piano practice, and a depleted bank account.

He was hardly broke. Years of wise spending and smart investments had protected his assets, and ever since *Arthur* he had negotiated a profit percentage of every one of his movies. He still had the Bentley that he'd brought over in the seventies – its London licence plates now replaced by the Californian proclamation 'TENDRLY' – but its value had dropped, and it was almost constantly in the garage being repaired. The good life did not come cheap, and he needed to work to maintain it.

DUDLEY: I wanted to take time off when I turned fifty. I thought, 'Wait a minute, isn't this the age when people sit down and do something important and their minds turn to re-evaluating and reorganising and all those things.' It just seemed a good thing to do in case I'd been driving along in a car with one wheel off for many years and not known it. I thought I'd do some amazing reassessment of my life or marinate in some wonderful creative juices and do something marvellous but nothing really happened. I thought, 'Well, I've got to stop something and I can't stop growing older so I'll stop work.' An amazingly effective remonstration! It was totally ineffective, of course. It just meant that I didn't work for two years!

For the last few months he had been making mild noises about returning to work. His earlier feelings of burnout had been replaced by a new vitality. He felt creative, and the desire – the need – to perform had returned.

The scripts had continued to pour in during his sabbatical but none had appealed to him. Now one did.

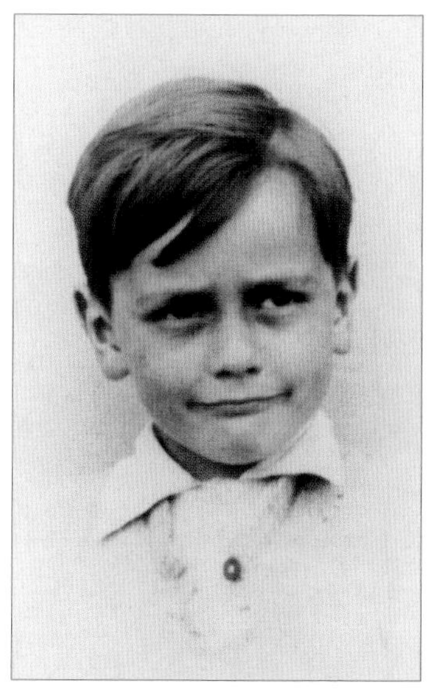

Top left: Dudley's favourite childhood photo, taken early 1940s *Photo courtesy Dudley Moore collection*

Top right: Newport Festival, England, 1961. Musician Harry Klein and students watch and listen to Dudley Moore at the piano *Popperfoto/Getty Images*

Middle left: Alan Bennett, Peter Cook, Jonathan Miller and Dudley Moore shaking up British comedy in the early 1960s in *Beyond the Fringe* *Terry Disney/Getty Images*

Below left: A classic 'Pete and Dud' scenario for *Sunday Night at the London Palladium*, 1967 *ITV/REX/Shutterstock*

Below right: *Beyond the Fringe* programme, 1964

Top left: With Peter Cook, performing the 'One-legged Tarzan' sketch for ITV's *Royal Gala Show*, November 1966

Larry Ellis/Daily Express/Hulton Archive/Getty Images

Top right: Lowered into the Thames with Peter Cook for a sketch in *Not Only But Also*, 1965

George Elam / Associated Newspapers / REX/Shutterstock

Above: Dressed as nuns in *Bedazzled*, 1967

© Columbia Pictures

Left: Dudley Moore and Suzy Kendall watch Patricia Routledge in a scene from the movie *30 Is a Dangerous Age, Cynthia*, 1968

© Columbia Pictures/Michael Ochs Archives/Getty Images

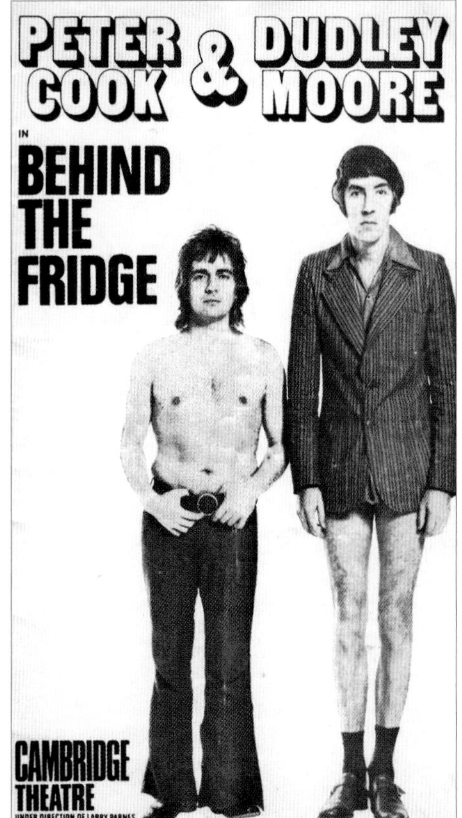

Top left: Dudley with his mum and dad, Ada and John Moore, 1966 *Popperfoto/Getty Images*

Top right: Programme for *Behind the Fridge* at the Cambridge Theatre, 1972

Middle left: With his first wife, actress Suzy Kendall, 1968 *Photo courtesy Dudley Moore collection*

Below: With author Barbra Paskin, at Dudley's house, 1979 *© Barbara Paskin*

Top left: Still from *Foul Play*, directed by Chevy Chase, 1978

© Paramount Pictures/Moviestore Collection/REX/Shutterstock

Above left and right: The movie that sealed Dudley's profile as a sex symbol: *10*, starring Bo Derek, 1979

(left) © Orion/Warner Bros/Bruce McBroom/Kobal/REX/Shutterstock

(right) © Orion/Warner Bros/Moviestore Collection/REX/Shutterstock

Above: On *The Muppet Show*, 1979

David Dagley/REX/Shutterstock

Right: Attending the 1984 People's Choice awards ceremony in Los Angeles.

Bill Nation/Sygma via Getty Images

Top left: Still from *Arthur*, 1981
© Orion/Kobal/REX/Shutterstock

Top right: With *Arthur* co-stars Sir John Gielgud and Liza Minnelli
© Orion/Kobal/REX/Shutterstock

Centre: Still from *Arthur 2: On the Rocks*, 1988 *© Warner Bros/Kobal/REX/Shutterstock*

Left: With Susan Anton, circa 1982 *© AMPAS*

Below: With Elizabeth McGovern, filming *Lovesick*, 1983
© Ladd Co/Warner Bros/Moviestore Collection/REX/Shutterstock

Top left: At the piano, 1980s *© Barbra Paskin*

Top right: Playing the organ in Las Vegas chapel pre-wedding to Brogan, 1988

Photo courtesy Dudley Moore collection

Middle left: With third wife, Brogan Lane

Photo courtesy Dudley Moore collection

Middle right: Rehearsing after conducting lessons from George Solti, 1990.

David Farrell/Getty Images

Right: On top of the Empire State Building with author Barbra Paskin, 1995 *© Barbra Paskin*

Top left: With Liza Minnelli during *Arthur* reunion tour, Boston, 1996 © *Barbra Paskin*

Top right: At author's apartment with her cockatiel, Dylan, 1997 © *Barbra Paskin*

Middle right: Pete and Dud reunited in the 1990s *Photo courtesy Dudley Moore collection*

Below: Pete and Dud hanging out at the Cobden Working Man's Club, London 1993, with Keith Richards, Ronnie Wood and Dave Stewart, *RICHARD YOUNG/REX/Shutterstock*

Above: Dudley with his beloved dogs, Minka and Chelsea, 1990s

Photo courtesy Dudley Moore collection

Below: With classical music partner Rena Fruchter, 1996 *© Arthur Paxton*

Above right: Dudley rehearsing with Rena in New York hotel 1995 *© Barbra Paskin*

Left: Dudley celebrates his 66th birthday with a benefit concert at Carnegie Hall. Joining him are (*left–right*) Bo Derek, Cleo Laine, Lauren Bacall and Chevy Chase

Richard Corkery/NY Daily News Archive via Getty Images

CHAPTER 22

Back to Work
1987–88

In March 1987 Dudley came out of his self-imposed retreat and returned to work on his first film in two years.

Like Father Like Son saw him as an ambitious surgeon and strict father to sixteen-year-old Kirk Cameron. Accidentally they drink a brain-transference potion and their minds become trapped in each other's body, with hilarious results. By the time they return to normal, they have gained new respect for each other and fresh understanding of the intense pressures each faces in their individual lives.

Dudley struck up an instant rapport with director Rod Daniel and was enchanted by his exuberance. Daniel, who had made only one previous feature, *Teen Wolf* with Michael J. Fox, had a hearty sense of humour and laughed constantly, making him a perfect match for Dudley.

He soon witnessed Dudley's ability to handle the unexpected. In one scene, after setting the living-room sofa on fire, Dudley had to push it out of the French windows into the swimming pool and walk away as it sank to the bottom of the pool. But, to Rod Daniel's chagrin, the sofa didn't sink. 'It stayed up there and burned and burned! It looked like a flaming battleship in that pool, but I kept the camera rolling because Dudley was still working and giving me one of those incredibly funny W.C. Fields reactions!

'People always said Brando was a pure improvisational actor, that it didn't matter what was scripted, he would always keep going. To me, Dudley was the same. If you didn't say "Cut!" the guy would still be going. He's the purest form of comic in the sense that it's never over for him.'

Dudley had a lot riding on this film – not least the resurrection of his wilting film career. He had been criticised for doing less than the best material, and he needed this movie to restore his credibility.

His music still played a vital role in his life and in early summer he performed two nights of concerts with the Los Angeles Philharmonic at the Hollywood Bowl, playing part of Beethoven's *Triple Concerto* and excerpts from his own film scores, followed by jazz with Ray Brown on bass and Jeff Hamilton on drums.

He was having fun – especially with his jazz. Long after the orchestra had been sent home, Dudley was still playing. The audience loved it, and so did the critics. 'He held forth respectably in both Beethoven and jazz,' claimed the *Hollywood Reporter*, 'and in general displayed the incredible talent that is Dudley Moore.'

Dudley had recently bought another house – in Toluca Lake, an affluent retreat near North Hollywood, just a few streets away from the estate where Bob Hope had lived for decades. It was a French cottage on two floors with a swimming pool and a small garden. Brogan decorated it with a warm, nostalgic touch, hanging dried flowers from the kitchen ceiling and old pictures on the walls, which gave it a quaint charm. They spent weekends there, when the beach at Marina del Rey became too populated, and then Brogan would fill the house with friends and the strains of Dudley's piano playing could be heard throughout the neighbourhood.

A few weeks after the Hollywood Bowl concerts, Dudley flew to New Jersey to perform Beethoven's *Triple Concerto* again, this time in the distinguished company of Itzhak Perlman and Yo-Yo Ma. He more than held his own with the two world-famous musicians. Of the three soloists, the *New York Post* noted that 'Moore seemed to have taken his job the most seriously'. 'The audience loved him,' agreed Perlman. 'He gave a really good performance, and we all enjoyed ourselves tremendously.'

Dudley loved the *Triple Concerto*. He found it sweet and touching, especially the deeply stirring middle movement. It had merriment and joy, and he had always been moved most by a sense of wit in a musical work. He had never considered a sense of comedy to be incompatible with music and once ventured that, given a few differences, Itzhak Perlman, who had been crippled by polio from the age of four, might have made a fine stand-up ('or, in his case, sit-down!') comic.

'I've always seen humour in life,' averred Perlman, 'and I enjoy and appreciate it and use it in my work. But one has to know when to apply it. In certain pieces of music a sense of humour and fun seems to fit, but obviously it depends on what you're playing. That's why it's particularly enjoyable to play with Dudley, who has so much humour himself and sees it in a piece of music.'

Dudley was now often to be found playing jazz at his restaurant in Venice, but one night he made a surprise appearance at The Loa, Ray Brown's jazz club in Santa Monica. 'It was amazing!' Brown laughed. 'The women were lined up for two blocks down the street! We'd never seen so many people in that joint before!'

Frank Sinatra and producer George Schlatter were among those who clamoured for a seat. 'Frank was a huge fan of

Dudley,' Schlatter enthused, 'and he thought his musicianship was astounding. He adored watching him play, and at the end of every number that night he stood up to give Dudley an ovation.'

When *Like Father Like Son* had its Los Angeles premiere at the famed Chinese Theatre on Hollywood Boulevard, Dudley hoped it would restore his ailing career. But the critics were scathing. *Variety* dismissed it as '98 minutes of benign drivel', although the *New York Times* differed in its opinion, declaring that 'Dudley and Kirk Cameron are so clever and charming that they turn a potential dud into a sweetly engaging film'. It was not the most auspicious return to film-making, but audiences enjoyed it and the movie became a financial success.

A few days later, Dudley was accorded the honour of his star being unveiled on the Hollywood Walk of Fame, just across the road from where his new movie was playing. He was now immortalised beneath millions of feet on Hollywood Boulevard, next to Louis Armstrong's star. It was, he told Johnny Carson on *The Tonight Show* that night, 'pretty amazing!'

Towards the end of the year, Dudley and Peter Cook were reunited on stage for America's *Comic Relief* television special, hosted by Robin Williams, Whoopi Goldberg and Billy Crystal. It was the first time they had performed together since the last *Derek and Clive* album in 1976. They resurrected their immortal 'One-Legged Tarzan' sketch, and it was clear to those present that there was still an enormous chemistry between them. Peter seemed to take perverse pleasure in causing Dudley to crack up the whole way through and they were harmonious and relaxed and wildly funny.

Robin Williams, a co-host of *Comic Relief* since its inception, was a lifelong fan of the duo but that night was the first time he had seen them perform live. He was ecstatic. 'It was wonderful to see them together! It's one thing to hear them on the albums and see their videos but quite something else to watch them together on stage and see how they played back and forth. I'd always appreciated them so much, especially in films like *Bedazzled* and *The Wrong Box*, which were really funny movies, like the next step up from the Ealing comedies.

'Peter and Dudley were obviously descended from the *Goons*, but they were great comics of their own who played off each other brilliantly. It was amazing for me to see them live and watch the two different energies at work – Peter's dryness and Dudley bouncing off of that on one leg. There was a real feeling of euphoria in the air that night, and they obviously enjoyed being back together again.'

Despite their triumphant reunion, there was no sense that the couple might reunite permanently. The gulf between their two lifestyles was too wide. Peter, every inch of his tall frame an Englishman, hated leaving London for any length of time. As for Dudley, he was firmly entrenched in his California nest.

> **DUDLEY:** I remember being slightly pissed off when someone in the British media said that I was on to a good thing with Peter. I mean, Peter could have been on to a good thing with *me*, for Chrissakes! Despite what some critics have said, I don't think Peter thought I was his creation. I remember Nick Luard, who owned *Private Eye*, always being very vituperative about me. They had a *Private Eye* cover showing a drawing of Peter with a doll of me on his lap and he was the ventriloquist. I think the other members of *Private Eye* were very embarrassed about that!

Age and Brogan were weaving a relaxed environment around Dudley, and it helped that financially he was secure enough not to feel pressured into accepting the next 'mediocre' script that came across Lou Pitt's desk. More than ever before, he sought peace in his life these days, understanding that his best music would come when he played in an atmosphere of relative tranquillity. He spent hours every day at one of the two grand pianos, usually playing Bach as soon as he got up every morning.

Director Stanley Donen was a familiar face at the Marina house. One evening Dudley jokingly revealed that he had never been paid for the extra work he had done on his *Bedazzled* score, and then was profoundly embarrassed when Donen made out a cheque on the spot for $3,000. Dudley returned it a few days later with a note. 'I guess having embarrassed you,' Dudley wrote, 'you did a wonderful job of making me feel more than small (!) by writing the cheque. I'm really sorry that I brought this up. I was only trying to be funny.'

Dudley liked pleasing Brogan with little acts of appreciation, and he particularly enjoyed buying her presents. Although frugal towards himself, he was extravagantly generous to others. He asked her to make out a wish list, and since what she wanted more than anything was to be Dudley's wife it was hardly surprising that this crept on to it:

'A front porch for Toluca Lake. A white fence. A trip alone with you. Old European paintings. A HUSBAND!! Pillows. Ring. A big hug. Car. Compassion. You. Teacup poodle. Portable telephone. Write me a song, perhaps play with a saxophone. You to be happy.'

Brogan's wishes were granted. All of them.

Ever since the overwhelming success of *Arthur* in 1981 there had been discussions about making a sequel, but nothing had ever matched the standards set by Steve Gordon, who had died tragically the year after *Arthur*'s release. Until *Arthur 2: On the Rocks*.

Andy Breckman, a comedy writer for *Saturday Night Live* and a devout Steve Gordon fan who claimed to know every line of *Arthur*, had been working on a new script for two years, and Dudley believed it did justice to the original. He was paid

$3 million to star in the film and also to be executive producer. Veteran comedy director Bud Yorkin, former partner of comedy producer Norman Lear, was hired to direct.

In December 1987 Dudley, Liza Minnelli and Sir John Gielgud – Hobson having been resurrected from the dead in a single, all-too-brief flashback – were reunited in New York.

Arthur 2: On the Rocks sees Arthur Bach and Linda now married and attempting to adopt a baby. But the father of Arthur's ex-fiancée has never forgiven him for jilting his daughter, Susan, at the altar. Bent on revenge, he buys out the controlling interest of the Bach family firm and manipulates the family into cutting off Arthur's finances. Convinced that Arthur can only be happy with money, Linda leaves him so he can marry Susan and have his fortune restored. Drunk, penniless and down-and-out, Arthur is on the verge of capitulating to escape vagrancy when he is visited by the ghost of his beloved Hobson.

'You're a spoiled little shit,' admonishes Hobson. 'I've told you before, you can do anything with your life that you want. Stop your drinking.' Fortified, Arthur sobers up and confronts Susan's father, who is ultimately forced to have the inheritance reinstated, leaving Arthur and Linda to be blissfully reunited.

Liza Minnelli was ecstatic about working again with Dudley. 'Here's this incredible genius of a man who doesn't really know he's attractive but who knows what's funny. He understands Arthur's innocence and what a good person he is. Because that's Dudley, too.

'It's an extraordinary thing,' she pondered to me back then. 'It's like we're less than lovers but more than friends. Sometimes we don't have to talk. We can just look at each other and know what the other is thinking. We went together so well.'

The success of the original film had been an immense surprise to John Gielgud. It had brought the unassuming 83-year-old actor an entirely new audience who had never known him through his stage work. And it elevated his earnings to a level he had never known before. When he arrived in New York to shoot his one scene, he was astonished by the reaction of the cast and crew. 'I turned up on this huge set under one of the bridges, and when everyone saw me, they all started clapping. I was very touched by that. I hadn't acted in New York for some years, and it was awfully nice to know that they still remembered me.

'I loved that butler, Hobson, and I was so very glad they found a way to bring him back from the grave to advise Arthur on his new troubles. It felt very good to be working with Liza and Dudley again, even for only a few days.'

Bud Yorkin, who had directed some of America's finest comedians, among them Dick Van Dyke, was fascinated by Dudley's originality. 'The first take is usually the most spontaneous, yet if I said, "Try it again," Dudley would have us all in hysterics. "Fuck it!" he would say, and then he'd say it again in nineteen different languages, from Pakistani to Japanese! He was very funny. And Dudley and Liza together were a perfect combination.'

In spite of his earlier contrary feelings about marriage, Dudley had decided he would marry Brogan, and in the back of his diary he scribbled out some prenuptial notes that included giving her the Toluca Lake house. On Valentine's Day, he formalised his decision and proposed to Brogan. One week later, as soon as filming had ended on *Arthur 2*, they flew to Las Vegas in the studio's jet. When the short service was over, they left the wedding chapel walking on a path of paper hearts. Dudley, wearing a wedding ring for the first time in his life, shouted, 'This time, this is the one!'

On the Monday morning after their weekend wedding, with opening night barely two weeks away, Dudley reported to work for first rehearsals of *The Mikado*. He had been looking forward to it for more than a year, not so much because he had never appeared on stage in Gilbert and Sullivan before – although he had played the violin in *HMS Pinafore* at Oxford and conducted segments from *The Mikado* in *Foul Play* – but more for the opportunity to work again with Jonathan Miller, whom he regarded as a remarkable talent. But he'd underestimated the amount of work the role entailed.

'He was rather ill-focused at the beginning,' Miller recalled, 'and hadn't bothered to learn it properly. It took some days for him to buckle down and really give it the same attention he gives to the piano. He thought he could wing it, and he often maddened his colleagues in the early rehearsals by not knowing the words or the music. We had to be very firm with him and tell him it wasn't something he could wing his way through. He suddenly realised it was a serious business and pulled his finger out, and once he learned it he did very well. He was a marvellously accomplished clown and he did a wonderful job.'

Dudley enjoyed the challenge, and found the stage surprisingly seductive now that he was treading the boards once more.

'Knock 'em out!' cabled *Hollywood Reporter* columnist George Christy on opening night. And Dudley did. 'A comedian of the first order,' announced *Variety*. 'His grab bag of physical gags is still immensely entertaining and he is not at all out of his element while singing.'

Most critics applauded Miller's *Mikado* for what it was – not another version of the traditional operetta but an innovative staging. 'A gloriously antic night of opera,' exulted the *Los Angeles Herald-Examiner*, 'a masterpiece of merry-making that preserves the work itself in all its romping, giddy glory. This is the triumph of Jonathan Miller's stagecraft and there is something akin to genius at work here. Moore is, in a word, wonderful and his Ko-Ko is first-rate stage invention.'

Any trepidation Miller might earlier have felt about Dudley was replaced by unequivocal admiration. 'I can't tell you what a pleasure it's been working with you again after all these years!' he wrote in a card to Dudley after the opening. 'It's a brilliant performance and there are moments when it takes my breath away.'

Dudley enjoyed doing *The Mikado* with Miller. It was a highlight of the three-month-long 1988 Arts Festival of Britain and he was sorry to bid it farewell when the Festival ended.

On Dudley's fifty-third birthday in April, Brogan threw a dinner party for fifty people and filled their living room with candles and four hundred balloons.

For director Rod Daniel it was one of the most sparkling dinner parties he'd ever attended. 'I sat next to Mary Steenburgen and Malcolm McDowell, and, when I turned around, Jack Lemmon and Arnold Schwarzenegger were at the next table! What was really impressive for me – and maybe it shouldn't have been – was the level of star power in that room to salute Dudley. It said a lot about him.'

Brogan's Sunday lunches were a popular tradition with their friends, who enjoyed her food as much as hearing Dudley play the piano while she was cooking. Like Suzy Kendall before her, she usually served Dudley's favourite rack of lamb with puréed cream carrots and roast potatoes with mint, followed by jelly. That's when the grand bottles of wines in the vault were gleefully uncorked. 'Dudley loved those festive gatherings,' says Brogan, 'and that's when that house came alive.'

Brogan believed in celebrating the past, and was always seeking to provide Dudley with pleasant reminders of his earlier days. One of his treasures was a handwoven carpet depicting Oxford University. Dudley had always loved a particular picture of Magdalen College, and Brogan sent it to weavers in New York who then hand-wove the carpet with its picture of graduates walking in the university grounds. 'When I unrolled it,' she remembered, 'he just fell all over it in sheer amazement!'

Another surprise had been harder to effect. With the help of Dudley's sister, she had tracked down and exported from England the old upright piano that had been in the Dagenham home since Dudley was a child, together with the rickety piano stool onto which he had first tentatively clambered at the age of five. Everybody has one most treasured possession in their life. For Dudley, it would always be that piano.

Visiting him at home, it was almost spooky to see the piano and conjure up an image of the five-year-old boy sitting on the precarious stool, playing with the keys. There, at that piano, is where his musical stirrings were cultivated.

DUDLEY: I couldn't believe it when Brogan unveiled it. It was amazing! Sometimes when I look at it I can imagine myself back in Dagenham, at the house in Baron Road where my parents remained till the end of their lives. It's not that I miss England but occasionally I'll see something and it will make me feel nostalgic. I don't crave the company of English people but I have a few English friends. So I don't really miss England but every now and then I'll buy things that remind me of being there. I've got a BBC video about England and I watch it on and off. I don't try and recreate England here but there are certain things that remind me of it, like the piano, of course, and my Bentley which I brought over from England. The grandfather clock is an English clock and I love that painting of a snow scene which I bought twenty-five years ago down the King's Road. But there are lots of things I never had then that I have now. We never had a Christmas tree in our house. Now I have two Christmas trees . . . both fake, of course, being California! . . . Did you eat all the biscuits that were on the plate?

BARBRA: No, I only had one.

DUDLEY: Ha! It must have been one of the dogs. Minka, maybe. Ah no, Chelsea has a very guilty look on her face. Look at her, I'll bet it was her. Little devils. They always try and act so innocent.

BARBRA: Did you always have pets?

DUDLEY: Always. When I was growing up we had a cat. Well, two cats. One died. It was very sad. It got stuck in the thing that housed the heater and it died. My first cat, Sparky, used to sit next to me on the piano stool when I came home from school and he was a wonderful audience when I played. Never so much as a miaow out of him . . . oh crikey, that's given me an urge to play the piano right this minute. I want to play this piece that I wrote years ago. I remember writing it. Gawd, it seems like yesterday in some ways. [Plays piano]

Early that summer, *Arthur 2* had its premiere, but despite everyone's expectations the film received catastrophic reviews. The dialogue was nowhere near as funny as its predecessor's, nor did it contain the haunting poignancy that had been so evident in the relationship between Arthur and Hobson. Dudley, who considered the sequel to be better than the original and had been anticipating his first film success in years, was surprised and disappointed.

The *New York Times* deemed it 'a lame sequel in which Arthur has become a clamorous bore', and *Time* denounced the film as a 'graceless sequel'.

When the film had been privately screened, it received the third most enthusiastic audience response in the history of Warner Bros. Convinced they had another huge hit on their hands, the studio poured their efforts into a massive and expensive publicity campaign. But times had changed in the seven years since the first *Arthur*. Alcoholism had become an immense social issue, and audiences were no longer able to laugh unashamedly at a happy drunk.

'Being drunk was not popular when *Arthur 2* came out,' Minnelli determined. 'Nobody was drinking – it was the time of non-alcoholic beer – and it was very unpopular to play a drunk.

Arthur's drinking wasn't the point of the film – just like it hadn't been with the first one – but that's how it was perceived because of the times. It went against the social grain.'

> DUDLEY: I thought *Arthur* 2 was better than *Arthur* in some respects. I thought the story was very strong and I liked it quite a bit. It was a very good story by Andy Breckman and we'd been meeting for many months about it. I told him not to be disappointed if he didn't meet the standards of *Arthur*. But I thought he did meet it. It was a very unique piece and I loved it. But I think people had been mesmerised by the performance in *Arthur* and just didn't go for *Arthur* 2. It was a different look but I thought there were some very funny things in it.

Spurred on by Brogan, Dudley was feeling an increasing urgency these days about mastering music. He found himself needing less in his life these days than ever before. As long as he had his piano and the forty-eight preludes and fugues of Bach, which he hoped to record one day, he was content. More and more his life was becoming centred around the piano, with a bit of acting thrown in.

Late in 1988 a magazine article quoted Peter Cook at his most acerbic. Peter ridiculed Dudley's lifestyle as vacuous, called him a 'munchkin' and mocked Brogan's efforts to get him to enjoy the great outdoors.

The British press seized upon the article as a fresh excuse to attack the Hollywoodisation of Dudley. Eager to say he had sold out and become plasticised, journalists suggested Dudley's brains had been baked by the California sun, assisted in no small measure by an army of psychotherapists. What serious man, they questioned, would live in a 'pink' house on the beach with personalised licence plates on the cars in his garage? Had he not committed intellectual suicide by living in California?

It was all right for David Niven to have lived in a pink house in the Hollywood Hills during his Hollywood heyday, but it was somehow ridiculous for Dudley to live in his terracotta home on the beach.

Even Jonathan Miller weighed in. 'He doesn't strike me as very happy, poor old thing,' he told me. 'He's always seemed to be searching for something in a rather peculiar way, and that's where California didn't help him very much. Because he was surrounded by all that ghastly West Coast new-age nonsense.'

'I think the British were cross with him for leaving England,' reflected his friend Lysie Kihl. 'He and Peter Cook were such a brilliant act that nothing ever was quite as wonderful again. In a way he was the bad guy for leaving. He spoilt our fun. This marvellous couple that we loved to watch wasn't there any more, and the British public was not happy about that.'

Over the years, whenever we had done interviews in my apartment, Dudley had expressed such nervousness around my birds, two budgies and two cockatiels, that I'd had to relegate them to the bedroom and shut the door. As his visits became more frequent he began to relax around them. The clincher came one afternoon as he was in the midst of discussing a future project. He suddenly looked up from his mug of coffee and exclaimed, 'You've got rats! In the bookcase, I can hear them!' I shook my head. 'No, that's the birds.' He wasn't having any of it. 'I know rats when I hear them. I'm telling you, there are rats there!'

For some months, the budgies had been making their nest behind the books in the bookcase, chewing on the pages to feather their nest. Once I got wise to their lack of appreciation for the printed word, I substituted old paperbacks that had been marked to discard.

'It's not rats, Dudley; it's the birds!' He was still disbelieving so I moved a few of the books to reveal the nest behind them. The two parent budgies looked up crossly, not pleased by the unwelcome disturbance, while four minuscule pairs of eyes and tiny beaks popped up simultaneously over the pile of shredded newsprint. Dudley was mesmerised by the sight. He lost his fear of the birds that day and from then on was happy to recline on the couch with one cockatiel perched on his chest while the other tried to pull digestive biscuits out of his mouth. He became so fond of the birds that he even appeared on British television with them, one on each shoulder.

Towards the end of 1988 a new album of Erroll Garner recordings was released. It was compiled from previously unreleased music, and Dudley was proud to be asked to write the liner notes, which he did at length and with unmitigated admiration. He wrote:

> Nothing in the arts has affected me quite as much, before or since I first heard Garner's music. He is not only a genius but a phenomenon with a uniqueness that is almost unbearably strong. I sag with the burden of gratitude. The optimism of life, of being alive, of feeling alive, of communication, of love . . . that's what Garner is and what he does for me and will always do for me. That's why I love to try and play like him. His music has got into my veins. To my mind, Erroll Garner is probably the most important pianist that I have ever heard. Passion . . . that's what he had. And that's what all great artists have. A sprinkling of the demonic, a yearning for the tender and a straight line to joy.

CHAPTER 23

The Great British Chicken Chase

1989–90

By 1989 the earlier blitz of filmmaking had subsided and the film scripts that continued to pour into Lou Pitt's office tended to be remakes of *10* and *Arthur*, from which Dudley shied away.

He was still playing jazz, although not as much as he had in the past. When Vic Lewis, his first employer, flew to Los Angeles to record a jazz album with an all-star band, Dudley agreed to play one number on it. As generous with his time as he was with his money, he never forgot those who had helped his career.

In March 1989 he played once more at Ray Brown's club. It would be the last time. Director Rod Daniel, who never missed an opportunity to enjoy Dudley at the keyboard, was on hand to cheer him. 'The guy was euphoric when he played the piano. That was his bliss. It was the place he went to be happy, and that's really when he came alive.'

Many among the audience – eminent *Los Angeles Times* jazz critic Leonard Feather included – might have been forgiven for thinking Erroll Garner had been reincarnated. 'There were many moments when it was possible to believe that he returned to us in the form of Dudley Moore,' reported Feather. 'He's a pianist for whom the art of swinging is clearly a triumphant *modus vivendi*.'

Oscar Peterson agreed, but yearned to hear more of Dudley's own style. 'I admired his own personality in his playing and I told him I was intrigued more by that than when he saluted Erroll Garner. I think perhaps he didn't have the opportunity he was looking for really to develop his own style, and that was a pity.'

In May, Dudley reteamed with his *Six Weeks* director (and restaurant partner), Tony Bill, for *Crazy People*, written by Robin Williams's award-winning *Good Morning, Vietnam* writer, Mitch Markowitz. As a harassed, burned-out advertising executive, he ends up in a sanatorium with mentally ill patients and enlists their assistance in writing 'no-nonsense' ads that grab the public's imagination and in the process turn the world of advertising upside down. One advertisement for an airline declares that 'Crashes are a fact of life and people die like crazy. But fly United,' it urged. 'More people arrive at their destination alive on our flights than others!'

Daryl Hannah was the inmate with whom Dudley becomes romantically involved, Mercedes Ruehl their sympathetic doctor, and Paul Reiser was Dudley's advertising partner. Dudley liked the script and thought it funny and tender in its portrayal of people who had difficulty in knowing how to handle their lives. The public, however, would ultimately disagree.

Soon after he began work on the film, Dudley struck up a close friendship with Paul Reiser. 'I'd been a fan of his for years,' Reiser enthused, 'so it was a real kick for me to work with him. We were filming on location in Virginia, and Dudley was friendly to everyone. I remember being impressed at how unfailingly gracious he always was to everyone in this small Virginian town who wanted to chat to him or get his autograph.'

The two men occasionally went to dinner together in a nearby restaurant club, and when Dudley took over the piano, Reiser marvelled at his ability to sight-read. 'He would just pick up a manuscript and play Beethoven right there on the spot and it would blow me away! I'm a pianist, too, but not at all at his level. A few times we sat and played together, and that was a real bit of heaven for me – although it wasn't easy to keep up with him, because he was quite brilliant.'

Reiser enjoyed these evenings – and not only for the opportunity to duet at the piano. 'Some of my fondest memories,' he laughs, 'were going out to dinner with Dudley and discovering what eight-hundred-dollar bottles of wine tasted like!'

On the personal front, Dudley's third marriage had hit seriously bumpy ground. Brogan had now moved into the Toluca Lake house, giving Dudley the space to be alone in the Marina home. Despite his deep feelings for her, Dudley once again felt trapped.

> DUDLEY: I experience relationships eventually as a form of death. I am attracted by someone who is sweetly and thoroughly focused on me and then I run like a fool who feels that he will die from a sort of strangulation.

Nor could he shake off his need for other women. Brogan recognised his compulsion but felt powerless. The phone constantly rang with women wanting to see him and Dudley did nothing to discourage them.

That summer, he flew to Europe to surprise sister Barbara on her sixtieth birthday. Barbara had no idea that her brother was in town and was flabbergasted when she returned home from shopping and Dudley suddenly stepped out of a room with a grin on his face and a huge laugh at the sight of hers.

While in London, he reunited with Peter Cook for *The Secret Policeman's 10th Anniversary Ball*, a charity benefit for Amnesty

International. Peter and Dudley's reprise in late middle-age of the 'One Leg Too Few' sketch from *Beyond the Fringe* seemed even funnier than the original. 'Good comedy never dies,' acclaimed *The Times*, 'it simply gets recycled for the next generation.'

For a while Dudley and Peter would be partners again. The BBC was assembling six half-hour programmes, each with a new introduction, to be broadcast under the title of *The Best of What's Left of Not Only . . . But Also*. The content really wasn't the best of the original series, but it was all that could be salvaged since the BBC had erased most of the programmes, and what remained had deteriorated badly. Of the twenty-one programmes from three series, only seven remained.

In November Peter Cook married his long-time girlfriend, Lin Chong, and called Dudley with the news. They talked often on the phone these days, and Dudley enjoyed their conversations immensely. Peter had a dry English wit that Dudley missed, and his caustic tongue had mellowed. The self-deprecating humour so characteristic of the British, which Dudley found both entertaining and philosophical, was in sharp contrast to American humour and he felt at home with the British attitude.

DUDLEY: We talk a lot on the phone these days. We've been fine since we came back together. Peter has mellowed and his tongue isn't as sharp as it was in the past. He's always sending me faxes if he reads something in the paper that he thinks would bother me. It's a strange thing, our relationship. We're so close, it's almost like a marriage with all the ups and downs. We've always been a bit wary of each other. And if I saw him coming into the room now there would still be this defence mechanism to go up. Maybe I've always felt a little intimidated by him, I don't know . . . I've got to go to the loo, I'm dying.
BARBRA: So am I.

DUDLEY: Well, you go first then.
BARBRA: No, no, you go first.
DUDLEY: No, no. It's your loo. I insist.
BARBRA: Okay, well, um, but if you go first that means I can have a cigarette in there afterwards and you won't smell it 'cos you'll already have been.
DUDLEY: Ah, right, then *I'll* go first!

Dudley had finally succumbed to Brogan's relentless urgings to record some of the music he had written over the years. His house was now equipped with a recording studio on the top floor, complete with piano, organ and synthesiser, and he had installed state-of-the-art music computers so that he could mix his own recordings.

She persuaded him to invite saxophonist Kenny G to the house to check out his music and play a few tunes with him. Kenny loved what he heard and was amazed by Dudley's sense of melody, which he considered the most important part of any piece of music. 'Song after song, each one of them had such a uniquely captivating melody,' he recalled. 'I don't know how he kept coming up with them like he did! He was a great musician.'

They played several pieces together that day, and recorded them on tape. 'We were like two guys who could play anything together, even though it was Dudley's music I was playing. I can remember the melodies even now, and I haven't heard them for years. That's how you can tell if a song is good – you don't forget the melody.'

Dudley shut himself up in his studio and spent hours working on compositions. The result, months later, was *Songs Without Words*, an exquisite album of ballads that also included the haunting themes from his *Six Weeks* score. It was his first album since the one he had recorded in Sydney with his trio in 1978.

The CD included an old track called 'Patrick' which, as Dudley wrote to his son, 'I dedicated to you and which I seem to remember writing mainly at a Playboy [Mansion] pyjama party!'

Declared broadcaster and musician Michael Pointon: 'This album is a worthy farewell from an unforgettable talent. *Songs Without Words* is an enduring testament to Moore's musical legacy. Its moods vary from romantic and tenderly pensive via bravado à la Liszt or Chopin to the gently reflective Garneresque piano touch contrasting with a self-mocking, melodramatic vein almost like the heavily orchestrated forties Gainsborough movie scores Dudley would have known in his youth. The whole album is a brilliant testament to his vast classical knowledge.'

In the spring of 1990, Dudley appeared with Bo Derek on the Academy Awards show. The audience was appreciative. Their earlier partnership in Blake Edwards's *10* had been one of Hollywood's favourite couplings. 'They presented the costume award,' recalled Bruce Vilanch, who wrote some of the comedy material for that year's Oscars, 'and Dudley told Bo, "It's funny that we're presenting for costumes, because what I remember most about you in *10* was that you didn't wear one at all!"'

Soon after that, Dudley was lured back to Britain and into commercials by Tesco, who spent £3 million promoting itself. A sizeable chunk of that went to Dudley – but not the million pounds that the newspapers claimed, although over the next few years it would amount to well over half that figure.

In a role perfectly suited to his physical comedy, Dudley played a Tesco buyer ineffectually chasing free-range chickens. There seemed little other work around and this suited him. He liked the farcical approach to the ads and, besides, commercials took only a couple of days to shoot, rather than the couple of months for a film.

The series of ads showed him crashing through a vineyard, falling into a vat, and haring after a hot-air balloon that had taken off without him, always in a futile search for chickens. The commercials were an immediate and sensational hit in Britain. They popularised Dudley among a new generation of kids and gave him a new lease on his acting life.

Back in Los Angeles, Dudley was now living alone in the Marina house, but was often to be found in the other home with Brogan. 'He loved being in the Toluca house,' she recalled wistfully, 'and he felt comfortable and happy. We had the best times there. We cooked, we danced, we played, and he loved it, he thrived on that. But then he would be this loner and go back to the Marina house and be the recluse. He needed that other side of himself that he was never able to shake off.'

Los Angeles, by nature and architecture, is a city that breeds isolation. Sprawling, with no real nucleus, it is a linear network of suburbs interconnected by freeways. Unlike most major cities, it is built entirely around the automobile, which makes every destination a chore to reach. Seldom can one simply walk down the road to the local market or go to a cinema or even hang out at a nearby cafe without getting into a car first and driving there.

In the Marina house, the fireplace spreading its warmth against a rare chilly day, Dudley mused about his proclivity to reclusiveness, aware of the trap created by living in such a sprawling city with no centre.

> DUDLEY: It's not like old Beethoven doing his work and then walking down the road and having a drink at the local bar, and I have to be very careful not to disappear up my own arsehole. It's all very well to ride my aerobic bike in the morning, but I used to ride a real bike and talk to real people. More and more one's life can be sustained in four walls.
>
> I'm living in a sense out of contact with people, but I *can* contact people directly I go out. The restaurant I'm involved in is five minutes up the road and so I can go up there if I want a gregarious time. It's so easy to talk to everyone

on the end of a phone. I've talked on that bloody phone forever . . . as a matter of fact I'm amazed it hasn't rung this morning. Nobody wants me. Of course they fucking don't! Who wants an ageing English dwarf with a club foot who's still worried about it!

BARBRA: Why do you *say* things like that?

DUDLEY: I say that because I don't really mean it. I say that because it makes me laugh. Because a) it's true and b) it's not true. So I'm ageing – I'm not really. So I'm English – yes I am, but I'm not really, I mean, I don't feel particularly English. So I have a club foot – yes, that's a physical thing. I say 'dwarf' because I've been called a dwarf so many times so I'm pre-empting the laughter in a sense. It doesn't matter in a way and yet it does. It's a philosophical sort of attitude that I find entertaining and sustaining too. Whenever I talk to Peter on the phone we get into endless laughter because of the self-deprecating stuff that goes on and it's fun, you know. Americans can be so fucking serious about themselves, although it's true to say that English people can go to the other extreme.

For a while at least, Dudley would be leaving the oppressive security of his Marina home. He was on his way to Europe to embark on a great musical challenge.

CHAPTER 24

An Orchestral Triumph and Another Chicken Chase 1990–91

In May 1990, accompanied by Brogan, Dudley returned to Oxford University to accept his M.A., which he had never collected after graduating in 1958. On the night of the ceremony he gave a small organ recital in his beloved Magdalen Chapel, then commandeered the piano to delight the graduates with some of his parodies.

Bernard Rose, his Oxford tutor, had always been struck by Dudley's contrasting musical talents. Many musicians had passed through his hands since the days when he had begun teaching in 1933 but Dudley, he ventured to me, was the only genius he'd ever encountered. 'The extraordinary thing is he has different talents both as a classical musician and a jazz pianist. But I think he hasn't really known which way to go, and that's been a great sadness.'

A few days later, Dudley flew to Hamburg to host the ground-breaking television series *Orchestra*! for Channel 4. It was a definitive and exciting introduction to classical music and, while explaining the role played by the various instruments, it also traced the history and evolution of the orchestra from its beginnings with a small group of players huddled around a keyboard into today's modern symphony orchestra of over a hundred musicians. Producer Jonathan Hewes wanted to present the six-part series in a way that would reach beyond the normal classical musical audience, and he knew that Dudley's warmth and humour would broaden the series' appeal.

He enlisted Sir Georg Solti, one of the century's great conductors, as the central figure of the programme that focused on conducting. 'But when we met him,' Hewes told me, 'he was so charismatic and such a wonderful old maestro with enormous energy that exhausted us all, we realised it would be daft to have him in just one programme, so we asked him to join with Dudley for the whole series.'

The combination was electric. Dudley had admired Solti since he was a youngster, and he was ecstatic, if somewhat intimidated, at the prospect of working with the veteran conductor.

Solti recalled with amusement that when they met for the first time, Dudley was very timid around him. 'I think he thought I would eat him! And I, too, was very shy, because I had seen him many times in films and had enormous respect for him.'

For a man of seventy-seven, Solti had an extraordinary vitality, and his abundant energy inspired Dudley. They filmed with the Schleswig-Holstein Festival Orchestra, an international group of young musicians, and Dudley, who had never before attempted such massive works, played sweeping pieces with Solti that included the first movement of Schumann's *Piano Concerto in A Minor*.

It would have been daunting for any concert pianist to play with Solti, and Dudley was understandably nervous. But he performed with a mastery that surprised even the maestro. 'He played the piano extremely well. He was quite frightened by it, but in a nice way, and he was never afraid to say so. I liked that about him.'

Dudley found the experience very grand. 'Solti was always a source of encouragement to me,' he enthused to Peter Cork, 'and has twice the energy that I have! He is very limber and a wonderful person to be with, probably because he didn't insist on cramming what he felt on to me.'

The programmes were immensely entertaining. Dudley's humour permeated the series without ever becoming irreverent, and he enjoyed a bantering camaraderie with Solti, himself a humorous man. "We both loved laughing,' recounted Solti, 'and I told jokes as much as him, so that was a strong common bond that brought us quickly together. I didn't know when we started that there would be as much humour as there turned out to be, but I think humour is necessary sometimes in music, and it worked very well in this instance.'

Dudley's absorption in and devotion to the music were apparent and he proved acutely knowledgeable about its history. Those who had formerly been convinced he had sold out to Hollywood had to admit now that they'd been wrong. No artist with baked brains could have tackled such a formidable task as *Orchestra!*

Dudley even enjoyed some free conducting lessons from Solti, and led the orchestra under the maestro's vigilant and critical eye. 'I was afraid he would be mortified,' Solti proffered, 'but he wasn't and he did very well. He was not afraid, and he never lost his sense of humour in the remarks he made about conducting.'

Dudley loved working on *Orchestra!*, which later won awards at festivals across the world in Russia, Montreux and the United States. The whole experience had been extraordinary for them all. 'I had a tremendous time,' Dudley wrote to Solti after returning to Los Angeles. 'Your passion and intensity, your resilience and determination were there for everyone to enjoy – me above all others. Thank you so much for a lovely time and for an inspiration that will never leave me. I send you my undying allegiance.'

With the series over, Dudley again felt himself to be at a

crossroads in his life. Should he pursue his music or concentrate solely on acting? Working with Solti had reminded him of the strenuousness of classical performance and how demanding an instrument the piano was. It took not only a great deal of concentration and technique but assiduous practice, and if he did not play for a day his fingers became a bit stiff.

'I think there are a lot of things that one leaves until late in life,' he wrote to Peter Cork, 'and I'm not sure that I'm not leaving my piano-playing too late. I'm doing a lot on my own, mainly trying to learn the [Bach] *48 Preludes and Fugues*, which is quite a task. I don't know quite why I'm doing it or who I'm doing it for, except for myself.'

> **DUDLEY:** I'm more interested now in learning a piece of music and pinning it down rather than just flipping through and idly sort of playing things. I've noticed my approach is different. I'm not so intimidated by a technical problem at the piano. I tend to practise more slowly, realising that the technique is very much at the service of the expression and that really you can learn anything if you split it up into little pieces. I'm focused more and more on something that is smaller and smaller, but it's the best I can do.

Dudley felt confused. He wanted to play the piano, but it was not enough. What he really wanted was a good movie and he still hoped for one, although without any great expectations. There had always been a conflict between his musical and acting talents, as there had between the audiences for each. Suzy Kendall had always been aggravated by people saying they loved his music so much and he should do more of it, or that they loved his comedy so why didn't he stick to that. Dudley, she declared, was blessed with being multitalented, and she found it offensive when people talked as if he should only concentrate on one rather than both.

In August 1990 Dudley returned to London to film a new series of Tesco ads. Arriving at London Airport, he was recognised by a couple of young boys and was amused to overhear them debating to each other, ''Ere, shall we ask 'im if 'e's found them bleedin' chickens yet?'

He hadn't. Filming beside the River Tay, he found salmon – but still no chickens. By now the ads had become so popular that, following the airing of each commercial, Tesco found its shelves stripped of chickens and whatever else it was that Dudley had managed to find instead of them, prompting Tesco chairman Sir Ian MacLaurin to announce his public pleasure in the daily growth of the Tesco brand. Dudley should have deferred his fee and accepted shares in the company – Tesco's profits were going through the roof.

So was his popularity in Britain. Ironically, the Tesco chickens – or absence of them – had brought him a new kind of fame and more success than anything he had done since *Arthur* almost ten years earlier. His appeal now spanned the generations. The older generations knew and loved him for the work he had done with Peter Cook, while a younger generation knew him only through his Hollywood movies. Now an even younger generation had come to know him through the commercials.

His reborn popularity coincided with the thirtieth anniversary of *Beyond the Fringe*. In those thirty years since first coming together on the Edinburgh stage, each of the four *Fringe* performers had achieved great things: Jonathan Miller, an incisive intellectual, had directed films, television and operas, written books and lectured all over the world; Alan Bennett had become one of the foremost social playwrights of his time. As for Peter Cook, he was one of Britain's greatest wits, dubbed by Peter Ustinov 'the funniest man in the world'.

Yet, once patronised by his fellow Fringers for being the least intellectual, it had been little Dudley, the one who carried the largest chip on his shoulder, with all of his supposed defects, who had become the cynosure of international attention and a sex symbol for women throughout the globe. He reminisced about the Fringers in my Hollywood apartment in late 1990.

> DUDLEY: It's strange because he's so good at it, but Jonathan has constantly said he doesn't like directing. Certainly we had a great time when he directed *Mikado*. Alan is one of the world's great playwrights and commentators and that gives me great pleasure. Even though he stopped talking to me at one point for a whole year. I went round to see him some time ago and there he was – chewing his tie as usual! It was like a night out of *Beyond the Fringe*. He always used to chew his tie. I don't know if it was from frustration or excitement. I couldn't tell and I never asked . . . Who's that munching on your papers? Is that Dylan? I thought so. Dylan, leave her questions alone. She needs them. You can't be chewing them up. Ha ha! Are the birds putting you off your stroke? I'm very happy with them here. They don't bother me. I think it's funny! It seems a bit like being in an aviary!

Early in October, Dudley performed at a tribute to Michael Caine in the presence of Princess Alexandra for the UK/LA Festival of Britain. Roger Moore hosted the evening, and Dudley turned some traditional English pub music into a 'Suite for Michael Caine', which he later titled *Fantasie-Impromptu*, in the style of Chopin.

Then it was back to London for a promotional blitz with Peter Cook to herald the BBC's video release and television broadcasts of *The Best of What's Left of Not Only . . . But Also*. Dudley and Peter appeared on every major talk show in Britain, and the newspapers were full of stories about the couple and their long partnership. The launch party attracted every leading alternative comic in Britain. Young or old, to them Cook and Moore represented two gods who had paved the way for the kind of comedy that now prevailed.

Italy beckoned next with the filming of two more Tesco ads. This time, Dudley found tiramisu instead of those elusive chickens. Some time later he was having lunch in Upminster with his sister and she served him a delicious dessert. 'What's this?' he asked her. 'Tiramisu,' she replied. 'I love it!' he raptured. 'Where did you get it?' She grinned back at him. 'Tesco's, of course!'

While he was in England Dudley tried to locate another important fragment of his past. He was fifty-five now, but he had never forgotten the person who, when he was seven, had shown him the first real affection he had ever experienced in his life. Now he tried to find her.

In 1942, Winifred House in Barnet had been the convalescent home where he had spent so many lonely anguished days and nights that had inexorably shaped his psyche. It was there that he received his first kiss from a woman when she had tucked him in bed. He wanted desperately to find Nurse Pat, the source of that early love. But the home's records did not go back that far and she was untraceable. Disheartened, Dudley instead made a sizeable donation to the institution, now a home for children with learning disabilities, in gratitude for the kindness he had carried with him from all those years ago . . . and had spent a lifetime trying to recreate in his relentless pursuit of women.

A few nights later, at legendary lyricist Sammy Cahn's house, Dudley took over the piano and also sang 'The Second Time Around', forgetting Cahn had written it. Suzy Kendall had always liked Dudley's singing voice and had urged him, without success, to record it on an album. Sammy Cahn obviously shared the same opinion. Faxing his appreciation to Dudley the next day, he said, 'I've heard my songs sung again and again but you were a joy to listen to last night. We were all wiped out by your singing. I know

I've tried to get you to do a piano album but now you must allow me to try and bring about a piano and "singing" album!'

Dudley was always punctual about returning phone calls. No matter where he was. I received calls from him in New York, London, Melbourne, Sydney, his bathroom. Even his car:

DUDLEY: I'm in the car on my way to a lunch date. I'm driving there. If I can find it. I'm going up 19th Street and I don't think I'm supposed to.
BARBRA: Are you in the wrong place?
DUDLEY: I think so. I don't know why. Anyway, you wanted to know about Sammy Cahn. I liked him a lot and went to his house a few times. What was really nice was that Sammy sang with me at one of his parties, both of us together . . . I think I'm lost! I turned off the freeway and now I'm in the wrong place. I thought this was straightforward. Better pull out the map here – I'm just talking to myself – hmm, Western Road, I should have got off at . . . ah, here's 19th Street, I need to go back there . . . Yes, Sammy wanted me to record an album of his songs, which I thought was very flattering . . . this is very illegal what I'm doing – I'm making a U-turn to get back to 19th Street . . . oh, flipping hell, I'm *on* 19th Street, for crying out loud!
BARBRA: So turn around and go back *up* 19th Street.
DUDLEY: Yes, if I turn around it might work. I think I've worked it out now. It's as plain as can be . . . Oh shit, maybe not. Where do I turn now? Left or right? Left, I think.
BARBRA: Are you sure?
DUDLEY: No, I'm *not* sure!
BARBRA: Turn the map upside down.
DUDLEY: I can't see the road sign, it's too high and it's blocked by the sun . . . but yes, let's go on, we were talking about Sammy Cahn . . . oh shit, it should have been right!

Oh, *there* it is! Bingo! . . . I think Sammy was trying to make me feel good about my voice because I always loved singing ever since I was a kid and I've missed it a lot . . . wait a minute, wait a minute, now I've gone past it! It's a recording studio. I don't get this, there's 1416 and 1414 but no 1412. It's got to be around here somewhere.

BARBRA: Park the car and find it.

DUDLEY: Yes, okay, I'm parking . . . Another thing I meant to tell you – I remember Carl Reiner wanted me to play Armand Assante's mother in drag. I filmed one day and the next day he told me it wasn't going to work and we'd have to drop it. So that was that.

BARBRA: I'm stopping you there. I don't know how you're managing to talk and drive at the same time if you're lost. Have you found the place?

DUDLEY: I haven't, no. It must be around the corner or something. Oh shit! Got to go. Talk to you later. . .

DUDLEY: It's me again. I've got to go back to Newport Beach! The numbers are all wrong. So we can go on talking. Where were we?

In January 1991 *Orchestra!* was transmitted on Channel 4 to resounding applause. 'I enjoyed it enormously,' applauded Itzhak Perlman, 'and I thought it was great that Dudley could be so easy with this great maestro and with such humour.'

As *Daily Telegraph* critic Max Davidson later declared of Dudley, 'The man is congenitally incapable of solemnity, which paradoxically makes him the ideal person to front a programme about classical music.' Although a few purists disagreed and found the jocularity between Dudley and Sir Georg Solti inappropriate, most critics felt it was a brilliant approach.

'I so much enjoyed the programmes,' Sir John Gielgud was moved to write to Dudley. 'I worked with Solti years ago in

Berlioz's *The Trojans* and found him extremely friendly and helpful as I am sure you must have done too.'

Dudley now found himself honoured at a gala tribute for the continuous support he had given to the local Venice Family Clinic, which provided health care to the uninsured, unemployed and homeless. Paul Reiser hosted the evening and Dudley offered some musical entertainment, accompanied by Kenny G on saxophone.

He had always felt it necessary to contribute in assisting people with no resources of their own. A firm believer in community activity, which he had enjoyed as a youth, he frequently helped the clinic by freely donating his time and money, hosting cocktail receptions at his house and restaurant and playing piano at benefit concerts to raise money for the organisation, which in the previous year had served over 50,000 patients.

He had always had an acute social conscience and felt guilty not to be doing more. He had always tried. From the early days of *Beyond the Fringe* in New York he had been making monthly payments to his parents for their wellbeing – a payment that he increased substantially over the years and continued until his mother's death in 1981 – and he gave endless financial gifts to family members and loans to friends.

DUDLEY: You're given a set of cards when you're born and you lay them out and think, 'Oh, I'm lucky, that's a good hand.' But there are those who don't have such good hands. I find it extraordinary that some people are more talented than others and are rewarded accordingly. I don't like that. I can't stand to see people on worse terms than I am.

I've been very lucky. I've lived comfortably all my life. Even when I came out of college and I was living on cornflakes I still thought I was having a great time. Because I hadn't been used to anything else. I felt I could always earn my living by playing in a bar or something and earn ten bob a night. In fact, that's the rent I was paying for my first flat in Hampstead. It was ten bob. It was a tiny room, the size of my little office here in my house, and it was my bedroom. I had everything I needed and I had a gas fire that I had to put money in. It was fine. I never felt deprived.

I think we have to be very careful about people who don't have resources. I'm a great believer in community activity, which is why I'm involved with the Venice Clinic here because people who go there have no money, no insurance. What do they do? It's very difficult to get yourself out from under. I help in different ways. I help with money, I help with doing TV appearances, charity concerts, fundraisers. As a matter of fact I'm having people over here to the house at the end of January when they have their art walk. I'm not some sort of amazing charitable phenomenon but if somebody moves me I'll try and do something about it.

Back in the seventies, when Dudley had bought a house in Islington, it had still been occupied by an elderly woman who was renting it from the former owner. Rather than evict her, Dudley bought her a flat where she could comfortably live out her days. She was a complete stranger to him, yet his conscience could not ignore her.

His contribution as a humanitarian was an aspect of his life that Dudley never discussed. He was reticent about his efforts and was embarrassed when they were acknowledged. A few years later it would come to light that Peter Cook had behaved in a similar manner. Charitable on a private scale, he helped a number of individuals and not even his wife had known. Only after his death, when those people wrote to Lin Cook, was his private generosity revealed.

In April 1991 Dudley returned to filming with a zany Disney comedy, *Blame It on the Bellboy*. An ensemble story of mistaken identity, it was directed in London and Venice, Italy, by Mark Herman, with Bryan Brown, Bronson Pinchot and Patsy Kensit rounding out the cast.

Bronson Pinchot, as an Italian bellboy in a Venice hotel, is given three envelopes to distribute to three guests with similar-sounding names. His poor English leads him to mix up the envelopes and turn the world upside down for Messrs Orton (a clumsy real-estate scout – Dudley), Horton (a small-town mayor turned Lothario – Richard Griffiths) and Lawton (a Mafia hit man – Bryan Brown). The hit man gets directions to a romantic rendezvous with a young woman whom he assumes to be his target, the amorous mayor is summoned to meet a lovely young estate agent whom he thinks is his dating escort, and the timid property scout turns up on the Mafia's doorstep believing their house is for sale and finds himself having to convince them that he is not their hit man.

Dudley's on-set behaviour was riotous as ever. Bronson Pinchot, who was starring in his own television sitcom, *Perfect Strangers,* claimed Dudley as his new idol. 'He had a genius for making everyone feel unbelievably at ease, and when he walked on the set each day, his first order of business was to do something droll with the first person he saw, whether it was the man pushing the tea cart around or the gaffer. I told everyone at the time I wanted to be just like him.'

The two shared a private joke that nobody else ever understood. Bronson had told Dudley a story that tickled his ribald fancy: his mother had seen a production of *The Sound of Music* with a thickly accented German woman playing the Mother Superior. When she asked Maria, 'What is it you can't face?' the last two words came out sounding acutely reminiscent of Derek and Clive. 'Dudley thought this was the funniest thing he'd ever heard,' laughed Pinchot, 'and after that he would always come on the set to wherever I was and say to me, "What is it, you cunt-face?" and dissolve into laughter! Of course, no one knew what to make of it, and to Dudley that was even funnier. Perhaps they thought it was an affectionate term that he was calling me a cunt-face!'

By 1992 Dudley's marriage to Brogan had disintegrated entirely. Still, they continued to spend time together, enjoying the companionship. Dudley felt frustrated and sad that he had been unable to make his third marriage work. It was pretty clear that he wasn't cut out to play the role of husband, though he had tried. But his despondency over their break-up didn't encroach on his unwavering pursuit of women. He was still playing the field and there was always a surfeit of available females.

CHAPTER 25
Musical Chairs
1992

'Movies are fun, music is work,' Dudley had often told Lou Pitt, 'and when I feel like working then I'll play the piano.'

As the year unfolded, music beckoned more strongly than ever. With Dudley reflecting on the future of his film career, he was sure he would never have another success like *10* or *Arthur*, and it was obvious that he was no longer an immediate choice for Hollywood's biggest film producers. Convinced that his film career was beyond resuscitation – at least to the heights of the past – he turned back to the one constant love of his life and scheduled a series of classical concerts across America and Canada.

Those who had always believed that his heart, soul and greatest talent belonged in music were glad to see this. 'I think he finds great happiness in his music,' Lysie Kihl mused. 'He's very lucky to have it, because he would be a very, very desperate man without it.' Choreographer Gillian Lynne also had always felt music was where Dudley channelled his greatest passion and where he felt most complete. 'When he's performing it, he's a totally rounded person, completely in command of his brilliance and his mind and his feelings . . . with no self-doubts.'

DUDLEY: I love playing the piano. I don't think I could live without the piano. Although to be honest with you, I would rather be a concert violinist because I love the violin so much. I've always wanted to play the violin professionally but I never felt I was good enough. I've played the piano for so long that I feel I can't suddenly turn my back on it. Maybe I should take up the violin as a recreational thing and stop talking about it . . . what's that noise from the bookshelf? One of the birds, I suppose.

BARBRA: It's Papillon. He's hanging out with the budgies behind the books in the bookcase.

DUDLEY: Ha ha ha!!

BARBRA: Don't laugh, it's not funny. There's not enough room there for them all.

DUDLEY: Ha ha HA!!

BARBRA: Hang on, I'll get him out. I have to remove some books to get to him. I'm glad you're amused.

DUDLEY: I am *very* amused! I think it's very funny! Oh God! Ha ha ha! It would make a great sitcom with all these birds flying around here and flying in and out of the bookcase!

While in London, Dudley joined the BBC Concert Orchestra and his former trio mates for his first ever British concert tour. He played classical music and jazz in Brighton, Manchester and Birmingham. The highlight was three electric nights at the Royal Albert Hall, which the BBC recorded, in a concert he would remember and cherish forever.

The tour reunited him with drummer Chris Karan and bassist Peter Morgan for the first time in fourteen years. 'I was so surprised to hear from him to ask if we'd be available,' Chris Karan recalled, 'and of course I said we'd love to do it. I'd more or less given up by then because so many years had gone by. It was a little rusty but the magic was still there and he still had an incredible feel.'

When Dudley opened at the Royal Albert Hall, a huge contingent of friends turned out to see him play, among them his sister and her husband, Suzy Kendall and her daughter, music editor Else Blangsted, who had flown in from her home in Switzerland, and theatre producer Alex Cohen and his wife, legendary actress Hildy Parks, who had followed him to London from New York. Lin and Peter Cook were also there and Peter, Lin saw, 'was terribly proud of him and so happy to hear the applause for him that night in that magnificent place. It was really quite moving.'

The year before, American pianist Rena Fruchter had formed Music For All Seasons (MFAS) with her husband Brian Dallow, a British pianist and early schoolmate of former prime minister John Major. Like Yehudi Menuhin's organisation in London, MFAS provided classical music performances for people confined in hospitals, nursing homes and schools for special children, and among the illustrious board members were Sir Georg Solti, André Watts, Maxim Shostakovich, Gian Carlo Menotti and Roberta Peters.

Fruchter had been a child virtuoso, making her debut as a soloist with the Philadelphia Orchestra at the age of six. By eleven she was performing with other notable orchestras and had achieved national recognition. After turning professional, she released several recordings of her work and had recently been writing a music column for the *New York Times*.

Dudley had met Rena during his 1987 concert with the New Jersey Symphony Orchestra. She interviewed him for a *New York Times* article and they had struck up a deep musical alliance which grew into a close friendship. She had for a long time been encouraging his talent and, in the same way that Robert Mann had been such an inspiration in earlier years, was pushing him to perform at public concerts. Wanting to pursue an active involvement with MFAS, Dudley was happy when Rena made him its president.

His film career might have been waning but he was still one of the entertainment industry's most popular performers and was turning down more musical requests than he could accept. Former First Lady Betty Ford asked him to appear at a charity celebration with Liza Minnelli for the tenth anniversary of her Betty Ford Center and was disappointed when he told her he had a previous commitment. 'Liza will be so disappointed you can't make it,' she wrote to him. 'You and she would make for a dynamic evening so I hope you won't mind if I keep my fingers crossed and pray for a schedule change.'

Dudley always acknowledged every invitation, even if he was unable to accept. Roger Moore had been after him for a long time to play at a UNICEF benefit, and Dudley apologetically explained in a long fax why he could not be there. 'To Sonny Moore from Roger Ditto,' Roger promptly faxed back. 'By taking the time to write you have confirmed that of which I was always certain and that is that you are a straight shooter and an all-around nice guy and you REMEMBER which is more than can be said for most of the pricks in our business . . . your name came up last night at dinner with the Sinatras, they spoke very highly of you and admire your talent and all that shit . . . "I know him," I bragged.'

The two Moores had shared a running gag for years. 'I always treated Dudley as my son,' Roger laughingly told me, 'and I introduced him as "My youngest son, Dudley . . . all the rest of them grew tall!"' They had been friends since the sixties, but Roger had actually known of Dudley long before they ever met. 'I kept getting his fan mail and I couldn't think why somebody was writing to me and calling me Dudley. It turned out that the BBC was mistakenly forwarding to me all these letters for Dudley from someone in Oxford who was besotted with him!'

Following the unprecedented success of *Orchestra!* Dudley embarked on a new six-part musical series and hosted *Concerto!* for Channel 4, which analysed and performed different concertos each week. Michael Tilson Thomas replaced the unavailable Georg Solti. It was an interesting combination since Dudley and Michael disagreed with each other all the time, but their passion for the subject worked well.

He was all over the globe these days. In Toronto, he performed in two cabaret shows at the ritzy Sutton Place Hotel. Coinciding with the opening of Toronto's annual film festival, his appearance became the talk of the town, enhanced by John Dankworth and Cleo Laine who joined him on stage. It was, the critics were quick to assess, 'a rare treat for the denizens of Toronto', and many turned down the opportunity to attend the festival's welcoming dinner for Robert Redford in favour of hearing Dudley.

'Something happens when he plays,' reported columnist George Christy, who saw lines around the hotel for each of Dudley's performances. 'A room comes to life and it's almost like a psychic magic in the air.'

But Dudley seemed incapable of totally feeling the appreciation himself. 'I don't understand,' he remarked to Marsha Berger, a fan with whom he had struck up a friendship and who ran his fan club, 'how I can be so popular as you say I am when I haven't had a hit film in ten years.' Marsha laughed. 'Not that I'm comparing,' she told him, 'but Jimmy Stewart hasn't had one in forty years!'

That month, September 1992, Dudley scrawled gloomily in his diary, 'Got divorced!'

'We should never have been married,' Brogan sadly reflected. They had been together for more than seven years and had shared something very special. Under Brogan's encouraging tutelage, Dudley had become outgoing and daring in a way he never had been before. And never would be again. In spite of the divorce, both were reluctant to relinquish their relationship. 'He was the love of my life,' Brogan told me wistfully. 'You don't throw that away because you get divorced.'

CHAPTER 26

Classical Movements 1992–93

The Brogan years had been gregarious ones, but towards the end Dudley found himself retreating into his cocoon of isolation. He had always exhibited the face of a clown and, like all clowns, he wore laughter as his mantle and kept the tears inside.

His friend Robert Mann recognised the different facets of Dudley's nature. 'All great clowns who can translate the humour and humanness of human vulnerability and error, whether it's a Chaplin or a W.C. Fields, have fairly brooding insides. Dudley's no exception.'

Jazz singer Barbara Moore had always been touched by 'an appalling sadness seeping through the notes in his music', and, however jolly the music seemed, she always caught the sound of anguish emerging from somewhere deep in the chord structures. 'You feel there's the little clown laughing at the world, but inside it's the Pagliacci thing. Deep down Dudley has never liked the thought of being the little man, because inside himself he's such a big chap.'

But these days much of Dudley's inability to feel peace within himself revolved less around his self-image than around an inherent dissatisfaction with his work – a feeling that plagues people with excessive talent. No matter how hard he strived, it never felt good enough to him. 'You would think somebody that successful would be able to sit back and feel good about it,' considered his first wife Suzy Kendall. 'But he never did.'

As Joe McGrath had earlier observed: 'He felt he was wasting his life. He really felt that music was very important and he hadn't fulfilled himself, he hadn't written the thing that he wanted to write. He didn't know what it was, but time, as he said, was just passing and he still hadn't got down to doing it.'

Over lunch in his restaurant, Dudley wistfully conceded to me his dissatisfaction.

> **DUDLEY:** I suppose I haven't made the dent in life that I hoped to. I think I've missed the boat a bit. Maybe I should have tried harder. But I have tried hard. I look at the stuff at the Royal Albert Hall and places where I played Mozart and I was trying very hard. I haven't become a full-out comedian or musician or composer. You could say I'm a jack of all trades, master of none. If I'd been a physically different person, I might have concentrated more. I guess the incentive isn't there, and I feel it's too late to do anything. I just hope the concerts will go on and I'll be listened to and recognised to some extent.

While still playing the field, Dudley had acquired a new girlfriend. Several years earlier he had met 27-year-old Nicole Rothschild when she had encountered him in the street and begged for his autograph. Never able to resist an attractive girl, they had begun an affair. Eventually, despite not having annulled her previous marriage, she married Charles Cleveland, a dark-skinned Creole and self-confessed drug addict, had two children, then divorced a few years later.

Dudley had helped them financially throughout their marriage. Now he moved Nicole into an apartment close to his home, gave her a $20,000 sports car and a monthly allowance. But he was still enjoying the company of different women, among them Quincy Jones's daughter Jolie. One girlfriend was rarely enough for him.

Since the early sixties, Dudley's friend Gillian Lynne had witnessed his insatiable appetite for women. 'Here was this brilliant talent, wonderful-looking, absolutely cuddly and deliciously wantable fellow but who had not been blessed with height and had been given a club foot, and I felt he was going after all the wrong people just to compensate for that. It was as if he was saying, "I might be little and I might have a club foot, but look who I can get!"'

Such a busy, gregarious life was exhausting and, giving his social exploits a rest, Dudley flew to London with Brogan, still a close companion despite their divorce.

At Buckingham Palace, Dudley performed at a royal charity concert presided over by Prince Edward. At the banquet beforehand, Brogan, who was sitting next to Edward, asked him, 'When are you going to show me around this place?' He smiled reservedly. 'There are rather a lot of rooms here,' he replied. 'That's all right,' Brogan smiled encouragingly. 'We can start with just one.'

Afterwards, Dudley played cabaret in the music room adjacent to the austere banqueting hall. 'The piano wasn't a great piano. I sort of expected better for Buckingham Palace.' Still, it did not spoil his performance. As Prince Edward later wrote to him, 'I have had nothing but enthusiastic feedback from those present about how much they enjoyed the evening and this is due in no small part to your marvellous entertainment. I hope you enjoyed the event as much as we all did.'

He and Brogan had indeed enjoyed it but were immensely disappointed not to take home any souvenirs. Checking out the men's room, hoping to spirit away a roll of toilet paper with 'Buckingham Palace' emblazoned all over it, Dudley found only the standard toilet tissue used by common folk. Nor were there any ashtrays bearing the royal insignia.

> **DUDLEY:** Brogan and I searched everywhere but we couldn't find a single thing to pilfer! There was nothing with the name Buckingham Palace. Nothing! Maybe they just had too many people taking that stuff. At least we got the menu, which Brogan ran back to retrieve as we were leaving.

Bordeaux now beckoned for a new Tesco commercial. It was the last one and finally Dudley located the elusive chickens. He found thousands of them at a French farmhouse and filled his car with them all. But driving home he was overcome with compassion and released the lot.

He had spent nearly three years in his search for those elusive chickens – a quest that had begun in the summer of 1989 and taken him halfway across the world. He had waded through rivers, careened over a cliff, swum in a vat of wine and trudged through the outback (actually Malibu Creek). Along the way he had found brie in France, salmon in Scotland, grapes in Italy, wine in Chile, Stilton in England and pizza in America, but not a single squawking chicken. Until now. With these final commercials due to debut on Christmas Day, the British papers were full of stories about his Tesco exploits.

The American television networks had long been considering Dudley to star in his own series. CBS had floated him earlier in *Dudley* as a twice-divorced father whose kids and ex-wives lived with him under the same roof, but the show was considered too risqué. Now they devised a new concept and *Dudley* was reborn. This time he was a pianist-composer whose wife (Joanna Cassidy) turns up out of the blue and dumps on him their rebellious teenage son, believing he will benefit from some paternal influence – a view not shared by either of the males. After the first show was broadcast, *TV Guide* applauded, 'Moore is cute and perfectly suited for sitcom silliness'.

Dudley liked the immediacy of television and coming up with a new show every week. He had always thrived on pressure. But he was being stretched to the limit, working five days a week, sometimes eighteen hours a day. He wasn't too sorry when the show was ingloriously cancelled after just a few episodes.

Meanwhile, the offers continued to pour in. There was another television show, this one in Britain. *Dudley Moore and Jazz with Friends*, a late-night light-entertainment programme, would have mixed comedy with songs, jazz and interviews with celebrities, but he turned it down.

He also rejected an offer from the Los Angeles Opera to do a new Gilbert and Sullivan opera with Linda Ronstadt. Dudley liked the singer, with whom he'd once performed at a charity benefit, but the idea did not appeal to him. The only reason he had done their earlier *Mikado* was because he wanted to work with Jonathan Miller.

A few years before, when the *Los Angeles Times* had run an article about celebrities' greatest wish lists, comedian Phyllis Diller, an accomplished pianist herself, revealed that her idea of heaven would be to hear Dudley Moore play jazz at her house. 'He read it and dropped me a note, telling me "any time",' she recalls. 'But it took about three years, because he was so busy. Finally we picked a date, and I asked if he'd mind if I shared it with a few close friends.'

Her invitations gave away her excitement. 'Come share my fondest dream come true,' she wrote. 'Dudley Moore is going to play jazz!' Thirty people showed up at her Brentwood home, including her closest friends, Bob Hope and his wife Dolores.

To her amazement, Dudley arrived with a bunch of sound equipment and a bass player. 'He treated it like an actual performance, as if he'd been hired to play a concert,' recalled

Diller, 'which I felt kind of bad about, especially since he was very shy and wouldn't mingle with everyone. But he was magnificent. I remember Bob sat on the floor and was completely enthralled by him. It was one of those wonderful evenings where you died and went to heaven.'

Dennis Koch, Dudley's dog walker, loved to hear him play when he arrived at the house. But the moment he walked inside, Dudley stopped. Aware of this, after walking the dogs, Dennis would return to the house and sit outside the front door for a while. 'The dogs loved his music, and I told them their daddy was playing and to be very quiet, and the three of us would just sit there and listen to him play. It was pure magic. I had all these free concerts. But I never told him I did that, because I knew it would embarrass him.'

In May, Dudley performed with the Toronto Symphony Orchestra. He was now earning between $35,000 and $50,000 a concert, and with some bookings spread over a couple of nights, it was no mean achievement for a man who had never believed he could sustain himself through playing classical music.

With the sole exception of his visit to Phyllis Diller, Dudley had not played jazz for a long time, partly because the kind of jazz he played required being part of a trio and, more significantly, because he felt he had lost the ability to create. 'It's a great pity,' regretted Oscar Peterson, 'because in my opinion he had a lot to say creatively and compositionally and I was hoping he would always continue in the field.'

DUDLEY: I'd probably find it very intimidating now to play jazz in public. I haven't played for so long. It's hard to believe I haven't played for such a long time. I don't know how it could have happened. But it's not because jazz is more intricate than classical music; it's as intricate as you want it to be.

In my early days of improvising madly I used to play a

lot and I loved it. I always played sort of slow Erroll Garner, which is about one hundred and twenty crochets a minute; it's a favourite tempo of mine. He's wonderful at that speed but he can play much faster. I can't.

I once considered buying his piano. Some bloke had it for sale and I went and played it. It was pretty exciting to be playing Erroll Garner's piano but I didn't buy it in the end. The guy was asking too much money for it and I also couldn't think where I could put it if I bought it. But it was a tremendous thrill to play it and to imagine Garner sitting there.

What Dudley really wanted more than anything was to create and play his own music, but he wasn't convinced he could make a living at it and he lacked the impetus to push it. While people paid him to perform other composers' works, it seemed the appropriate route to follow.

August 1992 found him in London publicising the Channel 4 series, *Concerto!* It was perfect timing for the launch of *Derek and Clive Get the Horn*, the video of the third album with Peter Cook that had previously been only fleetingly available to the public. Time had not diminished their public's appreciation and the launch was a huge success.

Robin Williams had always been a dedicated fan of Dudley's more ribald features. 'Nobody's ever written anything that Dudley and I could do together,' he reflected, sounding disappointed and asking me to put a 'job wanted' notice up on the BBC's bulletin board. 'I think we would be a wonderful combination for a film. My choice would be to make *Derek and Clive: The Movie* with him. I think we'd be fabulous!'

Returning to Los Angeles, Dudley reunited with Liza Minnelli in a film for HBO. *Parallel Lives*, directed by Linda Yellen, featured appearances by Gena Rowlands, Ben Gazzara, Paul Sorvino,

Treat Williams, JoBeth Williams and Robert Wagner. It was a loose story, entirely improvised, about a high-school reunion.

Liza Minnelli found it all rather strange, 'because not only were the lines improvised but also what happened to the characters, so we became the makers of our own destiny and never knew what the other person was going to say. Improvisation is a very frightening thing to do when you have no outline or idea of what a scene is about.'

However, she was exuberant at being around Dudley again, who to her was like 'a shot of adrenaline, and he always had me in fits of laughter'. Especially when he told her about the coloratura singer he had heard on the radio as a youngster, which so turned him on that he would masturbate whenever she hit the high Cs. 'I found that story so funny,' Liza laughed, 'that I wrote it into my computer later! It made me laugh so hard that I felt as if I'd done four hundred sit-ups. My stomach ached for days!'

Wanting to preserve his solitude in the Marina home, Dudley bought a house around the corner for his girlfriend, Nicole. He had always felt a responsibility towards the family and friends surrounding the women in his life, only Nicole had a rather large family. Dudley was helping them all and was supporting Nicole, her two children and her ex-husband Charles, who was HIV positive. He had bought cars for Nicole, her sister and Charles. And he had bought an apartment for Charles's mother in Las Vegas. It all seemed outrageously philanthropic but it was part of the obligation he felt when he was committed to a woman.

But it was a tempestuous relationship. It is said that opposites attract, and Dudley, meticulous, structured and rational, was indeed attracted to entirely the antithetical qualities in Nicole. But these very differences triggered endless fights between them, often resulting in Dudley emerging scratched and bruised. Yet somehow they always kissed and made up. In spite of his reluctance, Dudley eventually gave in to Nicole's pleading and married her after his lawyers had tracked down her first husband and had that marriage annulled.

Instead of a honeymoon, Dudley was happy to embark on a new television series, *Daddy's Girls*. He was paid $250,000 for the pilot episode and played the owner of a clothing business whose wife runs off with his business partner, leaving him alone to bring up three very modern daughters.

When it debuted in September 1994, the reviews were not kind, and ultimately the show was cancelled. Dudley was disappointed. He had liked it and hoped it would work. 'I don't know if my persona is something the great American public really wants to see,' he mused to me wistfully at the time. It was, but audiences wanted to see him in something that made the best use of his humour, and the show had given him no opportunity to express the physical comedy that his fans found so endearing.

At least there was still his music.

With music now the dominant force in his life, a new concert tour took Dudley across America and into Canada. He was averaging two concerts a month – an impressive record for a musician who, as he liked to put it, had come from behind. At that rate, he was guaranteed a long and highly lucrative career.

In New York Dudley faced a challenging return to Carnegie Hall in a benefit for Music For All Seasons. He had long considered expanding his repertoire and was particularly keen to play Grieg's *Piano Concerto* but had lacked the confidence to try. Spurred on and tutored by Rena Fruchter, he spent weeks solidly learning the work. She was impressed by his perseverance. 'He really didn't think he could do it because it's a tough one. It's intensely frenetic, and taking the decision to try it was a big hurdle for him to overcome.' He performed it exquisitely and EMI recorded it for a CD release.

Dudley and Rena had recently formed a production company to record concerts for video and television. They planned a solo concert for the following year – a retrospective in which Dudley would both play and discuss his career. They also launched a short-story competition for young writers, with Dudley agreeing to set the winning entry to music which he would play at a new concert at Carnegie Hall set for April 1996.

Earlier in the year I'd begun writing Dudley's biography. We talked constantly on the phone and he visited me with regularity, content to delve into his memory while birds flew overhead or rested and slept on his welcoming shoulders.

Towards Christmas, I had overnight houseguests and the morning of their departure they lingered over their breakfast, knowing that Dudley was coming for lunch and sending not very subtle messages that they hoped to meet him. That, I knew, would not go down well with Dudley. I needed to clear the breakfast table and start preparing lunch, his usual trout and Brussels sprouts (steamed for exactly six minutes; sometimes he'd stand over me, glued to the minute hand of his watch so that they didn't cook a second too long). But still my guests sat there, dawdling over their smoked salmon and cream cheese bagels.

Suddenly, with a whoosh of wings overhead, my mischievous cockatiel Papillon flew over and came skidding to a halt in the tub of cream cheese on the table. He promptly sank down into it and was trapped there, to the horror of my friends. They looked at each other in shock and with one matching thought got up from the table. I fished Papillon out of the cream cheese, which he was already checking out with his beak and clearly enjoying. As I cleaned his feet under the warm tap water I heard my friends leave. Top marks to Papillon. He had sensed my frustration and used his avian instinct to intervene and manipulate the situation.

Dudley was vastly amused by the tale when he arrived and, perching Papillon on his finger, he thanked him with what can only be described as a lengthy Derek and Clive-like discourse. And a heaped teaspoon of cream cheese.

CHAPTER 27

Goodbye-ee, Peter Cook

1995

In January 1995 Peter Cook died. At the age of fifty-seven, a light had been switched out in the corridors of British comedy.

Dudley was the first person Lin Cook phoned. 'It's almost impossible to define what Peter and Dudley shared together,' she pondered. 'It defies a simple explanation. They were part of each other's family, and there was a deep affection between the two of them. Dudley was the person Peter loved the most, but I think in the earlier years Dudley didn't realise how much Peter felt for him.'

Dudley felt disoriented. He could not imagine Peter not being there any more. Overcome by a need to hear his voice, he telephoned Cook's answering machine, but he felt even stranger when he heard it. A disconnected voice on the other end still in this world, yet the soul of the man who had put it there was no more.

Despite the shock of Peter's death, Dudley insisted on keeping our lunch date at his restaurant, where we were joined by his old friend from Oxford, John Bassett, who had brought the four

Fringers together in 1960. The restaurant was surrounded by TV crews and paparazzi but there was little that Dudley could tell them. He felt numb.

Peter's death was the end of an era, and for Dudley the cutting of a thread that had bound them together for more than thirty years. Theirs had been a marriage of sorts: two people loving each other but unable to live together, yet each willing to cross the world to help the other if asked.

First brought together in *Beyond the Fringe* in 1960, their ludicrous comedy in three series of *Not Only . . . But Also* had made them cult idols to millions of British viewers. Together they had made five films and a stage show that was seen on three continents, and they had given birth to Derek and Clive, two of the most obscene characters the world had ever heard.

A deep sadness engulfed Dudley and he was gripped by panic attacks that would wake him suddenly in the middle of the night. Sitting up in the darkness, he was weighed down by the thought that he would never be able to see or talk to Peter again.

At least there was work to distract him. *Oscar's Orchestra* was a futuristic animated series for the BBC about the orchestra. The series introduced the great classical themes in a form made entertaining to children. It offered an inspiring introduction to musical education and Dudley was delighted to adopt the voice of Oscar the piano.

With a new concert tour, he set off across the nation, throwing himself into Mozart and Gershwin, this year's choice, in symphony halls across the country.

In the midst of this, however, he faced a time of considerable change. He had just learned Nicole was pregnant. He felt calm about the prospect, although he'd always fretted about being a father and didn't feel he was particularly good at it. Though close in the early years, after his son Patrick became a teenager the two had grown distant. He wished it were otherwise but believed it to be inevitable; he was duplicating his own father's passiveness.

Impending fatherhood made him feel reflective and in his home one hot Californian day he sifted through more of the memorabilia he'd amassed over the years.

> **DUDLEY:** Oh, blimey! Just *look* at this photo of me with my hair plastered! I used to wash my hair and set it with melted-down Vaseline and it used to be an immovable rock for about three weeks! I don't know why. I just wanted my hair a certain way . . . and look, these are photos of my trio, for crying out loud! I recognise the sweater; I used to wear that sweater all the time! It's nuts that I kept all this stuff, I'm amazed by it . . . Oh, here's me with my Maserati! I loved that car but crikey it could go fast and I nearly got nabbed a few times by the police . . . that's a photo of my wedding to Suzy – I haven't looked at this lot in years – Oh Gawd, I'd forgotten about this: this is a letter from some girl who wanted me to adopt her! I was married to Suzy at the time and we went through a lot of stuff with that. She just turned up at our house and wanted to be adopted! She was about thirteen, fourteen. I got in touch with her parents and that's what I couldn't understand. Why did she want us to adopt her when she already had parents? . . . I have to laugh at some of all this because it's so awful! Some psychiatrist said it's terrible what people leave behind and it is in a sense. I guess like Gandhi says, we spend a lot of time doing things that aren't important but it was very important that we do them. And when we look back at what we've done it seems so empty.

In April 1995, Dudley turned sixty. It brought, oddly, a sense of relief. He was tired of being fifty-nine. He looked a good ten years younger than his age and still resembled the cute leprechaun of the 1960s when he was performing in Britain with Peter Cook. There were a few flecks of silver in his hair and the odd crease in his face, but otherwise time had been especially kind to Dudley. Fear of ageing had plagued him on earlier birthdays, but this one was remarkably free of trauma.

> CHICAGO – It's an overcast early evening and Dudley is performing for two nights with the renowned Chicago Symphony Orchestra, formerly home for twenty-two years to Sir Georg Solti. He's been rehearsing in his hotel suite all day, not even leaving the piano long enough to have lunch. It's a short hop to the orchestra's Symphony Hall and Dudley tells the waiting limo chauffeur that we're going to walk. We stroll down the busy street, Dudley filling my ears with tales about Mozart. Suddenly from behind us, a woman screams: 'It's *him*! It's *Arthur*!' Dudley glances sideways at me with a self-conscious, resigned smile, shrugs imperceptibly, then turns, beaming, to face two middle-aged women who have just pounced on him. They're gasping, stammering words of adulation. Dudley thanks them, shakes their hands, and we continue on our way. Depending on his mood, it's the dichotomy of the celebrity who is almost embarrassed to be treated in that way. There are days when he wants to retreat inside himself and not be 'on'. Today is one of them.

At the concert, Dudley earned a standing ovation for his performance of Mozart's *Piano Concerto No. 21* and Gershwin's *Rhapsody in Blue*. He topped off the evening with a few of his parodies and was a resounding success with one of the world's most musically knowledgeable audiences. Sir Georg would have been proud.

On the way back to the hotel, we stopped at a shop to buy

some items, then went to pay. The young man behind the counter took one look then said, 'Has anyone ever told you you look like Dudley Moore?'

'Yes, I've been told that before,' Dudley replied instantly as he pulled out his credit card. Behind us, an older man who recognised Dudley was frantically trying to get the young man's attention. Dudley handed over his card and the assistant looked at it.

'Oh my God!' he exclaimed. 'What a coincidence! Did you just change your name or is this a coincidence?' Dudley said nothing. He just smiled.

In London, at Peter Cook's memorial service, most of Britain's comedic community turned out to pay tribute to the extraordinary comic genius. Dudley told a few light-hearted anecdotes and at the end of the service he played their former signature tune 'Goodbye-ee', from *Not Only . . . But Also*, accompanied by the choir from Peter's old school.

There was a huge hole in Dudley's universe, and it would be a long time before he could fully come to grips with his emotions. For now, nearly six months after Peter's death, he could only reflect on the times they had shared and the work they had done, and wonder at the extraordinary scale and audacity of it all.

DUDLEY: After Peter's memorial service I rented a car and I drove over to Dagenham to the house in Baron Road where we had lived. The front garden has disappeared and there's now a carport there. My mother didn't drive. She never went anywhere. Never came out to visit me in Los Angeles. It was bad enough for her to leave the bloody door to walk up the road to the shops to get fish for the cat which she used to do. And she always wore the same coat; she wouldn't wear a different coat even though I put money in the bank every week. She always said, 'Oh no, I'm not spending that, dear, keep it for a rainy day, you might need it.' And apart from that, her rationalisation was that if you wore a new coat you'd probably get beaten up because it would make her look as if she had a few bob.

When Dudley returned from London, life suddenly gathered speed. He was delighted to join the renowned cast of a film for cable television. *A Weekend in the Country* was an ensemble piece with intertwining stories in which Dudley was joined by Jack Lemmon, Christine Lahti, Richard Lewis and Rita Rudner, wife of the film's director, Martin Bergman. Dudley played a vineyard owner romantically involved with Rita Rudner. It was not the first time he'd had an on-screen affair with a director's wife: in *10*, his girlfriend had been played by Julie Andrews, who was married to Blake Edwards; and in *The Wrong Box* he gave Nanette Newman, wife of Bryan Forbes, her first screen kiss.

He was also committed to a couple of concerts in Canada and America, and in between the weeks of filming, found himself flying back and forth across the two countries. His frequent-flyer miles were at an all-time high. Often he'd ring me from foreign locations, checking in to see if I needed new information for the biography I was writing about him.

DUDLEY: I'm calling you from Winnipeg. It's fine here. I'm my usual self. I'm in my hotel room with curtains drawn and I'm trying to rest after tonight's concert. I get focused on a performance, I suppose, and afterwards I feel pretty tired. I'm playing – surprise, surprise – the Mozart 457 [piano concerto] in C minor and Gershwin's *Rhapsody in Blue*. And of course my parodies.

BARBRA: You were worried about the Mozart. Are you feeling happier about it?

DUDLEY: Well, there's always something that goes wrong all the time . . . can you hang on a sec . . . it's okay, I heard

> the phone ringing but it was on the television! How pathetic of me! I had an amazing coincidence last night because it turned out the conductor, Bramwall Tovey, comes from Ilford! Right next door to where I grew up! So you can guess that we had quite a few things to say to each other. It doesn't happen very much at all that I encounter someone from my part of England . . . Actually, I'm calling you because I wanted to tell you something, but now I've forgotten what it was. Ha ha! I'll have to call you back when I remember. I think I'll probably go to sleep shortly so it will be tomorrow.

Two months after his sixtieth birthday, Dudley became a father for the second time. He was too squeamish to watch the actual birth of baby Nicholas and stood at the head of the bed filming the delivery – what he could see of it.

After years of being pursued by advertisers, Dudley made his first American commercials for National Car Rental. It was a series concept that tapped in to his comedic talent, just as the British Tesco ads had done. If audiences had been bemoaning the fact that they hadn't seen much of Dudley in recent years, that changed when the ads began running on national television.

Meanwhile, film scripts continued to arrive. Dudley was still in demand, and major directors were pursuing him. One of them was Barbra Streisand.

She offered Dudley a small role in *The Mirror Has Two Faces*, in which she was not only the star but also the director. Dudley was ambivalent about the part, but Lou Pitt urged him to do it. Pitt could be bullish when he chose, and this time when his agent spoke Dudley gave in. He would make the film, and maybe it would revive his dormant acting career.

In November 1995 Dudley began work on the Streisand film.

CHAPTER 28

Into The Darkness 1995–96

The past month had been a busy one for Dudley. He had played numerous concerts, filmed the first commercials in his near million-dollar deal with National Car Rental, and had hosted a two-day American memorial tribute in Los Angeles to Peter Cook.

His role in *The Mirror Has Two Faces* was not a large one, but it was likely to be hugely significant. For too long, he had been accused of appearing in second-rate works that had not made enough of his considerable talents. Now he had a chance to turn that around.

The romantic comedy marked Streisand's first return to directing since 1991's *The Prince of Tides*, and boasted a stellar cast that teamed her with Jeff Bridges, Pierce Brosnan, Lauren Bacall, Brenda Vaccaro and Mimi Rogers. Dudley had one of the several elite cameos as Jeff Bridges' best friend, while Streisand was playing a dowdy college professor who transforms herself to bring some passion into her platonic marriage.

> **NEW YORK** – It's the day before the start of filming and the cast has assembled in the Manhattan production offices for a full script reading. Streisand looks and sounds ebullient. She's wanted to make this film for years and her unrestrained enthusiasm fills the room. She must be exhausted from months of pre-production work, but looks fresh even without make-up. Her shoulder-length hair bobs from side to side as she chats with everybody grouped around an oval table. Some of the actors are meeting for the first time, and Streisand hosts the gathering like a mother hen, introducing everyone and making sure there's plenty of food and refreshments on hand. Dudley has asked me to remain but I opt to wait in the green room, aware of Streisand's baleful eyes constantly focused in my direction. Afterwards, Brenda Vaccaro came to me. 'He was wonderful!' she enthused. 'He gave the most fabulous reading! He was really funny and everybody loved what he did.' Dudley seems less than satisfied but he's relieved the reading went well and that he's come through it unscathed.

That night, Dudley rang me from his hotel room at midnight. I was startled. It was very late for him. Was something wrong? When he wasn't working his typical bedtime was early evening. He told me he'd just finished reading the last half of the biography manuscript I'd handed to him earlier. I hadn't expected him to read right through it but he had. 'I can't believe how much there is of it!' he exclaimed. No less, I told him, than the size of his substantial life.

The next morning, Dudley was fretting. Nicole had rung several times throughout the night to tell him she was moving the household immediately to Telluride, a small mountain town in Colorado. At Nicole's request, Dudley had already put down a deposit on a house there but she didn't want to wait. With the limo waiting to take us to the set, Dudley tried to clear his head of the chaos taking place in California and concentrate on the job at hand.

> NEW YORK – On location in the grounds of Columbia University Dudley runs through his lines with Streisand. An exacting director, she pays enormous attention to every detail, and though intensely focused on what she's doing at each moment, is simultaneously aware of everything taking place around her. She sees me watching and asks why I'm there. I know she never allows the press onto her film sets and expect to be banished at any moment. But to my surprise, she gives me a half-smile and allows me to stay.
>
> Dudley's tendency is to learn his lines loosely, then deliver a slight deviation from the script. But Streisand is punctilious about the written words and Dudley can't remember them. Even writing them on giant cue cards hasn't helped. The more frustrated Streisand becomes, the harder Dudley is finding it to focus at all. He's deeply concerned and doesn't understand why he can't remember his lines. He's so upset that he forfeited lunch and remained holed up in his trailer.

Dudley was relieved when the limousine arrived to whisk him to the airport for his flight to Montreal. His performance the next night with the Montreal Symphony lacked his usual verve and fluency. Distracted by Nicole's actions on the home front, for once Mozart and Gershwin could not command his full concentration.

Returning to New York the next day he met privately with Streisand, who was worried about him. Was he okay? she asked. In truth, Dudley would have been vastly relieved to be released from the film but he felt it would be unprofessional to tell her since he had already committed himself to it. He told Streisand he was fine and would have his lines memorised by the time he returned to film more scenes the following week.

The truth was that he was drowning in the morass of his marriage and becoming increasingly depressed. 'I just want to play the piano and have everyone leave me alone,' he told Rena. But with all the angst over his marriage, also the early symptoms of PSP had begun to materialise. Dudley knew things were wrong. 'Something is happening to me and I don't know what,' he told us both.

Flying back to Los Angeles, Dudley was anxious at being unable to reach Nicole on the plane's telephone. He had arranged for her ex-husband to collect their children and baby Nicholas from her sister who was babysitting them, and to fly them to Telluride, where they would all be living together. It wasn't until later that night that he learned everyone had safely reached the new home.

He was not surprised, nor disappointed, when Lou Pitt rang a few days later to tell him that Barbra Streisand was cutting him loose from the film. He had not wanted to make it in the first place, and was relieved not to have to face complicated flights back and forth to New York from Telluride. Still, the professional in him felt bad that he had not performed to the best of his acting ability. And he didn't understand why.

In Telluride, surrounded by the chaos of Nicole's family, Dudley abandoned his daily piano practice. Rena Fruchter flew out a few times and encouraged him back to the keyboard. They had a crammed schedule: there was work to do for MFAS, and they had several concerts to perform together in the months ahead, including a January concert in Washington with the National Symphony Orchestra. Dudley worked well in Rena's presence. She rekindled his passion and was a tremendous influence. He depended on her for the security that was otherwise lacking in his life and, with her encouragement, Dudley finally settled down to composing for the first time in fifteen years.

Their glittering gala benefit concert for MFAS at Carnegie Hall was only a few months away, and he applied himself to scoring the poem that had won their production company's young writers' award.

> **DUDLEY (phone message):** I'm still in Telluride. I'm not coming back to LA for a few weeks. I want to ask you . . . wait, I've got something in my eyes. I just saw a bit of protein float down, which you can see through your eye when you get older. I remember asking a doctor, 'What is that stuff I see, that strange, descending wheel-shaped thing?' And he said it's just protein coming off the eye. It's a normal age thing apparently. Charming, isn't it . . . Hang on, Emil has just clambered all over me! All the dogs are here. Christ, oh bloody hell, stop it! They fight CONTINUOUSLY! The big sheltie is bullied by the small Pomeranian and the dachshund. They're fighting now as we speak. There are massive jaws snapping here! And now I've forgotten what I was going to ask you! I'll call you back later when I remember.

They had been in Telluride barely two months when Nicole decided they should move back to Los Angeles. She had wanted to open a shop for children's clothes and furniture and Dudley had borrowed over $60,000 for her to buy merchandise and satisfy her latest whim. But, as so often happened, she changed her mind and the shop never opened, despite the amount spent on it. Life these days was confusing, to say the least. But Dudley always gave in, so back to the Marina it was. He wasn't sorry. Mountain life wasn't for him.

But he felt himself drowning in the turbulence of his life. He felt trapped and helpless in a continual cycle of abuse, remorse and apology but obliged to take care of Nicole and her family. There were endless rows and Dudley kept moving in and out of the house. Not for another few years would he come to understand that it was addiction, not love, that kept bringing him back.

For some time he had known he was in a financial predicament but he was horrified to learn that his business manager, Hugh Robertson, to whom he'd given power of attorney, had borrowed heavily against the equity in his house, which once had been valued at around $4 million. Dudley was now living off that loan. Robertson had also dipped into the trust fund Dudley had set up for his son. Dudley knew he'd earned nearly $40 million over twenty years and couldn't understand where it had all gone. Only later, after a lengthy investigation, was it learned that Robertson had been brought up on previous charges of defrauding his clients.

In an effort to recoup some finances, Dudley sold the house he had bought years earlier for Susan Anton. But when he tried to sell the flat he had bought for Nicole's ex-husband's mother, she sued him. In the end he paid her $25,000 to leave, even though thanks to his kindness she'd been living there free for years.

During their marriage, Brogan had often voiced suspicions about his business manager, but Dudley's loyalty would not allow him to believe them. It was yet another sad case of a manager embezzling the earnings of a Hollywood star.

PALM SPRINGS – Dudley is laughing uncontrollably. We're inside his hotel suite in Palm Springs where he and Rena are rehearsing for a concert later in the evening. There's an easy camaraderie between the two pianists as they work on Saint-Saens's *Carnival of the Animals*. Suddenly, in the middle of 'The Swan', the most serious and beautiful movement of *Carnival*, the pedal of Dudley's piano has begun to develop a loud squeak that sounds like a duck quacking. Its musical incongruity becomes increasingly funny, until the two of them can no longer play, they're doubled up with laughter.

That night, minus a squeaking pedal, Dudley performed *Carnival of the Animals* and Gershwin's *Rhapsody in Blue* to a standard that surprised and satisfied even Rena, his sternest critic.

Less than a month later, the gala benefit for MFAS took place in Carnegie Hall. It was the third time Dudley had performed in that hallowed auditorium. The evening was a major triumph for MFAS, assisted in no small measure by Dudley, who had been involved from the start with Rena and her husband in planning the programme.

Accompanied by the New Jersey Symphony Orchestra under British conductor Christopher Seaman, Dudley and Lynn Redgrave narrated Sir William Walton's *Facade*, in which Dame Edith Sitwell's zany poetry is spoken against a series of musical settings. 'Moore was funny,' reviewed the *New Jersey Star-Ledger*, 'and Redgrave was enchanting.'

Dudley was in top musical form and his new orchestral composition received particular commendation. *Fantasy on a Gypsy Breeze* was his score for the children's poetic saga that had won their short-story competition. Lynn delivered its verses with panache while Dudley's melodic score, with its jazzy, syncopated rhythms, captured every sense of the spirit communicated by the title. It was, said the *Star-Ledger*, 'a real honey'.

It was the first piece of orchestral music Dudley had composed since the *Six Weeks* score fifteen years earlier, and he was secretly rather excited with it, although outwardly he would only admit to its being 'okay'. He seemed to Rena reluctant to acknowledge his pleasure. 'Maybe if he admitted how good it was and how much he'd enjoyed doing it,' she contemplated, 'he might then have had to answer the question, "Why aren't you doing more of this?"'

The evening ended with Dudley and Rena playing *Carnival*. It had all been a huge success for MFAS and for Dudley in particular with the debut of his latest work.

'I think Dudley is only really alive when he's at the piano,' observed Rena. 'There's an intensity and caring about his music that doesn't exist anywhere else in his life. Only through music is he able to show real emotion and achieve genuine happiness. And when he's involved in it, there's nothing else that's really important.'

In July 1996, Dudley Moore and Liza Minnelli reunited for a concert tour in a fifteenth anniversary tribute to *Arthur*.

It had been eight years since they'd made *Arthur 2: On the Rocks*, and Liza had been trying ever since to persuade Dudley to do a concert tour with her. This reunion would take them to five main cities on America's East Coast. The deadline for my biography had been extended so it was arranged that I would join Dudley for the tour. It would make an appropriate additional chapter.

> **DUDLEY (phone message):** Hi, Barbra, I'm alone at the airport. It's the first of July and I don't think there'll be any problem if you wanted to come out to New York on the second of July. I think I'm having the same suite set up in the hotel so you're more than welcome to crash down on a sofa or whatever, a foldaway bed, whatever they have there, but anyway I'll hope to see you at four-thirty tomorrow. I don't know if you'll be in time for the four-thirty rehearsal but maybe you can catch the end of it . . . mmn, I'm having my first cup of coffee of the day, which feels quite nice actually, and I am travelling alone without anybody to distract me. See you tomorrow.

An unexpected crisis kept me in Los Angeles and it would be a few more days before I was able to fly to New York. Phone calls between us flowed back and forth, Dudley updating me with news from his end, culminating in a call on 4 July, America's Independence Day.

DUDLEY: Liza is impossible! She is so hyper and she has changed a bit. She seems to be very aware that she is fifty now. She's sort of proud of it but I don't think she likes it. She told me she didn't like it as much as she thought she would. I don't blame her at all . . . I've been watching Wimbledon. I think it was right that Tim Henman got beaten [by the USA's Todd Martin].

BARBRA: Why? Oh . . . because today's July the fourth and we lost the War of Independence!

DUDLEY: Yeah! Ha ha! And I saw Sampras and Krajicek. Oh, bloody hell. That was exciting! . . . Now . . . what about a ride to the hotel from the airport when you arrive at JFK tomorrow? I'll book the limo for you.

The following evening I joined Dudley in his multi-roomed suite at the St Regis in New York. He got up briefly to welcome me and settle me on the sofa bed that he'd had brought up to the living room. In the morning, he ordered a heap of different dishes for breakfast, pouncing on a dish of berries and dumping them in his sink for a soaking, 'just to be quite sure they're clean'.

We were first at the theatre for a rehearsal. Liza arrived late but wasn't in a good mood and didn't say hello. In performance that night, Dudley led the first half of the show and displayed his immense versatility at the piano and as a composer. He also powerfully conducted the orchestra in the second movement of Mozart's *Concerto No. 21*, playing the piano with one hand and conducting with the other. Liza took over the second half and then the two joined together on stage for the finale – Dudley at the piano, dressed as Arthur. Together they sang the *Arthur* theme, but the orchestra drowned out Dudley's piano and Liza drowned out Dudley's voice. At the end of the act, they both took a bow but Dudley bowed too far and his Arthur top hat fell off into the audience, who applauded appreciatively, thinking it was intentional.

> **ROCHESTER, NY** – For the next leg of the tour, we're ensconced in a sumptuous suite on two levels linked with a winding iron staircase. Dudley has bagged the upstairs bedroom and goes up to rest. After an hour he comes back down. 'It's very lonely up there,' he says plaintively, and stays with me for the rest of the afternoon. He isn't happy with the way the tour is turning out. It's been an uphill struggle for him to entertain the audiences, who seem less than thrilled by him. And Liza's unaccountable curtness is making him feel very self-conscious. 'I don't want to be her warm-up act, it's demoralising,' he'd told me earlier. Liza is treating him with disdain and has been very dismissive. It's made Dudley uncharacteristically angry and he says he never wants to perform with her again after this tour. For tonight's concert he wants to include the theme to *10* but can't remember the music. I've persuaded the hotel to dig out a VCR and to rent the film; both arrive within the hour. The moment the film begins, Henry Mancini's poignant music comes flooding back to him. I record it, and Dudley accompanies the recording several times until pronouncing himself satisfied. Then to the theatre. We don't like the limo driver. He's never ready and tonight he locked himself out of the limo – with us inside it! Again!

In the first four cities Dudley had to face predominantly Liza audiences. He sensed their apathy and his jokes fell flat, punctuated with long pauses while he tried to conjure up some witty repartee that would pull the audience over to his side. Only at the end of these shows, when he came back on stage in the guise of Arthur to join Liza, was he feted and warmly applauded.

Still, the tour was allowing him a new sense of direction. Distance from his warring wife gave him a more optimistic perspective. Travelling with him I saw that, although he liked to retreat into solitude, at times he also liked to come out from his isolation and seek companionship. Away from the turmoil of home, he played and practised at the piano more in those days than he had in a long time.

Rena Fruchter joined us in New York and together she and Dudley practised Gershwin's *An American in Paris* for their upcoming Australian concert tour. With Rena, Dudley was more focused and alert than he had been for a long time. Astute and studious, he pounced on mistakes in the score and corrected them to his satisfaction. He was in absolute command, confident and self-assured, and when they played the entire piece all the way through for the first time he was excited and thrilled. Not yet perfect, to this ear it sounded quite wonderful.

> **BOSTON** – The hotel has given Dudley the presidential suite. I can't help wondering what they've given Liza. We've been holed up in the hotel for two days because of a massive storm that's created tremendous damage throughout the city, but the afternoon of the concert is remarkably bright and clear. From a distance, the outdoor shell of the performing arena flanked by Boston Harbour resembles the Sydney Opera House. It's brought back fond memories and Dudley has been gazing at it wistfully from his hotel window for the past two days while the storm raged.

If the previous four cities had belonged to Liza, Boston belonged to Dudley. He was stopped everywhere: in the hotel, in the street. Fans had learned where he was staying and grouped outside the hotel to catch a glimpse as he exited. Everybody wanted to greet him. For once, the windows of the limousine were not opaque and passers-by waved as they peered inside to watch Dudley as the car manoeuvred slowly through the heavy traffic. It was all there still. The applause, the adulation, the sheer unadulterated love for this man.

When Dudley stepped on stage at the Arts Center in Boston Harbor, there was a palpable excitement. The audience were thrilled to see him. With every joke they roared and with every piece he played on the piano they applauded wildly. Dudley reacted, as he always had, to the audience. His jokes became funnier and funnier and he took them further than scripted. He bantered with the audience and they loved it. Producer Ed Kasses was beaming. 'That's the man I've always loved and found so funny!' he exclaimed to me. 'He's back! Where's he been?'

Where had he been indeed? He had been sucked into a black hole over his turbulent marriage and slowed career for a long time. Yet the audience's tumultuous response had erased that, at least for now. There had been some who perceived Dudley Moore's career as over and there were others who insisted it was not. That afternoon in Boston, Dudley proved the latter group to be right.

He had become resigned to the belief that he had no real place in entertainment any more. He had lost confidence in himself and had told me often lately. 'I know it's sad because I have so much to give, but I've tried to come back and people don't like what I do. I'm resigned to that.'

Boston breathed new life into him. Dudley knew that he had recaptured it. He needed to perform to feel alive. Knew too that he could. All his focus and concentration had been diverted to his personal life but if one thing was able to rise above that it was public acclamation. In front of his audience he felt loved and wanted. The feeling was so powerful that it swept away his self-doubts.

Dudley was back. That afternoon he was the man he had always been, the consummate performer his audiences had always adored.

His fans clamoured at the stage door for autographs. Security guards tried to ward them off, but Dudley, ever appreciative of his public, insisted on greeting them. As his limo drove us away – after the chauffeur again locked himself out of the car with Dudley and me already inside it – crowds of people flanked the road to shout to him and wave and blow him kisses. He smiled back, drained and almost embarrassed.

And yet, despite his exhaustion, there was a new spiritual energy about him. The resignation that his career was over had been replaced with a hope that had been kindled by the overwhelming response the Boston audiences had shown him.

For far too long, Dudley's world had been wrapped up in his personal life. Now it was time to take care of himself and focus on all that he held dear: his work – the longest love affair of his life.

Two weeks later, he left his fourth wife and filed for divorce.

CHAPTER 29

Tragic Revelation

1996–99

The summer of 1996 was a rebirth of sorts. Dudley had been signed for a new film in Europe, concerts were scheduled through spring of the following year, and there was the Australian concert tour in November.

His heart was in his work and there was a new vitality about him, a subtle rejuvenation. He felt more alive than he had in months. The desire had returned, along with the urgency, the passion to perform.

Throughout the autumn of 1996, Dudley concentrated on the imminent five-week Australian tour with Rena Fruchter. They were to play in four main cities, with additional concerts set for Hawaii, New Zealand and Hong Kong, and he hoped it would prove a resurgence of his career. It would be his first appearance in Australia in twenty-five years.

DUDLEY (phone message): I'm at the Grand Hyatt in Melbourne and I'm registered under the name of David Marks. I can't work out what time it is there but can you call me back? I have press interviews in five hours and I'm bound to get asked about the biography and it's difficult to know what I should say. So the Grand Hyatt is where I am and Los Angeles is where you are. Ha! Talk to you soon.

DUDLEY (phone message): I'm talking to you from Melbourne, of course, just a few minutes later. I just want to say call me back and you can call collect of course. What else, um, did I have to say? I did have something to say but I can't remember. The main thing is, what am I going to say to the press? Buzz me.

A few days later there was another call from Dudley to update me.

DUDLEY (phone message): 'Hi, Barbra. The concert went well last night and we have another tonight. Rena is actually seven minutes late for breakfast. I shall have her guts for garters . . . and Bob's your uncle! What time is it there? It's seven minutes past nine here so I presume it's seven minutes past two in the afternoon the day after . . . or is it before? Before I think. I'm not sure. I can't bear to make the calculation again! I'll try you later but we're both okay, although I woke at one-fifteen this morning and wasn't able to go back to sleep. Wonderful, here's Rena. I'll talk to you later.

The tour progressed but there were hiccups along the way. Dudley was having difficulty with one finger on his right hand and it sometimes resulted in playing wrong notes, which the critics could not fail to notice. He was also not communicating too well with some of the Australian press; more than one outlet hinted he was drunk when he sounded almost incoherent.

> LOS ANGELES – Dudley is on the other end of the phone. We're discussing his next concerts but he doesn't sound right. Sentences begun sometimes become rambling and he keeps losing his train of thought. 'Are you all right?' I ask, when he seems not to be making sense. 'No, I'm *not*!' he shouts in frustration without knowing why. This is alarming since his usual response would be 'I'm *fine*!' – his way of dismissing how he really feels. He's been concerned about his increased mental confusion for some time, yet his doctor says everything is okay. But his prowess at the piano, which in earlier tours had provided such memorable highlights for Australian audiences, is now becoming less than optimal. There seems no explanation for this loss of musical acuity.

In April 1997, after a series of concerts across the US, Dudley returned to Carnegie Hall and performed at MFAS's annual benefit concert. The gala coincided with his sixty-second birthday and his narration of *Peter and the Wolf* was a resounding success.

But something was now clearly amiss with his playing. Sometimes he sounded good, other times it was as if his fingers simply refused to play the notes he instructed them to play. He pushed himself harder to practise three or four hours a day. No matter how tired Rena got, he would urge her on.

In retrospect, the signs had been there two years earlier in New York when he'd had difficulty in remembering his lines for Barbra Streisand's film. He'd put it down to the confusion surrounding the turmoil of his home life. But just a few months later, on the *Arthur* reunion tour with Liza Minnelli, he'd been concerned about some of the notes he was playing at the piano. And I saw him trip twice on the stage at rehearsal and have difficulty in keeping his balance. When I quizzed him about it he said he thought it was his eyesight and put it down to needing new glasses.

After the Streisand film and his inability to remember the lines,

Dudley had gone through a barrage of tests which had ruled out every obvious brain disorder. The doctors were mystified. We were left to believe that his erratic behaviour, obvious confusion and memory loss were the product of his emotional turmoil.

Dudley tried to apply himself to working with Rena on an album of Gershwin music. The album was never completed. Two days after starting work on the intricate piano pieces, he phoned me from New York early one morning in distress. 'My fingers on my right hand won't go where I tell them to go; they don't play the right notes,' he mourned. 'I don't know what's happening.' No matter how hard he practised, his fingers would not obey the messages being sent from his brain.

The next day he entered the world-famous Mayo Clinic in Minnesota for a barrage of tests.

Almost by accident, they found a small hole in his heart, a blocked artery and a hiatal hernia but nothing else. A referral took him to Dr Gizzi, a specialist in the rare disease progressive supranuclear palsy (PSP), a distant cousin of Parkinson's. Dr Gizzi was certain that he'd found the answer when he saw horizontal movements in Dudley's eyes, a main symptom. Other doctors disagreed and Dudley wouldn't accept his diagnosis of PSP. So the testing continued while Dudley remained in New Jersey under the caring attention of Rena and her family.

It was while he was at the Mayo Clinic that he was diagnosed as having an addictive relationship with his fourth wife. At last he came to understand this was not love. It was a disease every bit as destructive as substance addiction. He agreed to undergo medical treatment, realising at last that he was a victim of abuse who showed all the classic symptoms of an abuse victim.

Meanwhile, disturbing rumours about his health continued to swirl in every direction. He'd had a series of strokes, they wrote, he was an alcoholic like Arthur, falling down drunk and slurring his words. Dudley, through it all, kept silent. What was there to say, after all? Even he didn't know what was wrong. 'I wanted to wait until I knew without doubt what was wrong,' he shrugged. 'It seemed kind of nuts to say anything until then.' The few people who knew of the unfolding tragedy were sworn to secrecy and they respected Dudley's need for silence.

Early in 1999, to cheer him on his sixty-fourth birthday in April, nearly three hundred people from the world of entertainment sent me letters to assemble in a monumental collection that I bound in two huge albums. Among them were a David Hockney original painting in the form of a birthday card, Paul McCartney's parody on the Beatles hit 'When I'm Sixty-Four', Leslie Bricusse's mini-musical on rolled parchment, Paul Anka's dedication of his 'My Way' song sheet, Phil Collins's three-page fan letter, Quincy Jones's entire spiritual collection of jazz, letters from Dudley's heroes – surviving Goons Harry Secombe, Eric Sykes and Spike Milligan – a Rolling Stones caricature of Dudley with their ribald comments scribbled around the face, loving epistles from Kenny G, Elton John, Bette Midler, Whoopi Goldberg, Neil Simon, Milton Berle, Jack Lemmon, Mel Brooks and hundreds more. I had revealed little about Dudley's health. All anyone knew was that he was not well, and they offered inspiration and messages of love to the man who had given them so much pleasure through his music and his humour. And they reminded him how much they held him dear and in their thoughts.

Dudley was overwhelmed. The next month, accompanied by Rena, he flew to Los Angeles and came to see me. They had flown in from New York to supervise the packing of his possessions from his Marina house, his home for twenty-five years, for his permanent move to New Jersey. With Rena's aid and that of his faithful cane ('Maurice'), he climbed the stairs to my first-floor apartment with great difficulty but without faltering. He looked frail but less tense than I'd seen him in years as he shuffled through the front door. Leaning back on a couch, one of my budgies perched on his hand; it was a reminder of so many earlier visits.

He was deeply moved by the outpouring of affection shown to him by so many of his friends and colleagues, even some who hadn't known him.

'I found it enormously touching. I thought it was extraordinary that they would write me letters that expressed their feelings about me and it was quite overwhelming. Such a surprise. It was amazing. I was very moved by certain people – Goldie Hawn, Mary Tyler Moore, Phil Collins – their letters were immensely touching.'

I hadn't seen him for several months and by then his speech had become more discordant. He watched with a faint smile as I introduced him to the newest member of my avian flock – a tiny blue budgie who I'd named Blue. 'What do you think?' I asked him. 'The name seems to fit. Do you like it?' He gazed at the little bird who boldly returned the stare. No, he didn't like it. 'Sapphire then?' That worked for Dudley, and Sapphire he became.

It reminded me of our last trip to New York, when I'd left him and Rena in the St Regis hotel suite to practise for the next night's concert and had gone on a buying spree. 'What do you think?' I'd asked on my return, pulling a pair of pink high-heeled sandals out of a box and dangling them in front of him. 'Do you like them?' He regarded them soberly, then, 'No, I don't!' Strangely, I never wore those shoes. Not even once.

While he was in Los Angeles, Lou Pitt – his agent and close friend who was like a brother to him – threw a party to reunite him with many of his former colleagues and friends. Dudley was thrilled, if somewhat apprehensive, knowing how his speech had deteriorated which made conversation difficult. The guest list was astounding, a *Who's Who* of Hollywood. And as Dudley took the place of honour in a huge armchair, his friends embraced him, among them Blake Edwards and Julie Andrews, Bo Derek, Paul

Reiser, Raquel Welch, Brooke Shields, Cate Blanchett, Nastassja Kinski, Susan Anton and ex-wife Brogan.

Just a few weeks after his visit, a final symptom led to the confirmed diagnosis of PSP, fifteen months after Dr Gizzi had first diagnosed him. Dudley was neither shocked nor surprised. Though he'd been dreading this, he had already accepted that he was living with a degenerative condition. One that afflicted less than three people in 200,000. Finally, now he could silence all those who had believed him to be drunk when his voice became slurred and his movements faulty. For Dudley, it was almost a relief after four years of uncertainty to know definitively what was wrong and to put a name to it. He decided to make a public announcement and typically injected some humour into it.

'I understand that one person in 100,000 suffers from this disease and I'm also aware that there are 100,000 members of my union, the Screen Actors Guild, who are working every day. I think therefore it is in some way considerate of me that I have taken on this disease for myself, thus protecting the remaining 99,999 SAG members from this fate.'

Progressive supranuclear palsy is a distant cousin of Parkinson's and attacks the motor functions. 'It feels as if I have something on the tip of my tongue but I can't quite get at it,' Dudley told me. 'I start to say something but by the time I've said it, the rest of the thought has disappeared.' Hardest to accept was his difficulty in playing the piano, though he continued to perform an occasional concert with Rena. But his playing had become very disjointed as the fingers on his right hand failed to respond to the messages sent from his brain.

I saw him one more time. He had always promised an interview with me once he had a confirmed diagnosis. He kept his word. At last the full tragic story would be revealed to the world.

In October 1999 I flew to New York to visit him in New Jersey where he was living next door to Rena Fruchter's family who had been caring for him for the last two years. He'd been living with them until recently when the next-door house had fortuitously been put up for sale. Dudley bought it the same day the sign was erected. He put no limits on our interview, asking only that I not divulge his home and to say he was still living with Rena's family. He still feared reprisal from his volatile last wife, even though they were now divorced.

I stayed in his house and woke the following morning to find Dudley sitting on the edge of my bed, a half-smile on his face. For a brief moment it almost felt like déjà vu. All those times when I'd kipped down on sofas in his sumptuous hotel suites while accompanying him to performances across the country. But there was nothing similar about it. The next few days were gut-wrenching as I witnessed the tragic depth of Dudley's illness . . . and his constant vacillating between hope and despair.

Dudley's health had already been the focus of endless discussions between us for a couple of years. Since early 1995 there had been signs of neurological disorder. He had begun to appear unsteady and sound confused. Time made balance and speech increasingly elusive. By the end of that year, early aberrations had led to neurological tests but they all proved negative. PSP is so rare that it is easily missed. Meanwhile, his speech had become slurred and his balance unsteady; at any given moment he would trip while walking or climbing stairs. He had developed a tendency to fall backwards and his eyesight had become impaired. He was having trouble focusing and was suffering double vision. In hindsight, the signs had been everywhere, but they always ended up being attributed to the emotional turbulence and confusion he was suffering as a result of his tumultuous lifestyle at home.

Taking part in conversation had become difficult. Invariably by the time he'd formulated his thoughts and was ready to speak, the conversation had moved on elsewhere. Sometimes he would begin expressing a thought but would lose the rest of it before he could get it all out. It was frustrating and enervating and he found it easier to listen than participate. 'I'm trapped inside this body,' he told me repeatedly.

> **NEW JERSEY** – We're in Dudley's house, next door to Rena Fruchter's family where he had been living for the last two years. Rena's daughter has moved in to help and he also has a cook/housekeeper. All of his possessions have arrived from the Marina home and many decorate the vast basement living room. He now has three grand pianos and his childhood upright but only plays when no one is around.
>
> I venture his decision to release a statement about his medical condition had been courageous. 'I felt it was necessary,' he says softly. 'So many stories that were circulating were misplaced and a lot of them were downright untrue. There were stories put around that I was drunk, which was not true, and never had been. I was disappointed that it was the way people understood it.' There's a long pause while he struggles to locate the words to continue. He gives up. 'I do want to add something to that,' he sighs, 'but l can't.'

He felt tremendous gratitude towards Rena and Brian, who had taken him in and cared for him. 'They are remarkable,' he told me hauntingly. 'It's an extraordinary thing that Rena and Brian have done these last few years and I'm very grateful for it. They're like the family I've never had. I feel very comfortable here. Life is very quiet and nice and extremely supportive.'

> **NEW JERSEY** – Around his household, Dudley is surrounded by three cats and a dog. An animal lover who has always owned dogs and cats, he's become deeply attached to them all. Walking unexpectedly into the living room, I almost fall over him lying on the floor, where he's slowly stroking

and playing with Jasmine, a sable and chestnut calico cat. She purrs in feline bliss. The animals adore him, waiting patiently for the attention they know he'll give them.

As Rena drove us home from the restaurant after lunch – a daily ritual – Dudley played his *Songs Without Words* CD and as the music swelled to a haunting crescendo, his eyes filled with tears. It was his evocative score from *Six Weeks*, arguably his most outstanding composition. He spent a great deal of time now listening to his own music. It was as if, no longer able physically to play the music, listening had become his substitute. His ears had replaced his fingers. Dudley had become one of us, a viewer and listener. And for the first time in his life, he had become able to sit back and regard his work with genuine appreciation.

DUDLEY: I don't find that I'm missing the beat of a concert. I don't visualise myself at concerts and I'm not obsessed by images of myself at the piano. You get used to the idea of saying, 'Goodbye, goodbye, practical world.' I was there for a while and I don't feel the need to remember some moments concertising. But there are regrets. It's very hurtful not to be able to produce that irresistible sound and to realise that one can't function in the same way ever again. So I just listen to my old records and feel it's something unachievable by today's standards, but it was achievable in the past.

While conceding that his acting career was over, he still hoped to do more narration and in that way at least hang on to a remnant from his past life as a performer. The spontaneity of acting now defeated him but with persistent speech therapy he felt more confident about learning lines for narration where he would not have to rely on body movements.

But he did miss acting. Looking back at his career, his face lit up when we reminisced about special moments – landmark comedy he had provided with Peter Cook in *Not Only . . . But Also* and the early films they had made together. And then there was *Arthur*, his lovable millionaire drunk. Gleefully he quoted specific lines that he still remembered with particular fondness. It was ironic that his movie career had declined because of *Arthur*. The public had wanted more of him in that persona.

> **DUDLEY:** Arthur happens to be the one character that I love. It was an outrageous performance but I think it wouldn't have worked if it hadn't been outrageous and it wouldn't have put in the mind of so many people that I was alcoholic myself.
>
> I really would have liked to have been like him. Less drunk. He was a very attractive man, very, very humorous and I liked that part of him. Not so much the intoxication but the wit, the wit! That was what was so attractive about him – that wonderful wit!

It was striking to find his mind so sharp. Even if he couldn't verbally complete his thoughts, they were there nevertheless. I was recording our conversations with my compact BBC equipment. He was fascinated by the small minidisc recorder and wanted to know how it worked. After just over an hour he looked at his watch – a lifelong frequent habit – and remarked that we must be close to the end of the minidisc, which I'd already told him ran seventy-four minutes. He'd been timing it in his head, which I thought was pretty remarkable. His instinct for time had always been uncanny.

In one of my last memories of Dudley I asked if he would play for me one last time. In the old days, it had taken little persuasion to get him to the piano. But that was then. Now he was afraid of what he would produce. Finally, he was cajoled into attempting something from his exquisite *Six Weeks* score. No, it didn't sound the same. But the sound was there nevertheless. The ability from his left hand ensured that and, transported by the possibility, he kept on playing. And just as occasionally in his conversation, a flash now of the old Dudley materialised in the music. When he couldn't sustain the classical sound, he suddenly transformed it into a moment of improvised jazz, as he used to do with his irreverent Bach parodies.

The left side of his body was not affected; as he put it, thoughts reached his left hand in a straight line. I asked if he would consider playing only with the left hand and reminded him that Ravel and Bach had written music specifically for the left hand. He shook his head. 'It's not my bag, it's not what I've done. It's maddening as it's the one thing that I really regret saying goodbye to – the ability to play with two hands – but it's impossible to get the hands together to play the right speed.'

After three days in New Jersey, I returned to Los Angeles. I left the same way as I had arrived. With a long, tight hug from Dudley and his face puckered into that boyish pixie smile. I'll always remember the last picture of him in my mind. Ever the caretaker, he'd stood at the door, leaning on his supportive cane, watching solicitously as I slid into the limo he had arranged to take me to the airport. As I was sped away down the tree-lined avenue, I looked back through the window.

Dudley still stood by the front door, watching and waving to me, his face wistful. And the words of his earlier unanswerable cry echoed in my ears. 'Why me? Why someone who has so much still to offer the world with his music? Oh Gawd, why me?'

Letters to Dudley

FOR DUDLEY..........

This Is (Moore than) Your Life!

Happy Birthday!

From your friends and colleagues
around the world!

Album Cover

Dear Dudley,

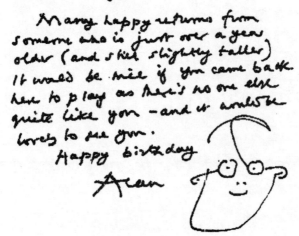

Many happy returns from someone who is just over a year older (and still slightly taller) It would be nice if you came back here to play as there's no one else quite like you – and it would be lovely to see you.

Happy birthday

Alan

Alan Bennett

Alan Alda

Dear Dudley,

I'm an exhuberant fan of yours and have been since the first time you made me hit my head on the seat in front of me as I collapsed in laughter in a Broadway theater.

I couldn't be more delighted than to be wishing you a happy 64th. A year from now I'll be 64, and I so look forward to a letter from you telling me how much you adore *me*. Either way, I adore you.

Alan

Alan Alda

ALEC BALDWIN

April 19, 99!

Alec Baldwin

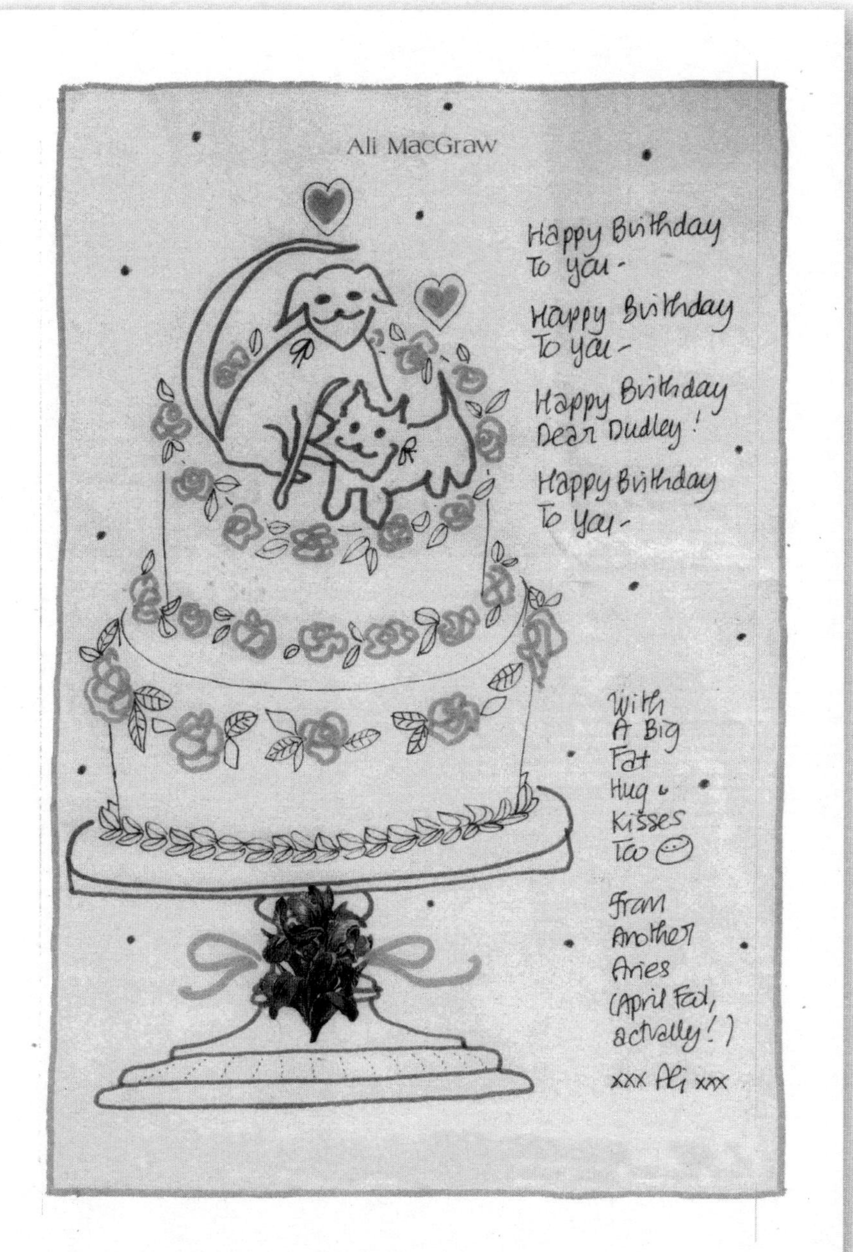
Ali MacGraw

Happy Birthday
To you -
Happy Birthday
To you -
Happy Birthday
Dear Dudley!
Happy Birthday
To you -

With
A Big
Fat
Hug &
Kisses
Too ☺

From
Another
Aries
(April Fool,
actually!)
xxx Ali xxx

Ali MacGraw

Alys Kihl

April 19th 1999

To Dudley for your birthday album
with much love from Lysie

So many good and funny memories... here are a few. You - playing your beloved Bach on your Hammond organ that joined our piano and harpsichord in the music room at 69 St Augustine's Road, and playing Beethoven and Mozart sonatas with Robert Mann while George and I listened with the upmost pleasure and admiration; me listening to George and you playing jazz together with the whisky and the jokes flowing; you and me playing Mozart piano duets; you calling to Stanley, your Persian cat "come on 'Steainley' in your most nasal Dagenham voice as you emerged from your little basement flat that you were renting in our house; the endless discussions about psychotherapy, guilt, depression and then the shouts and screams of laughter as you clowned, mimicked or imitated an accent, a posture an overheard remark.

Farting, that made us laugh till we cried. The way we addressed each other as 'man'. "Hallo, man, how are you man?" said very straight, not cool at all. Conversations peppered with 'man'. Don't know why it seemed so funny.

Oh dear little Flo
I love you so
Especially in your nightie
When the moonlight flits across your tits
Oh Jesus Christ Almighty
(sung in Edinburgh accent)

Taught to you by George who learnt it from Alastair Reid.

Happy Birthday, man.

Alys Kihl

Happy Birthday,
dear, dear, dear
Dudley

4/99

I love you SO much—
But then, you know that!

Missing you
Holding you
Hearing you—

Angie
(Dickinson)

Angie Dickinson

April 26, 1999

Dear Dudley,

I've told so many people, so many times, that I had the thrill and honor, of meeting you and spending the day with you when we worked on Mr. Bob Hope's 80th birthday t.v. Special.

I'll never forget how important you made me feel when you joked and visited with me, while we were "in" that long line of "stars" rehearsing all day.

You are so wonderful and sweet, and believe me, it meant the world to me! I'm a huge fan of yours and you made me feel like a friend.

I hope that your birthday was great. and again, You are so talented and such an amazing person.

Thank you for being so thoughtful and sweet to me.

Love,

Barbara

Barbara Mandrell

From The Desk of Dame Edna Everage

18th April 1999

Dearest Dudley,

Why do we keep missing each other?

You once told me that it was me who gave you a taste for statuesque women and I've been blaming myself ever since. I just want you to know that my embezzling manager Barry Humphries and I are thinking of you on your birthday and every other day and hope we can all get together when I come to America in September. Now it's hard to believe we're both a couple of senior citizens. Don't forget we can get discounted rides at Disneyland and Magic Mountain.

Huge hugs,

Dame Edna

Edna x

Barry x x x

Barry Humphries

April 12, 1999.

I have always had a weakness for comics with a dancer's grace and Dudley is the very definition of that.

I remember that he spoke at a benefit I attended; I may even have been the honoree. His performance from what were basically cue cards handed to him ten minutes before the event was astonishing - the effect was hilarious, relaxed and completely spontaneous. I never forgot it, I never figured out how he did it, and although I tried mightily, I never achieved the effect that he did that night.

He is my hero.

All Love and aloha from,

Bette Midler

THE ST. REGIS
New York

April 28 '99

Dear Dudley -

I don't know if you remember a date you had with my ex-wife Christie Brinkley back in 1983. I recall that she brought you back to our recording session in New York and made you sit and listen to some of the songs I was writing at the time. It was all very romantic and silly and awkward at the time - but I never got to tell you what an aficionado I was of your work - both in the musical + comedic genres. Anyway, I just wanted you to know that your 'Derek and Clive' period provided us with delicious material which we still quote to this very day.

THE LUXURY COLLECTION

Billy Joel – Page 1

THE ST. REGIS
New York

I have also admired your improvisational pianistic skills for many years, and I know that they are based on a solid knowledge of study and practice. I'm not much taller than you and I think I understand how uncomfortable it can be carrying around an over-sized set of balls with such short legs.

Anyway - Thank you for all the laughter and peverse pleasure you have given us over the years. It was much needed and appreciated. I remain a huge fan - Love, Billy Joel

THE LUXURY COLLECTION

Billy Joel – Page 1

Dudley —

Happy Birthday

my Beautiful Friend!

Love,

Bo

Bo Derek

fax from bob monkhouse o.b.e.

barbados, west indies.

date: 19·4·99

In The Sunday Times last year I wrote:

"I'm a devoted fan of three great comedians : Buster Keaton, Cary Grant and Dudley Moore. No other screen performers connect with me with comparable humanity, talent, charm and individuality.

Just a few lucky fans get to meet their heroes and I've been triply fortunate, having worked with Buster on the U.S. version of Candid Camera in the 60s, chatted with Cary over dinner in The White Elephant, Curzon Street, and encountered Dudley at a party in New York and again when he graced a space on Celebrity Squares in the late 70s. Of the three marvellous men, Dud rates highest in my estimation.

He is a bijou national treasure; a dreamer, vulnerable and flawed, touching the heart and soul with the grace of his comedy; disclaiming his own profound value with a public modesty that belies his private beligerence.

He is the greatest of the trio because, while Buster and Cary can never quite conceal the industry behind their magnificent performances, Dudley's gifts are part of his existence. What he does is what he is, whether at the keyboard or dropping his top hat or flinging beach towels under his sand-burned feet.

He is the perfect comic actor because he doesn't act, he behaves. He inhabits the music and occupies the jokes. His genius in performance is all one with his nature, as full of silliness and outrage and caring and helplessness as his entire life.

Buster and Cary are great because what they *do* is uniquely peerless; Dudley is the greatest because what he *is* is uniquely peerless. We can only pray to the Gods of Laughter to preserve him for us to continue loving him. Because that's what we do, isn't it ? We look at him and we love him. If there's anything in good vibrations, let's send our most heartfelt to Dudley as our thanks for all the laughter."

Bob Monkhouse...

Bob Monkhouse

SURREY.
ENGLAND.

13.4.99.

My Dear Dudley,

Many Happy Returns for your Birthday. A day that will go down in History with a Musical smile!!

Although I am now in the twilight of my career, some of my fondest memories are working with you – you little Ad Libber!!

It's been too long.

Hope to see you soon.

With love,

Wilnelia and Bruce

(FORSYTH)

Bruce Forsyth

BURT BACHARACH

Prod. ______ Title ______ Page ______

Arranger ______

For Dudley

wishing you all the best, and all good things possible for you and a Happy Birthday to you

Love + Affection

Burt Bacharach

Cmaj7 | D/C | G2 |

when you get caught between the | moon + N.Y. | City | I know its

Am7 | | Gadd2 |

Crazy | But its | true |

JUDY GREEN MUSIC Hollywood, CA 90028 (213) 466-2491 PG 1325

Burt Bacharach

April 19, 1999

Ms. Carol Burnett
In Residence

Dearest Dudley —

I might've known you'd be an "Aires!" Humor, personality, guts, musical talent... and sexy.

Have a wonderful birthday.

I send you my love.

Now & Always

Carol

Carol Burnett

CHEVY CHASE

My Dearest
Darling Dudley,

My Dad's birthday is also April 19. He will be 80 yrs. old. He is the funniest man I've ever known, but you come in a close second. Working with you on "Foul Play" was a <u>major</u> moment in my life!

As I write, I am trying to convince Harold Ramis, the director of

Printed on recycled paper to protect the environment.

CHEVY CHASE

"Caddyshack", to give me the part of Satan in the re-make of "Bedazzled", the funniest movie I've seen.

Dudley, I know these have been tough years for you, but you must pull out of it, and <u>never</u> forget the great influence you have had on people such as myself over the years. You are a brilliant mind, a world class pianist, and

Printed on recycled paper to protect the environment.

CHEVY CHASE

remain in my heart as a warm, intelligent and kind woman.

I wish you a terrific 64th, and hope if you ever need anything (a few bucks, some sleezy sex) you'd call upon me. I shall make myself available – for a price.

Your good friend
and greater admirer.

[signature]

Printed on recycled paper to protect the environment.

Chevy Chase

Christopher
Cross

April 19, 1999

Dudley –

You have given our hearts the joy of laughter, our souls the gift of your music and artists like myself great inspiration through your talent and grace.

Happy Birthday my friend give us 64 more.

Christopher

Christopher Cross

Dear Dudley,

Have a smashing Birthday.

you're a truly luvley Guy.

we all miss you and your great talent in Britain. so when are you coming Home?

lots of luv,

Cilla

xx

Cilla Black

Cleo Laine
John Dankworth

October 24, 1998

Dearest Dudley —

We have just both finished an hour or so here at the Old Rectory (which you know so well), talking to TV cameras about our relationship with you over the last half-century (getting-on-for!) It all evoked some happy memories of the times we spent together both here at our old shack and elsewhere in the universe, and I hope that the overall effect was a communication, however inarticulate, of the joys we have all shared together.

It all reminded us that we haven't seen you for some time now – it must add up to years by this time – and we would dearly like to get together with you some time, even if it were just for a chat on the phone. Unfortunately all the secret numbers we had for you at one time seem to have lapsed, and over the recent past we have made many aborted attempts to catch up with you. It would be just wonderful if we could get a call from you, or even just an address where we could pick up our lost threads again: however this opportunity of writing a little note to you seemed a very good opportunity to start the ball rolling again.

We both love you very much and wish you health and happiness in the future years. We have both now past the three-score-years-and-ten benchmark, and although the "degenerative process" (as our doctor puts it) has its cares, we still both manage to get a lot of fun and fulfilment out of life.

Our joy would be complete if we found it might be possible to spend some more time with you some day – we just hope it will happen!

— with much love from us both

Yours ever

Cleo + John.

Cleo Laine-John Dankworth

SIR CLIFF RICHARD

Dear Dudley,

this is just to wish you a very happy Birthday and a better year as far as "health" is concerned.

I don't really know you - but I am one of millions who love & respect you & your work and I'm glad of the opportunity to add my good wishes to all the others.

God Bless

Cliff +

Cliff Richard

Dave Brubeck

April 17, 1999

Mr.Dudley Moore,
c/o Barbra Paskin,
1560 N. Laurel Ave., #201,
Los Angeles, CA 90046

Dear Dudley,

I am told you will soon be having your 64th birthday. I hope it will be a joyful one. I am aware that this has been a tough year for you, and I hope and pray that in the coming year answers will be found and your health restored. Selfishly speaking, I want to hear some more piano playing from you!

I am sending to you two CDs that are perhaps different from what you may have of my recordings. The solo album is a rarity for me. I prefer to play with my own group and rhythm section, but once in awhile it's fun to just sit down and play for the fun of it. I did this at the end of one of the current quartet's recording sessions and the people at Telarc caught it on tape, then insisted on more, enough for the album, "Just You, Just Me". The mass "To Hope!" speaks for itself. People have told me that they have found the music to be healing and uplifting of spirit. I hope it proves to be for you.

Best wishes for a very happy birthday.

Yours sincerely,

Dave

Dave Brubeck

Dave Brubeck

DAWN FRENCH

5.5.99

Dear Mister Dud, Sir,

- VERY HAPPY BIRTHDAY indeed, oh yes, VERY HAPPY and also quite late I'm sorry to say.

So, you are 64 – and I am 41 – I find it odd that we never married. We could have been quite a pair, don't you think? At least I wouldn't have had to put up with neck-ache from kissing husband what is too tall if it had been you. I am averaging at about 5' ½" – how about you? I've got a sinking feeling I'm not going to grow much more now. Not upwards, anyway.

Yet again, big huge Birthday wishes & rest assured that we adore you. A lot.

Dawn xx

Dawn French

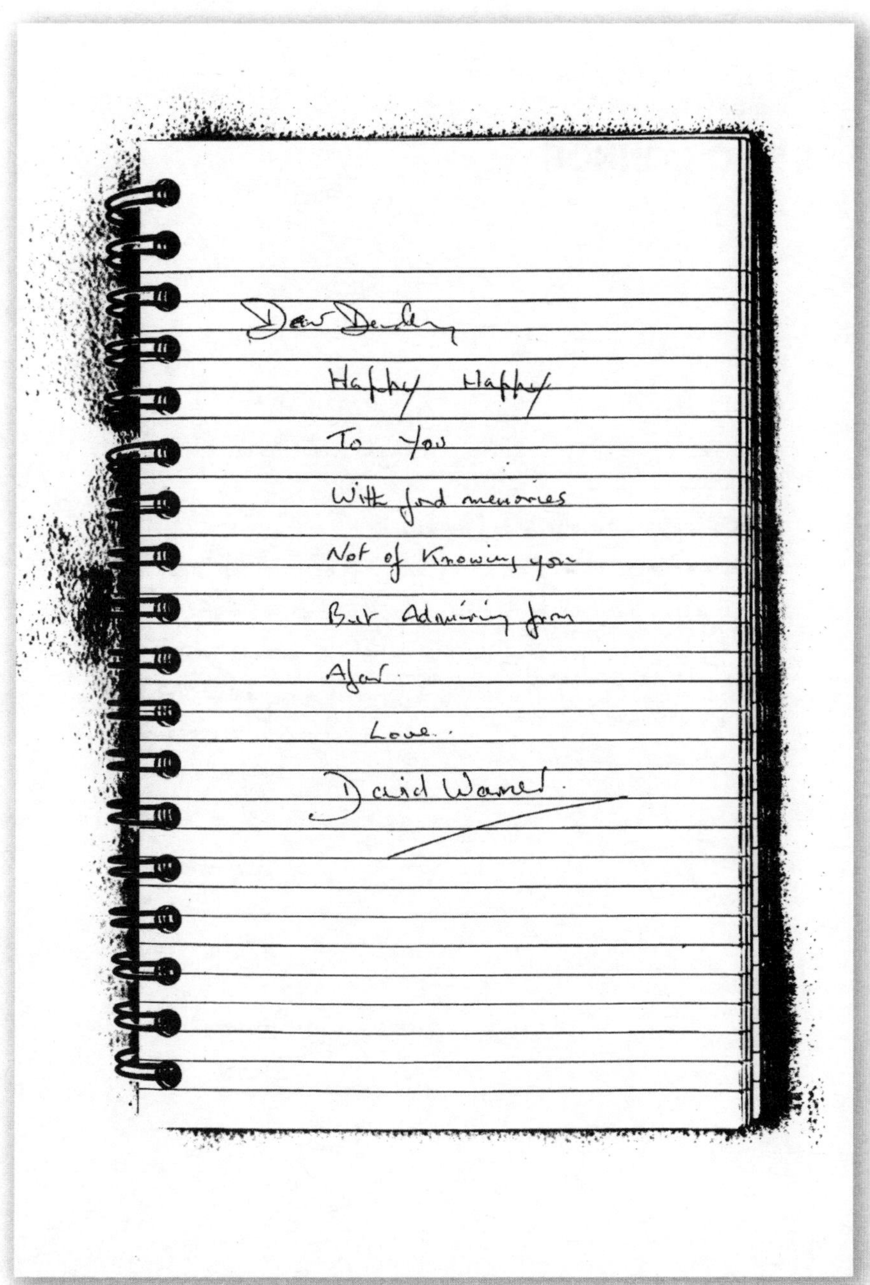

Dear Dudley

Happy Happy

To You

With fond memories

Not of Knowing you

But Admiring from

Afar.

Love.

David Warner

David Warner

DES O'CONNOR

13th April 1999.

Dear Dudley,

Happy Birthday to the Dagenham kid.

I remember you telling me on my show, what your mum said when she saw you nude in the film '10'. "Oh Dud I saw all your bits and pieces and I haven't seen those since you were a baby.... and you haven't changed a bit"

I am still getting laughs in concerts with that story.

Have a happy day Dudley.

Get back soon, we miss you.

As ever,

Des.

Des.

Des O'Connor

April 7, 1999

Dear Dudley,

I don't think I ever laughed more than when we were making 'Not Only...'. If you remember, we recorded the shows on Sunday nights, then went off filming the next morning, usually with horrible hangovers. We'd planned a sequence with Dud and Pete taking an off-peak holiday at Felixstowe in February. As the train headed north from Liverpool Street I looked out on fields of white and could hardly believe my luck.

So we were able to film you and Peter in deck chairs looking out to sea, then reveal you trudging back to the hotel through virgin snow. When we got to the fairground the man in charge of the roller coaster looked very worried. 'There's ice on the rails,' he said. 'She might never make it to the top of that second riser.'
My eyes lit up at the possibilities. 'Let's just take a chance'.

The light was fading as the car containing the lonely figures of Dud and Pete, muffled up against the cold, was ratcheted to the top of the roller coaster, rattled down, almost made it to the top of the next summit, then fell backwards into the trough. The luckiest shot I ever made, totally unplanned at the beginning of the day.

Many Happy Returns, Dudley, Dagenham's favourite son!

Warmest regards

Dick

Dick Clement

Dolly Parton

April 9, 1999

Dear Dudley,

I just wanted to be one of the many millions of friends and fans that you have to say "Happy Birthday to You." I will always treasure the time that I spent with you. Hopefully you will remember, as well, when you had your restaurant and I would occasionally come by. I thought it was wonderful when you used to perform.

You have always been and will always remain one of my very favorites. I've always wished we could do something together. Maybe by our next birthday, we might.

Good luck and God bless you. Again, Happy, Happy Birthday.

Love,

Dolly

Dolly Parton

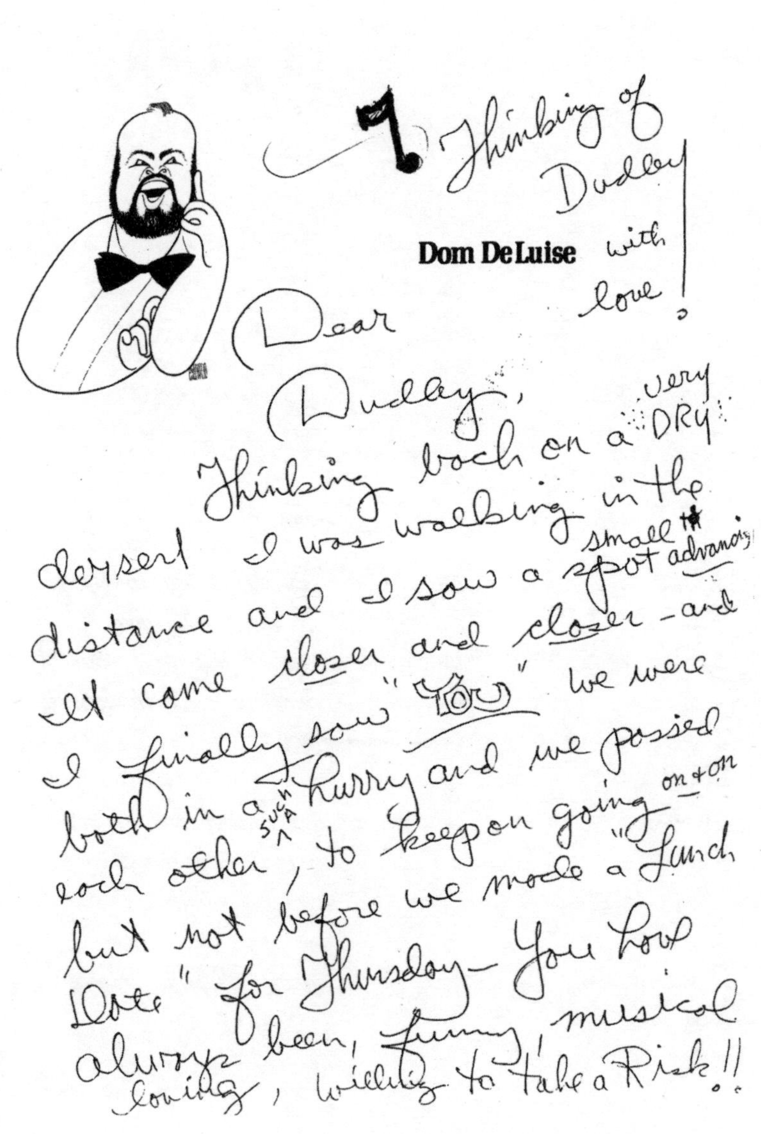

Thinking of Dudley with love!

Dom DeLuise

Dear Dudley,

Thinking back on a very "DRY" desert I was walking in the distance and I saw a small spot advancing
It came closer and closer - and I finally saw "YOU" We were both in a such hurry and we passed each other, to keep on going on + on but not before we made a "Lunch Date" for Thursday - You have always been, funny, musical loving, willing to take a Risk!!

Dom de Luise – Page 1

Even playing in the "Mikado"
You have charmed your way into all the hearts you came in contact with and mine especially — dance on this!!

Carol and I send you all our birthday love and "then some" which is a delicious chinese Dumpling!
Happy Birthday to you XX
Dom + Carol De Luise '99

Look at this → Dudley Moore!! !!
more!! !!
encore! encore!! Bravo!! more more!!

Dom de Luise – Page 2

Precious Dudley —

My sweet friend!! I just want to send you warm hugs and rousing cheers for your birthday and everyday!! I miss your presence — All my love and always.

Your forever fan and friend

Dyan Cannon

Dyan Cannon

Eartha Kitt Productions Inc.

Dear Dudley,

I came in every night from *The Talk of the Town* to see you at *The Establishment* and laughed my way through every performance. Even then I knew you would be a very important asset to our business, which has proven to be true. I loved you then, and I love you now.

All the best,

Eartha Kitt

Eartha Kitt

Eartha Kitt

Edward Asner

April 15, 1999

Dear Dudley,

I feel as if I know you, having worked seven beautiful, wonderful, creative years with your mother, Mary Tyler.

She spoke of you often, and every time I got to see you, you were my own personal trip to Disneyland. But you certainly didn't inherit Mary's ample tits and mouth. No matter.

But to get back to our subject - you. I have thrilled to your wit, wisdom and éclat from the time you shot onto the scene, and I've loved you ever since. You sir, are a non-pareil.

I hear you've been ill which distresses me and explains why I've been denied the pleasure of your art. I hope for your speedy recovery and the ability to giggle with delight at your talent once more.

Sincerely,

Ed

Edward Asner

Ed Asner

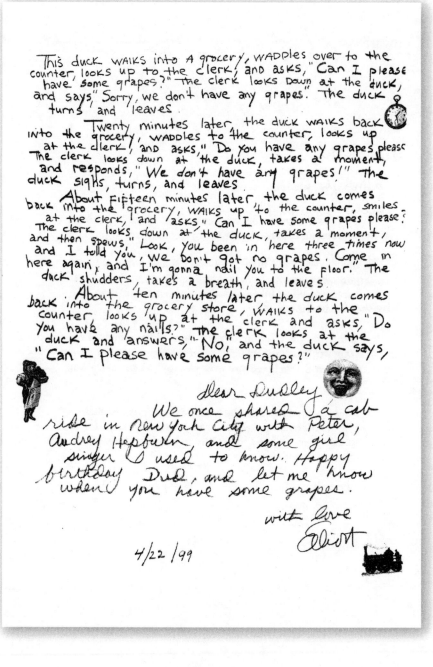

This duck walks into a grocery, waddles over to the counter, looks up to the clerk, and asks, "Can I please have some grapes?" The clerk looks down at the duck, and says, "Sorry, we don't have any grapes." The duck turns and leaves.

Twenty minutes later, the duck walks back into the grocery, waddles to the counter, looks up at the clerk, and asks, "Do you have any grapes please?" The clerk looks down at the duck, takes a moment, and responds, "We don't have any grapes!" The duck sighs, turns, and leaves.

About fifteen minutes later, the duck comes back into the grocery, walks up to the counter, smiles at the clerk, and asks, "Can I have some grapes please?" The clerk looks down at the duck, takes a moment, and then spews, "Look, you been in here three times now and I told you, we don't got no grapes. Come in here again, and I'm gonna nail you to the floor." The duck shudders, takes a breath, and leaves.

About ten minutes later the duck comes back into the grocery store, walks to the counter, looks up at the clerk and asks, "Do you have any nails?" The clerk looks at the duck and answers, "No," and the duck says, "Can I please have some grapes?"

Dear Dudley

We once shared a cab ride in New York City with Peter, Audrey Hepburn and some girl singer I used to know. Happy birthday Dud, and let me know when you have some grapes.

with love

Elliot

4/22/99

Elliott Gould

Emma Thompson

Dear Dudley —

although we've never met I've always been slightly in love with you. I'm forty on April 15th. It occurs to me that Arians don't take well to the notion of ageing. Is that why you haven't bothered?

Arrantly flirtatiously yours

Emma

Emma Thompson

DEAR DUDLEY,

MANY HAPPY RETURNS ON THIS YOUR 64TH YEAR.

ALTHOUGH WE HAVE NOT HAD THE CHANCE TO SOCIALIZE TOGETHER IN THESE PAST FEW DECADES, I WANTED TO TAKE THE CHANCE TO WISH YOU GREAT HEALTH AND HAPPINESS IN THE MILLENIUM TO COME.

I HAVE ENJOYED YOUR CAREER FROM THE EARLY DAYS WITH PETER COOK AND I WAS HAPPY TO SEE THAT FLOURISH INTO A SOLO MOVIE CAREER.
"ARTHUR" CONTINUES TO BE ONE OF THE CONSUMMATE ROAD MOVIES. WHENEVER THERE'S A TOUR BUS INVOLVED AND MILES OF UNENDING ROAD TO COVER, THERE'S "ARTHUR." PLAYING ON A ROTATING SCHEDULE WITH "AUSTIN POWERS" AND "MIDNIGHT RUN." ALL THE LINES ARE, OF COURSE, MEMORIZED BY BAND AND CREW. YOU'RE IMPERSONATED CONSTANTLY AND THERE CAN BE NO GREATER COMPLIMENT.

PERHAPS WE CAN HIT A KAROKE OR PIANO BAR THIS DECADE...YOU PLAY, I'LL SING AND WE'LL SPLIT THE TIPS.

BEST OF BRITISH,

ENGELBERT

Engelbert Humperdinck

Oh shit, it says it's my birthday!

Happy Birthday Dudley
and thank you for making it all possible

Eric Idle

Eric Idle

eric sykes

My dear Dudley,

I don't think it's quite appropriate to wish you Happy Birthday but as soon as you are better I'M your man, you only have to ask, even if its only turning over the pages whilst you play the piano.

Love,

Eric

ERIC SYKES

Eric Sykes

ERNEST FLEISCHMANN

April 14, 1999

Dear Dudley:

I understand that on Sunday you will be reaching an important milestone in your life, i.e., you will be ten years younger than I am. In sending you my very best wishes on this auspicious occasion, I remember with infinite pleasure some of the marvelous musical escapes in which you participated with the Philharmonic. In particular, I recall those nights at the Hollywood Bowl when Dudley Moore the Renaissance Man, was in full flower – as pianist accompanied by the Philharmonic, as raconteur, and playing a mean piano with your jazz trio – and just as happily do I think about a time when you played chamber music with Lynn Harrell and members of the Philharmonic. I trust these are good memories for you, too.

In any event, it is my fond hope that your 65th year will be a really good one for you, and so will all the others to follow thereafter.

My warmest regards,

As ever,

Ernest Fleischmann

Ernest Fleischmann

Francis Megahy

April 12, 1999

Dear Dudley

Excuse the typing — it would take a hieroglyphics professor to decode my handwriting.

So... It's your birthday.

I've so many memories of you, from when I walked into that party in Upper Berkeley Street in 1958 and heard you playing — to when you and Bob Mann entertained me and Liliana the Polish Witch on Ocean Front Walk — and what seems like dozens of evenings, from the Establishment to 72 Market Street.

Remember those organ-shattering evenings in the kitchen basement in Hampstead, when Peter would repeat yet again his terrible Elvis Presley imitation?

Well, old friend, I miss you terribly, and all the music and laughter you've brought into my life since my adolescence. I wish you long life and laughter and happiness — and I'd like to see you sometime!

Love

Francis Megahy

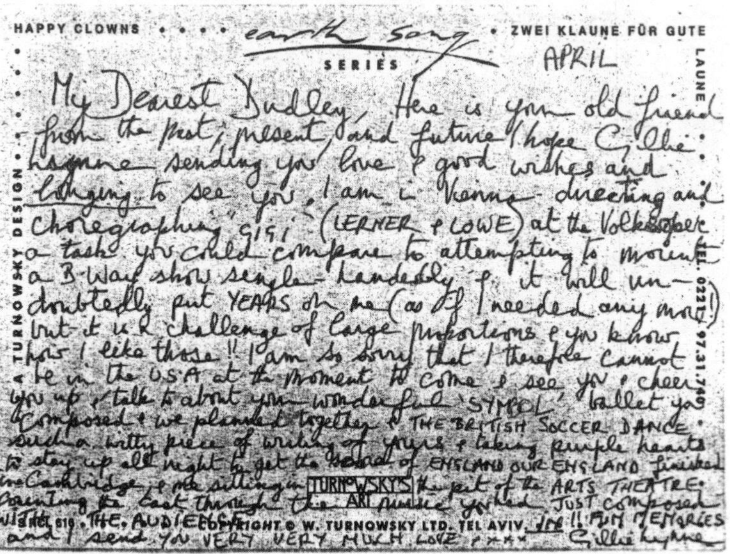

HAPPY CLOWNS • • • • • *earth song* SERIES • ZWEI KLAUNE FÜR GUTE LAUNE

APRIL

My Dearest Dudley, Here is your old friend from the past, present and future I hope Gillie Lynne sending you love & good wishes and longing to see you. I am in Vienna directing and choreographing "GIGI" (LERNER & LOWE) at the Volksoper a task you could compare to attempting to mount a B-Way show single-handedly & it will undoubtedly put YEARS on me (as if I needed any more!) but it is a challenge of large proportions & you know how I like those!! I am so sorry that I therefore cannot be in the USA at the moment to come & see you & cheer you up & talk to about your wonderful 'SYMBOL' ballet you composed & we planned together & THE BRITISH SOCCER DANCE such a witty piece of writing of yours & taking purple hearts to stay up all night to get the [illegible] of ENGLAND OUR ENGLAND finished in Cambridge & me sitting in the pit of the ARTS THEATRE screaming the cast through the music you had JUST composed WITH THE AUDIENCE [illegible]!! FUN MEMORIES and I send you VERY VERY MUCH LOVE & xxx Gillie Lynne

A TURNOWSKY DESIGN • TEL. 0221 97.31.740

TURNOWSKY'S ART

619 COPYRIGHT © W. TURNOWSKY LTD. TEL AVIV.

Gillian Lynne

My dear sweet freind.

Happy, Happy birthday baby! You know my daughter Kate's birthday is on the 19th of april so now I know why I feel such a kindship to you over these years. You are both wild and crazy. She was just a little angel waiting to come in. I love that day. Sorry I'm a little late in wishing you good tidings, I hope you forgive my tardiness.

I have the greatest memories of our time together on Foul Play. You know that was one of the best time I have ever had making a film. I had you on ones side and Chevy on the other and I was in heaven! I remember when you were doing your scene with that blow-up doll and I was waiting outside the door for my entrance and I laughed from my gut every single time you did it. I remember being amazed at how you could be funnier every single time! I discovered your genious! I recall and treasure our talks about life and relationships. We shared a lot during that time.

I always judge my films by the experience I had making them. Some are successes and some are failures but the time making them is what's valued or not. That's a great way to live life I think. The experiences are what's important and <u>you</u> fill a great one in my life.

I want you to take this love and wrap it around you and let it make you feel comfortable and safe. Take these arms of mine and imagine them surrounding you with love and light and joy and feel perfect because YOU are! in everyway. infact take all the love and devotion and adoration that's coming your way.

I kiss you all over and send you healing light. You precious, precious man.

Please forgive this typing but my writing is much worse.!

Kisses, hugs, big, big bear hugs.

Goldie

XXOOO

Goldie Hawn

Sir HARRY
SECOMBE C.B.E.

14th APRIL/99

DUDLEY MOORE

HAPPY BIRTHDAY DUDLEY -
FROM ONE OLD CROCK TO ANOTHER!

LOTS OF LOVE,

Harry Secombe

Harry Secombe

For Dudley Moore
From Hayley Mills.

April 23rd 1999
New York.

Dearest Dudley —

Happy happy Birthday 3

I hope you have a really lovely day.
It's been so long since I saw you — do you
remember a quite mad lunch we had in Los Angeles
20 years ago? I'd flown over from London with Peter
and what a flight that was! You picked us up
at the Beverly Wilshire Hotel in your white
Rolls Royce, I was very impressed. It was a very
lively, funny meal. I seem to remember Pete
giving you a hard time about — well, most things
really and you laughing alot and not taking
any of it very seriously.
I'm so glad for this opportunity to be
in touch again.
Get well soon — you're loved + missed

Hayley xx

Hayley Mills

August 19 1999

Dear Dudley,

A brief message to wish you all the best on your birthday. So far as I recall, we're only met twice – most recently by surprise at Winifred House, just along my road, and, many years earlier, when you interviewed me on your show.

I have a nasty feeling that I may have giggled through both meetings – you and Patrick Campbell have been the only two people I've known who have made me start giggling before they have uttered a word, and I thank you for it. Such ready laughter is invaluable therapy!

On my now thirty-year-old jazz programme on the Beeb, I once ran a miniature series called 'Pick me ups', inviting listeners to nominate pieces of music were guaranteed to raise their spirits and bring balm to the soul at the end of a tiring day. High among the pianists who were chosen were Erroll Garner, Mel Powell and yourself.

To have a single talent that can make people laugh, feel good and be lifted above themselves, if only for a while, is a rare gift. To have two or more suggests favouritism on the part of the Creator!

Among your friends and fans – and, as you just suspect, I am numbered among the latter and would like to have been among the former – there is much love, admiration and gratitude. In other words, have a bloody good birthday!

Humph (Lyttelton)

P.S. I hear you say "If that's a brief message, thank God he didn't send a long one

Humphrey Lyttelton

ITZHAK PERLMAN

April 19, 1999.

Dear Dudley.

I hear congratulations are in order for your Birthday So "A very Happy Birthday and many happy & healthy returns!"

Hope to maybe see you one of these days to play music or just tell jokes.

Be well.

Itzhak.

Itzhak Perlman

JACK LEMMON

April 19, 1999

Dear Dudley,

I am sure that this particular birthday is not the happiest one you've ever known, so I want to wish you a Happy Birthday for next year. That one's going to be a hell of a lot better.

Needless to say, I was sorry to hear you've been ill. However, there is one truism that I firmly believe in, because I"ve seen it happen to my friends so many times. So often it seems that people with extraordinary talents are extraordinary in other ways also. They seem to have an inner strength beyond that which most people have. I know damn well you are one of those people and I hope you'll feel fit as a piano (fiddle?) as soon as possible.

Speaking of inner strength, if I could put up with William Morris for forty years before I wised up, you can kick the shit out of whatever it is.

Felicia joins me in hoping you have a speedy recovery and we both send love. We miss you.

Always,

Jack

Mr. Dudley Moore
c/o Ms. Barbara Paskin

Jack Lemmon

April 14th, 1999

Dear Dudley:

I miss you! It's been a long time since I have seen you, and I have heard you are not in the greatest of health, so I wanted to send you wonderful warm birthday wishes, and a return to good health as speedily as possible!

You are truly one of a kind, and I look forward to seeing you back on the T.V. or movie screen again soon -- because you're unique! Keep on doing the things that make everyone so happy when they watch you. And, once again, fondest birthday wishes.

Love and kisses,

Jackie
xxx

JACKIE COLLINS

JC/vw

Jackie Collins

April 17th 99.

Hello Dudley -

It's been a long time since we've crossed paths. I haven't been around much in L.A. on the "circuit", have been trying to keep my life together in general. It's not easy is it! Anyway I just wanted to say a little "Bonjour" and wish you a happy birthday and better times to come - You're a great guy Dudley and don't you forget it -

with affection

Jacqueline Bisset

Jacqueline Bisset

Jane Asher

April 99

Dear Dudley -

How you've always managed to be brilliantly funny, a wonderful musician and incredibly sexy all at the same time has always amazed me. We miss you dreadfully: hurry up & entertain us again - Love & Happy Birthday Jane xx

Jane Asher

Jeff Bridges

Happy Birthday to the
world's funniest man —
My piano misses
you ... & so do I
love —
Joan

New York NY 10155

Joan Rivers

Joanna Lumley

London
April 9th

Dearest Dudley — I remember, in the late 1970s, being at the Inn on the Park to hear a famous country and western singer – I sat at your table and you were being (silently) pretty funny about something and I started to laugh like a drain and you got worse and worse until I was nearly sick and we both sat there weeping with suppressed hysterics — Lordy!! you are the most fabulous person!! This brings you all the love in the world and sloppy birthday kisses, you great star,

from Lumley XX

Joanna Lumley

Christmas 1998.

Dear Old Dudley,

Spent a lovely day in Oxford looking at our "initial" meeting places, that came before our long association, and the launching-pad of the Fortune Theatre that sent you into the stratosphere of the entertainment world.

Magdalen Chapel (where we met, courtesy of Anthony Page) and even saw your rooms (where we once listened to Errol Garner, before going to so many Festival Hall Concerts) then to the Union Cellars (where you took the stage with such confidence to play a music that was still a slight mystery to you, along with John Mumford, Dick Heckstall-Smith, Duncan Lamont, and a full selection of British Jazzmen).

Of course I still pass the Edinburgh Festival Offices in St James' Street, (where you met Jennifer

John Bassett – Page 1

and I met Johnny D + Cleo when they wanted a pianist (!)) and I still pass the building that once housed The Establishment (where you played like the man you are – totally inspired) plus all the myriad little things + places that are far too numerous to mention here. At all events, for me, you are a part of the best part of my life, and there's not a day goes by that I am not reminded of all the fun you made, and that we shared together.

When things are better, and the dust has settled, and you are yourself again and in charge of life, cliché (click click click as the Labour politician Manny Shinwell said) let me know where and how you are, and maybe we'll meet again. No American girl-friend now, so you are my only "excuse" to come to the States.

Best wishes + all love

John
Your Old J.B.

John Bassett – Page 2

I read your biography of Dudley with great interest, and have such very pleasant memories of my short time working with him on the two Arthur films
I am greatly saddened of his bad times lately and can only hope that the future may hold a premise of restoring his star prestige and remarkable talents

Sincerely
John Gielgud

John Gielgud

Facsimile message from

To: Dudley Moore, Esq

From: Sir John Mills, CBE

Date: 22 April 1999

No of pages: 1

My Dear Dudley –

I have just heard from Juliet that you have been under the weather lately, in fact feeling absolutely lousy.

It is very easy to sympathise and understand, particularly at the moment. I was doing my one man show in Hollywood a couple of weeks ago and had rather a bad fall and crushed a disc. I have spent the last twelve days in bed but am now up and hobbling around the house with a stick! I talk to Juliet every week so I shall have reports on how you are getting on.

America's gain was England's loss, we have missed you very much over here.

Mary joins me in sending our love and best wishes.

Get well soon.

John Mills

Dearest Dudley –

We all love you!!!..

If it wasn't for your genious,

we'd be alot less happy!

So – Have an amazingly

warm and loving

BIRTHDAY!!..

from

Jon Voight

+ everyone

else in the

whole world!

Jon Voight

Karen Black

April 12, 1999

Dear Dudley,

Well, this is going to be easy. Because I'm writing to tell you what I've had a lot of practice saying about you: that you are the only real thing when it comes to comedy on film. NOW, before you say oh Karen you're being hyperbolic, or you're just trying to flatter me, hear me out!

I've noticed that there are comics who are very good on stage, but when it comes to film they lose their panache big time. I've wondered about this. And here is the answer I've come up with: On stage you get to go , "Hey, audience, nudge nudge, I'm only kidding, I'm really not this sap . I'm the sharp guy, the one showing you the sap." And that's on stage, or even on tape; it's kinda cute, it pays off. But on film! Now that's a whole different story. Film itself promotes the possibility that this is actual. That what you are widnessing is indeed real. Therefore the comic on film has to live the part. Has to experience what the character is experiencing as the character, NOT as the brilliant observer presenting the character. Because otherwise the audience is saying to itself, "self? How come that person who should be scared in that very real situation isn't really scared? How come he's only SHOWING me somebody who is supposed to be scared? I would be scared." See?

And it's so few who can get the laughs they might design the performance toward getting on film! Because comics won't BE the part.

But you will. And you do. And you are a complete genius at this and I can't think of anyone who compares to you. I can think of funny people on screen, but I'm sitting there along with the rest of the audience thinking, "Gee that's funny". (notice no one is laughing.)

You are a dear, open, communicating friend. I love our little lunches together for various reasons-(do you remember when I said, should I take my shoes off?) THAT was the lunch at the Beverly Hills. I had a crush on you that day, a pretty bad one, but I never told you.

I guess that's all. I don't think anything in the physical universe can possibly interrupt your talent. It's there forever and that's a fact.

Lots of love,

Karen

Karen Black

AMALFI
KATE & STEVEN SPIELBERG
FAX TRANSMITTAL FORM

TO: Dudley Moore.
FROM: Kate Capshaw.
DATE:
TIME:
PAGES:

MESSAGE: 15 April, 1999.

Dear Dudley! Dudley!
My darling Dudley!
What the heck is going on
in your life?
I miss you on screen...—
I miss you on those ivories
and ebonies. I think of our
deliciously naughty chats
on the set. of "BEST DEFENSE."
PS. You were the only reason I did
that movie! BE WELL
DEAR FRIEND
Love Kate XOXOXOXOX

come back
come back

IF THERE ARE PROBLEMS WITH TRANSMISSION, PLEASE CALL

come back
come back.

Kate Capshaw

Here's Wishing the Magnificent
Dudley A Very Very
Happy Birthday!!
We Hope you Have
A Wonderful, Plumpshus
and Discomknockerating
Time!!!
Thank you for all the
Joy and Happiness
you Give!!
Sincerely
Ken Dodd and All
your Diddymen at
Knotty Ash. U.K.

Ken Dodd

April 12th 1999

Dear Dud,

Happy Birthday you young fart, which I say with authority as I am 1 year older and therefore an old fart

But the joys are yet to come – one more year and you'll qualify for the Holy Grail, which comes in the form of a Bus Pass, ever useful in the Canyons of Beverly and Hollywood Hills. And secondly the State Pension which will cover the Newspaper and milk Bill for life – so not to be scoffed at.

Meanwhile have a super 64th and Remember that you are the only one of our age group who became a world superstar, and thoroughly deserved.

Yours Lance Percival

Lance Percival

LARRY GELBART

4.19.99

Dudley dear-

Pat and I were so excited when we heard you were turning six four- until we learned it was your age and not your height - Oh, well, we love you anyway - and always will -

Larry

Larry Gelbart

Lauren Bacall

Dudley dear -

Still listening to your wonderful music - Would so love to be sitting in that little cafe with you and the piano making those fabulous Dudley sounds - I'll never forget it!

thinking of you - get well and hurry up and come to New York -

Affection always -

L. Bacall

Lauren Bacall

Lenny Henry

Dear Dud

I just wanted to scribble a quick note to you on your birthday. However ,as my handwriting is crap, (You could probably get a *very nice* prescription made up from one of my self penned efforts) I thought you'd appreciate this type written thing.
I seem to have been a fan of your work for most of my life, from watching you with Pete on 'Not only but Also) to enjoying Derek and Clive : My Mom came into my room..etc. So imagine my complete and ubridled joy when I was asked to appear for Amnesty international, You and Peter were top of the bill. I don't think I said very much to you. I was too nervous –I think. I remember we had to do photo's for the press to publicise the show –you looked like you weren't enjoying that aspect of the whole thing..you were there to do the show.
I loved what you did in the show , Frog and Peach –where you managed to corpse throughout the entire sketch ,but still actually *ask* Pete the relevant questions,and the magnificent Colonel Bogie sketch ,which had the audience on their feet.
It was an honour to be in the audience that night .

Thank you,and have a facking great birthday.

From a fan.

Lenny Henry.

Lenny xx

Cheers mate –
We Love you!!
(Told you my writing was crap.)

Lenny Henry

Dear Dudley
I remember the night
of Susan Anton's Birthday party.
You were so wonderful — I
fell in love with you
instantly! You had taken
care of every single detail
including having her hair and
make-up person on hand to
touch her up so that she
always looked perfect for
the cameras. What a guy!
As the cake came out
you jumped up onto a chair
to sing her Happy Birthday.
I know it was her night
but my eyes were on you.
What a guy!

Linda Gray – Part 1

I watched you weave magic into that evening, just as you weave magic into everything you do. I love and appreciate your talent and all of us you touched by your love of your craft.

Happy Happy Birthday dear Dudley. I miss your face — in person or on screen. Please get well. You deserve to receive the love we all have for you. I send you love and I will always keep you in my heart! What a guy!

Love
Linda Gray

Linda Gray – Part 1

LIZA MINNELLI

April 19, 1999

Dear Dudley,

Simply you are the best, the brightest, the funniest and dearest person I know...and are you cute!

We need you baby.

Love,

Liza

Liza Minnelli

"WHAT EVER HAPPENED TO HAROLD SMITH"

PRODUCTION OFFICE
2nd FLOOR, GLOBE II BUSINESS CENTRE, 128 MALTRAVERS ROAD, SHEFFIELD S2 5AZ
TEL: 0114 249 6363 FAX 0114 249 4144

14th April '99'

Hey babe,

I hear its your birthday and your feeling poorly.
Well Tom Courtenay and i send you big hugs and kisses from sunny Sheffield where we are filming 'Whatever happened to Harold Smith'
You know i love you!

Tons and tons of blessings too!

Love Lulu.

P.S. Stephen Fry also says hi!

Lulu

lynn redgrave

Dearest Dudley
Wishing you the
most fabulous
BIRTHDAY!!! Hooray!
Congratulations –
Much love /
Lynn

Lynn Redgrave

Mary Tyler Moore

April 13th, 1999

Dear Dudley,

Did you know that my
father and you share the
same birthday? Of course you
did! You've simply blocked
the weight of it all. But a
hugely happy day to you on
the 19th of April.

There's more — I have a
12 year old dog — to be exact,
a petite basset griffon Vendeen
who's mission since the 16th
century is to hunt rabbits. He's
low to the ground, basset like
with long, tri color hair.
I named him Dudley for-

Mary Tyler Moore – Page 1

getting that when he's formally introduced his name is Dudley Moore. I trust you don't mind.

I hope you're feeling well and that you'll soon be doing your magic again on screen.

I miss you, as do your other millions of admirers, but I have these memories of working with you, too

Love,

Mary

Mary Tyler Moore – Page 2

MEL BROOKS

April 19, 1999

Dear Dudely:

It's better to be better than not, so get better! Happy Birthday!

All the Best,

Mel

Mel Brooks

CULVER STUDIOS. 9336 W. WASHINGTON BOULEVARD, BUILDING B, SUITE 202, CULVER CITY, CALIFORNIA 90232
PHONE (310) 202-3292 • FAX (310) 202-3225

Mel Brooks

19th April 1999

My dear Dudley,

A Happy Birthday to you.

Every week when I go to Langan's I think of you as I sit at the table in the corner where you and your trio used to play for us. You are one of my favourite people and the funniest great piano player that I ever met.

We miss you here. Come and see us soon.

Much love

Michael Caine

Dear Dudley –

Happy Birthday and

many more 64 ths !

from a fan —

Michael

(aka M. PALIN)

Michael Palin

April 1, 1999

Dear Dudley,

Happiest of birthday wishes to you. I have been missing your irreverent and erudite spirit and trust that you are gathering strength, concocting dazzling cadenzas of one liners, snappy comebacks, double entendres and not to mention hemi, demi, semi-quavers. Many happiest returns of the day. I look forward to seeing you in the future.

All my very best,

Michael T. T.

Michael Tilson Thomas

MTT:mk

Michael Tilson Thomas

MICK JAGGER

Dear Dud,

Someone told me it was your birthday so I'm dropping you a note to wish you a very happy one.

I haven't seen you for ages – not since we had dinner in Venice with Eric Idle some time back. I'm quite often in LA – I'd love to see you sometime – or in London, or wherever.

Again wishing you all the best –

Mick.

Mick Jagger

MILTON BERLE

Dear Dudley,

My very best wishes for your birthday and the years to come. I hope to see you soon. I have always loved your work as an actor, but what I most admire about you, is your ability to play the piano and talk at the same time. And doing it so well.

My wife Lorna joins me in singing:

" HAPPY BIRTHDAY TO YOU
HAPPY BIRTHDAY TO YOU
HAPPY BIRTHDAY DEAR DUDLEY,
HAPPY BIRTHDAY TO YOU....
and many moooore. "

You are truly an original, and we love you dearly.

Love you,

Milton

Milton Berle

NEIL SIMON

Dudley Moore
Dear Dudley,

I hear your 64th birthday is coming up. Well, it's better than other things coming up.

I also hear you're feeling under the weather. A flight on the Concorde at 50, 000 feet will get you above that.

I just wanted you to know that you made me laugh so hard the very first time I saw you in London...and I don't speak English all that well. "Ten" was brilliant and I never understood why they didn't go ahead and make "Eleven".

I suppose my. favorite sketch of yours and Peter was the one legged man auditioning for the Tarzan movie. I tried to tell friends who had never seen it, by trying to do it myself. After falling to the floor for the tenth time, I realized that comedy is not only timing, it's also balancing.

I send you my love and best wishes on your birthday.

Warmest regards,

Neil Simon

Neil Simon

NORMAN LEAR

April 20, 1999

Dear Dudley Moore,

Although we've never met, I always feel I know those people very well who have made me laugh. You are certainly one of them. It's a great kick to be able to wish you a Happy Birthday and also to tell you that 64 is just a number.

Thanks for the good time you've given me.

Sincerely,

Norman Lear

NL/la

Dudley Moore
c/o Barbra Paskin

Norman Lear

My dear Dudley,

I'm down here in Oz, and a little birdie tells me that it is your 64th birthday! Wow! Good on yer mate! It seems like yesterday that I met you on a T.V. show in Sydney when you were here with 'DUD + PETE' and we had such a fun time – I have always been such a fan of your talent and musicianship, and I send you love + hugs for this milestone birthday, and 'thank-you' for all the pleasure you've given the world, the laughter + the tears, and congratulations for making it to this very auspicious age! – Much love,
Olivia Newton-John

Olivia Newton-John

DEAR DUDLEY (IF I MAY BE SO BOLD),

WE HAVE NEVER MET – MY LOSS. BUT I WAS IN THE AUDIENCE AT, I THINK, THE SECOND PREVIEW OF 'BEYOND THE FRINGE' AT THE QUEENS (THE GLOBE?) THEATRE IN 1961. I WAS THEN IN THE SECOND YEAR OF MY ACTING CAREER, SO AS PROS. WE SPAN IDENTICAL DECADES. DURING THOSE DECADES YOU HAVE GIVEN ME MORE PLEASURE, FUN, DELIGHT THAN ANY PERSON MIGHT EXPECT. THANK YOU – AND A VERY HAPPY BIRTHDAY.

Patrick Stewart.

Patrick Stewart

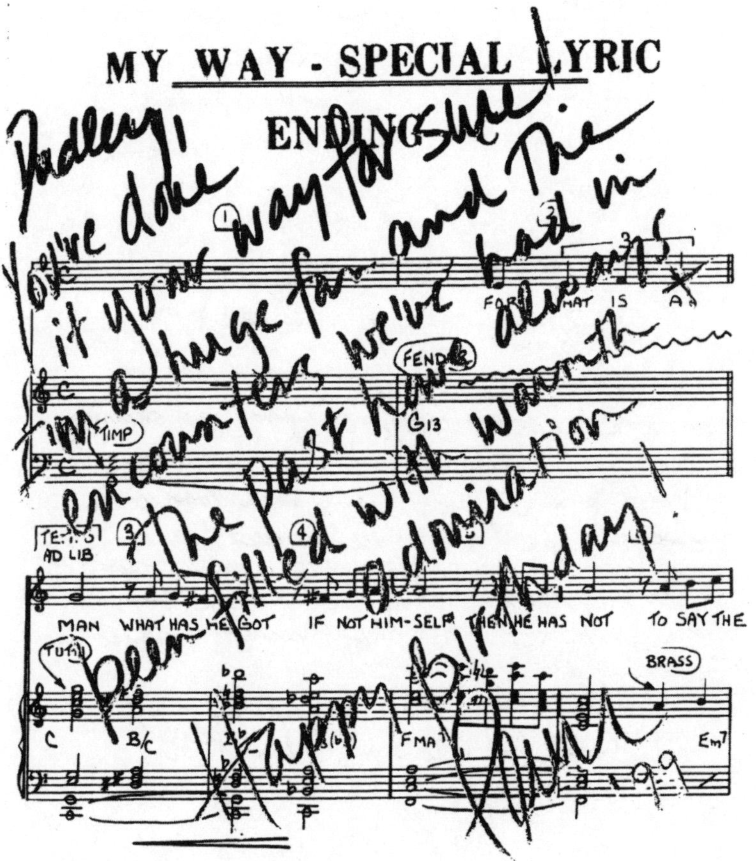
Piano Conductor
PAUL ANKA
MY WAY - SPECIAL LYRIC
ENDING
FOR WHAT IS A
MAN WHAT HAS HE GOT IF NOT HIM-SELF THEN HE HAS NOT TO SAY THE
Dudley,
You've done it your way for sure!
I'm a huge fan and the encounters we've had in the past have always been filled with warmth and admiration!
Happy Birthday!

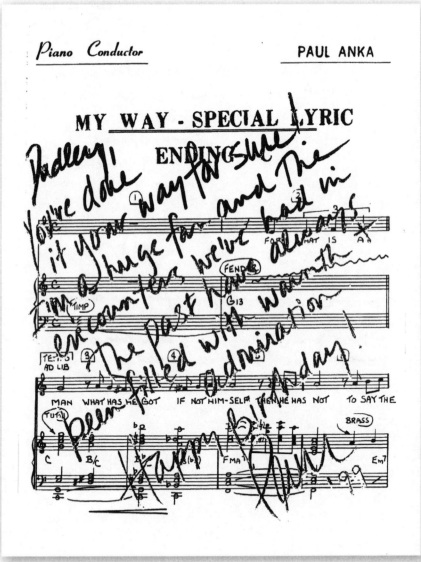

Paul Anka

Upton-on-Thigh
MECKLEWARLE

Dear Duddles,

I wish I had the ability to make up a song about your birthday – cleverly including in it your upcoming age, but I just don't have the gift; .....

There was an old one I heard in the Sixties what was appropriate though. It had in it the following marvellous words

will you still need me
will you still feed me!

well ... laugh? we piddled ourselves when we first heard that!
then it finished
when I'm 64!

well ----- It's so fitting I had to tell you about it.

love,
Auntie Paula (McCartney)
xx

Paul McCartney

PAUL SIMON

Dudley –

Have a happy birthday in 1999. Seems to me that we last saw each other briefly in Café Des Artistes in N.Y a few years ago. Now I understand that you're not feeling well and I'm so sorry to hear that. I hope its something that will pass soon. My best to you

Paul

Paul Simon

PETER FALK

April 15, 1999

Dudley,

We miss you! Could use a few laughs! Get your ass in gear!

Love,

Peter and Shera Falk

UNIVERSAL STUDIOS, 100 UNIVERSAL CITY PLAZA, UNIVERSAL CITY, CALIFORNIA 91608

Peter Falk

23rd April 1994
Ahmanson Theatre
L.A.

My dear Dudley –

Just to say Happy Birthday!

– I haven't seen you for years but remember you with much affection – particularly in those early years.

– I always think of you as the master TIMER – whether it be of a musical phrase or a line – that dangerous moment (often only a split second) when the phrase or the joke is delivered straight to the audience's heart. Have a great Birthday – You're a master.

Ever Peter (Hall)

Peter Hall

PETULA CLARK

DEAREST DUD

WHERE ARE YOU —?

WE MISS YOU, + YOUR TALENT, YOUR MUSIC – EV'RYTHING ABOUT YOU!

WHAT WAS THE NAME OF THAT RESTAURANT JUST OFF BOND ST.? I USED TO EAT THERE ALL THE TIME (MOSTLY BECAUSE YOU'D PLAY PIANO THERE NOW + THEN!)

HAVE A GREAT BIRTHDAY.

I LOVE YOU.

Petula

xxxxx

Petula Clark

Dear Dudley,

We've never met, but I feel as though I know you. Besides the wonderful stuff with Peter C. and the movies you've done, I recollect a night in 1964 at a party on stage for 'Oliver'. You played with the trio, and I was the Artful Dodger at the time ... I watched in wonder at you, Pete + Chris I was a musician even

Phil Collins – Page 1

then .. well a drummer anyway
and I just sat and enjoyed
the music.

I know it's your birthday
and I know you're a bit
under the weather at the
moment, but I just wanted
to let you know you've
touched people everywhere!
(if you know what I mean!)

Have a great day!

luv Phil Collins

Phil Collins – Page 2

QUINCY JONES

BELOVED DUDLEY______

I'M SENDING WISHES, LOVE & PRAYERS TO YOU, FOR YOU TO "GET ON UP, SO WE CAN GET DOWN" :)

I'M ALSO SENDING THIS PIECE OF MY LIFE TO SHARE WITH A GREAT MUSICIAN: YOU!

I'M SO PROUD THAT WE ALSO SHARED WORKING CLOSELY WITH JOHN & FAITH HUBLEY. THE LINE IS ONE OF MY FAVES. WE ALSO IN THE COMPANY OF BENNY CARTER & DIZZY - GOD BLESS YOU

LOVE & RESPECT

Quincy Jones

from the desk of Red Buttons

Dudley My Boy –

Sixty Four is not Old

Old is if you stopped buying Green Bananas –

Old is if you order Two Minute Eggs and they ask you to pay in advance –

Old is if you forget your Twin Brother's Birthday.

Thats Old – Sixty Four you are still a kid – Happy Birth Day

A Hug

Red Buttons

P.S. My desk wishes you the best.

Red Buttons

Dear Dudley

We have never met
but I've been a rabid
fan of yours for many
years.

Have a lovely Birthday
and love and luck to you

Richard (BRIERS)

Richard Briers

ROBBIE COLTRANE
C.D.A

Dear Dud,

I hear from Barbra that you are a few coupons short of a toaster, health wise, at the moment, and what with your Bus Pass being imminent, I thought I'd just send you Fraternal Birthday Greetings.

I shall not claim to be your Best Pal, as we only worked together once, at that Cambridge Circus week that Jack Cheese organised a few years ago; I can, however, claim that you were a seminal influence on my early years, as you were on all my chums, stuck as we were in the Highlands of Scotland, being turned into Perfect Little Gents, as our parents hoped. Little did they know.

Suffice to say that I still remember all the words and music for "When you're feeling glum, stick your finger up your bum", a song that has helped me through many a dark hour. I have been teaching it to my son, now six, and he cannot BELIEVE that anyone as talented as your good self could write anything so vulgar withour being arrested. Who says the Young are unshockable?

I am off to do an hour-long Parkinson Special shortly, you should do the same; you get to show off non-stop for a whole hour, with Parky asking kind questions. You owe it to all of us this side of the Pond who miss you dearly,

Happy Birthday, you old Bastard,

R Coltrane (Mrs).

Robbie Coltrane

ROGER MOORE

1st April 1999

My dear Dud — A little bird (feathered variety) told me that my little son Dudley was going to be 64 on the 19th of this month ———

Have a wonderful — PTO

Roger Moore

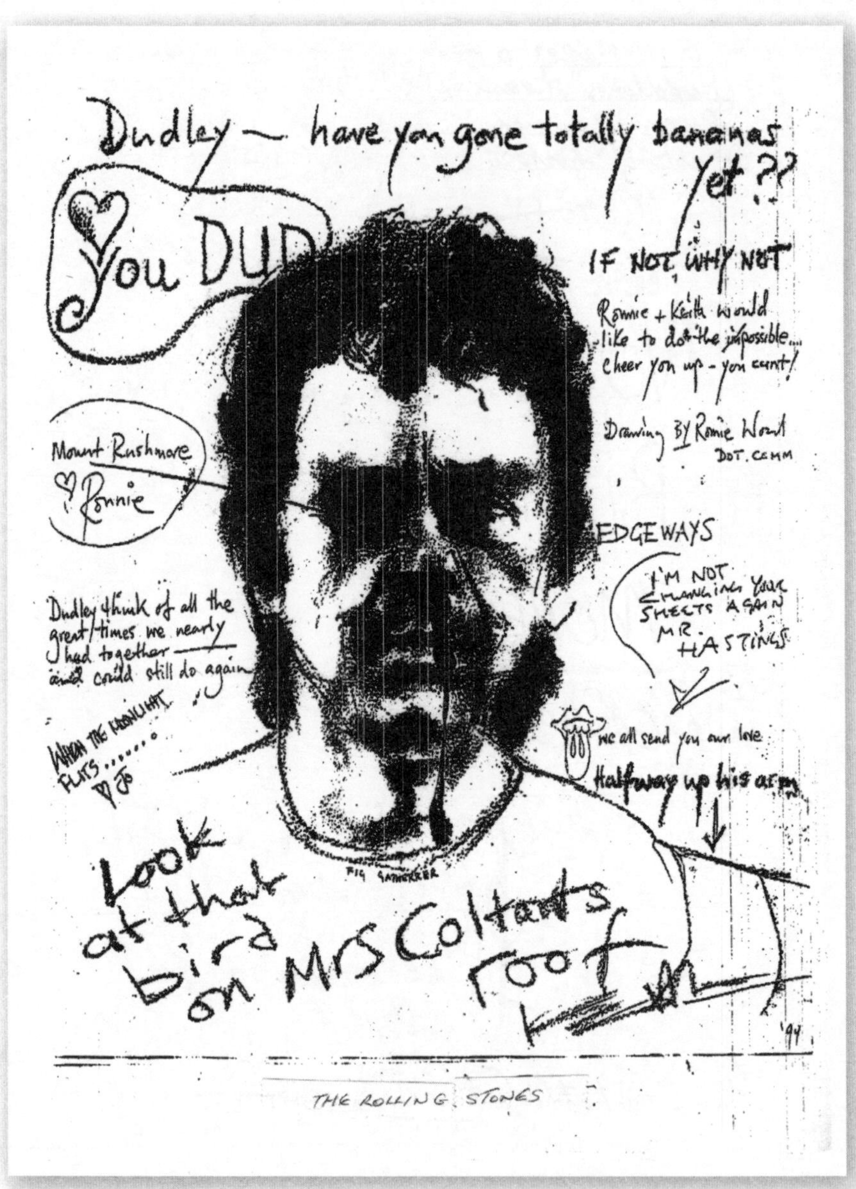

Rolling Stones

Here's a greeting from "The News Huddlines" team, now the longest-running comedy radio series in broadcasting history – 25 years! Cast: Roy Hudd
June Whitfield
Chris Emmett

DUD

NOT SO MUCH
A BIRTHDAY WISH
MORE A
COMEBACK SOON!

[signature]

June Whitfield Chris Emmett

Roy Hudd

Sid Caesar

Dear Dudley

I must tell you how much I have enjoyed you through the years.

You can't hide talent like yours.

Thank you for all the laughs through the years, and many, many more

With Love & Laughter.

Sid Caesar

P.S. You are Great

Sid Caesar

Spike Milligan

My dear Dudley,

A Happy Birthday to you and your piano playing and I'm looking forward to hearing that playing when you are back over here.

Love,light and peace.

Spike

SPIKE MILLIGAN

Spike Milligan

STANLEY DONEN

Dear Dudley—

The Best is Yet to Come!

And I hope you are about to
as well—

Happy Birthday +
Love—
Stanley

Stanley Donen

Stephen Bishop

Ap. 19, 99

Dearest Dudley,

Hello my friend. I'm so glad to be a part of this birthday celebration for you. I hope this greeting finds you in good spirits. I sure do miss your cute face and beautiful music. I pray you feel better soon so we can all, once again, enjoy your special gifts.

Just know that wherever you go & whatever you do, my love & friendship go with you.

Happy Happy Birthday dear Love

Ouch!

Susan

A.K.A Sooo-San

Susan Anton

SUZANNE SOMERS

Dear Dudley:

As I commemorate your birthday, I remember that the last time I saw you was several years ago in the *Black Forest of Germany*. You were dragging Susan Anton's luggage into this little Inn while The Pointer Sisters were bitching. Whenever I think of you, I remember that scene and it puts a smile on my face.

Thanks for all the smiles you have given me over the years.

I saw a TV special where you gave a piano concert that was truly exquisite. You have been given so many gifts; your talent in every arena is superb.

I will keep you in my prayers for recovery. Keep thinking good thoughts. Thought is powerful. The mind – body connection is truly magical. For those who doubt the power of the mind, think of the word: erection!

Happy Birthday dear friend.

Love,

Suzanne

Suzanne

Suzanne Somers

9th April 99

Dear Dudley

May your socks be full of fish and your mice be golden. May rivers of antelope droppings bless your chickens, and may the cynosure of your chilblains shine like a beef-loaf turnover in the dark galley-kitchenette of our wash-basins for ever.

Thinking of you and all yours.

love from

Terry Jones

PYTHON (MONTY) PICTURES LTD. REGISTERED NUMBER 1138069 ENGLAND. REGISTERED OFFICE · 68A DELANCEY STREET [illegible]

[illegible] · TERRY JONES · MICHAEL [illegible]

Terry Jones

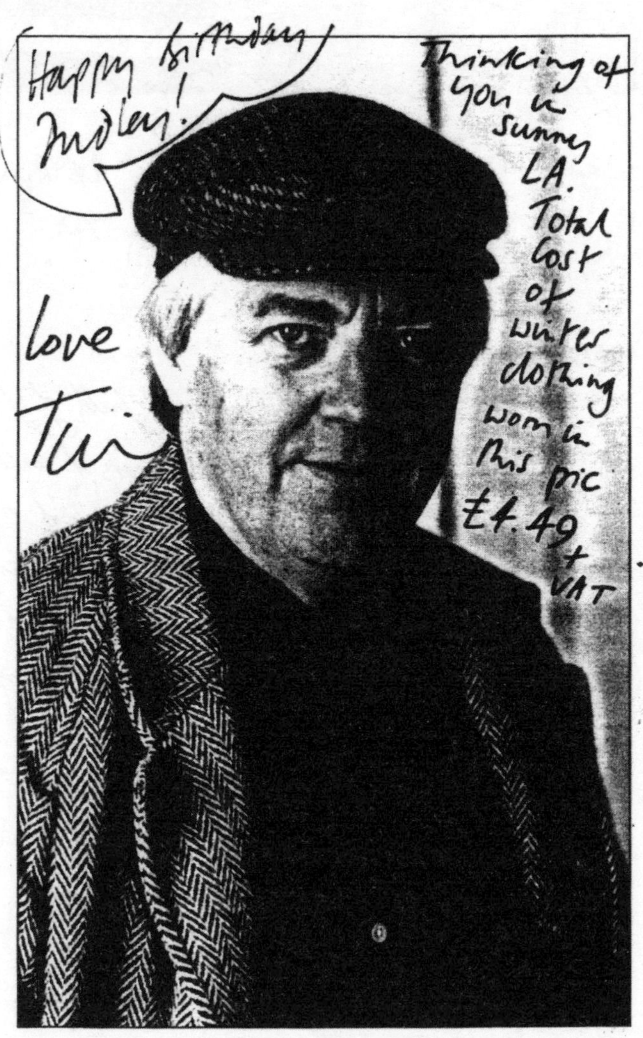

TIM RICE

LONDON SW13 0NR

Happy birthday Dudley!

Thinking of you in sunny LA. Total cost of winter clothing worn in this pic £4.49 + VAT

love
Tim

Tim Rice

Allan McKeown / Tracey Ullman

Dear Dudley,

(to be sung)

"We still love you

Now your 64"

Happy Birthay!

64 is a dangerous Age, Cynthia

Lots of Love

Allan and Tracey. XXX

Tracey Ullman

Dearest
Cuddley Dudley
Wishing you a Happy Birthday
& all sorts of good things for
the next year —
lots of love
Twiggy ♡
x x
x

Twiggy

Whoopi Goldberg

Dudley,

Happy, Happy, Happy, Happy Birthday Baby!

Hurry up and get better so we can see your face more often. . . I miss you!

Love,

Whoopi

Whoopi Goldberg

Woody Allen

April 1999

Dear Dudley,

Heard that you were under the weather and so figured you'd be able to appreciate all the physical problems I've had. Beginning with sinus pains I've had a torn rotator cuff, intestinal reflux, a touch of glaucoma, and mild skin cancer. Add to this several bouts of flu and stomach virus, not to mention a slight hearing loss in my left ear and you see what I've been up against. Sorry to burden you with all this but I feel you'd understand. Get well, stay healthy, and Happy Birthday.

Woody Allen

Woody Allen

CHAPTER 31

Facing The Challenge 1999

In his own way, Dudley fought back. He was resolute about working. In spite of his debilitation, and in a move that could only be described as gutsy, he agreed to give a charity performance in Philadelphia in November to benefit MFAS, with him and Julie Andrews narrating alternately Ogden Nash's verses to *Carnival of the Animals*. He threw himself enthusiastically into working towards the gala concert. He was glad to have something to look forward to and was particularly thrilled that he would be performing again. He had missed the applause of a live audience.

> **DUDLEY:** I'm looking forward immensely to doing this. With acting you have to be more spontaneous and you can't wing it. With narration, you learn the words and the expression of them and it's a fairly simple thing. I'm not nervous about it. Julie is going to be with me and she'll take over things I can't say. I actually feel quite excited about doing it.

With the help of his speech therapist, he worked assiduously for several weeks on the narration of *Carnival of the Animals*. Rena and Brian played piano and Julie joined Dudley in the narration. It was a resounding success and he was ecstatic to be facing an audience once more, the first time he'd been on stage in two years. It was not the way he could ever have foreseen his last public performance as an entertainer, but the standing ovation he was given was immeasurably warming. His public, like the piano, had been an enduring love of his life. And he, theirs. When he was spotted at airports in his wheelchair, people applauded him. The sound was music to his ears.

The latter few years were lived in the loving protective cocoon provided by Rena's family. Rena, her husband, daughters, son and grandchildren became Dudley's family. And although his body was failing him, Rena was uplifted to see that his spirit seemed to grow stronger. And there was still laughter. Dudley's earlier fart machine, Handi-Gas, had now been replaced with an electronic version that played six different sounds. He had never lost his impish delight at the sound that had ruined so many takes in his filming days.

Life settled into a routine filled with speech and physical therapy, daily excursions to the local restaurants for lunch, rented movies every evening, holidays at the family's Nova Scotia hideaway and even a week's cruise to Bermuda. With them at last Dudley was able to find a peace which had eluded him for so much of his life.

It was a life that had been filled with wonderful relationships and then the dreadful last act of a depraved marriage – 'a union created in hell', as one friend described it. Before he finally left, for the eleventh time, Nicole had broken in and smashed up his house, leaving it resembling a bomb site, burned and destroyed his cherished memorabilia and precious irreplaceable sheet music, left him bruised and scratched and threatened endlessly to burn down the house. He fled several times, to New York, even to

London and Australia, but she always tracked him down. Helpless against what he later discovered was an addiction for which he was eventually treated, he always returned, hoping each time that it would be different. It never was.

It had been a tragic contrast to much of his life, rendering him an abused husband involving endless divorce filings and restraining orders which were disregarded, forcing him to seek protection and surround himself with bodyguards. The last time he went back saw him terrified in his own house while she went berserk outside. After just one day he left, never to return; in 1998 his divorce became final.

Dudley was still very involved with Music For All Seasons and the production company he had formed with Rena. He worked assiduously with her in producing a CD of his 1992 concert at the Royal Albert Hall in which he'd performed classically with the BBC Concert Orchestra and as jazz pianist with his trio. Part of his UK tour, he always regarded that concert as his greatest success. He titled the CD *Live from an Aircraft Hangar*, his reference to the cavernous and venerable venue. Assembling and editing the CD from different recordings of the concert took several months and Dudley was painstakingly precise about the tracks to use and how it would sound. The result was a wonderful tribute to his pianistic mastery, topped off with his extensive liner notes.

In April 2001, three days before his sixty-sixth birthday, dozens of celebrities came together to mount a tribute to Dudley at Carnegie Hall, scene of his earlier triumphant concerts. The tribute was titled 'A Man for All Seasons', with proceeds going to MFAS and Dudley's PSP research fund. Among the many performers were Eric Idle, Chevy Chase, Bo Derek, Lauren Bacall, Mary Tyler Moore and trio members Chris Karan and Pete Morgan. Dudley was especially proud that his violinist friend Robert Mann had assembled a string quartet to play two movements of Dudley's *String Quartet No. 1* with Rena's son Joel as cellist. It marked its New York premiere and was only the second time Dudley had heard it played since he'd hurriedly composed it in his last year at Oxford. The concert was a resounding success and the long standing ovation Dudley received at its end left him in no doubt about his peers' affection and admiration. A few hours later, more than five hundred friends and performers joined him in celebrating as he cut his birthday cake.

Over the years Dudley had received countless awards and accolades but none equalled the pride he felt when he was awarded the CBE. The honour conferred upon him by the Queen cemented his role as one of Britain's national treasures. Despite his frail condition, in the autumn of 2001 he insisted on making the arduous journey to London, accompanied by Rena and Brian. At Buckingham Palace, he was wheelchaired in to meet Prince Charles, who spent several minutes speaking with him. A man with a great sense of humour, he had always enjoyed Dudley's comic work. The occasion itself was not without humour. Echoing shades of *Arthur,* Dudley had organised a silver Rolls-Royce but when his wheelchair would not fit in the boot a second car had to be ordered especially to transport it.

Celebrations afterwards took them to the Savoy for lunch with Dudley's long-time friends Cleo Laine and John Dankworth, for whom he'd often performed at the famed annual jazz concerts at their Wavendon home. He spent time with Suzy Kendall and her daughter Elodie, and his sister Barbara and her husband Bernard. When he said goodbye to them he knew it was for the last time.

At the end of January 2002, Dudley saw Cleo Laine and John Dankworth once more. They were performing at Michael Feinstein's club in Manhattan and he was excited to be able to attend. They had always been two of his favourite people, ever since they had first discovered him as a student playing jazz at Oxford. And he never forgot the kindness they had shown him when he joined John Dankworth's band.

In his last years, Dudley came to experience the one emotion that had always eluded him. Contentment. He had never fully recognised nor appreciated his talents. But now he revelled in them. He watched his movies, laughing with them. And he listened to his music, music he had composed over the years for films, stage, concerts. And there was bliss in his ears.

At last, Dudley Moore was able to appreciate what we had known forever. That he was a brilliant talent who had brought joy and entertainment to millions around the world. And who, in his final years, was able to enjoy that talent for himself.

At the end of March, just a few weeks before his sixty-seventh birthday, Dudley lost the battle he'd so courageously fought for the last five years.

Dudley's life was cut short far too soon, but we can give thanks that he has left us with a rich and glorious legacy. His amazing facility to switch between jazz, classical music, acting and comedy, that made him one of the most versatile and multifaceted performers of our time, is captured for posterity on records, CDs, tapes and film. In none of those arenas did he perform with mere adequacy – rather, he was outstandingly brilliant. He was one of the world's most gifted and adored performers and his work as a classical and jazz pianist and his exquisite compositions and film scores have inspired today's musicians who continue to play his music.

He touched people's hearts, both young and old. He was embraced by the world in a way that is rare for any performer. His music charmed presidents, queens, princes and princesses, and his movies enchanted audiences across the world.

It was Dudley's lot in life that he never knew in which direction to travel, save that he never really wanted to follow only one path, and it was the resulting fragmentation of his talents that instilled in him a sense of unfulfilment. If he had pursued classical music alone, he could have become one of the world's great pianists or violinists as he would have loved, yet we would have missed out on his extraordinary comic gifts. How could we imagine Pete without Dud? Or Clive without Derek? Inconceivable. And a cinema without his Arthur? What we would have missed! So he followed it all – and lucky for us that he did. And in the end he accomplished more than most of us can ever hope to achieve in a lifetime on any one of those many paths on which he travelled.

Postscript

Dear Dudley,

All these letters you received were my attempt to cheer you up on your sixty-fourth birthday and bring you some joy at a time when you knew you were ill. Wanting to remind you how much you were held in esteem and in the hearts of so many people. I never wrote one myself. But if I had, it would have said this:

Thank you for the kindness you always showed me, not only as your biographer but as an irritatingly persistent journalist who continually bombarded you for interviews over many years. Interviews which you always gave willingly and with enthusiasm.

Thank you for the largesse of your heart, which always made room for others and was always so caring for those less fortunate.

Thank you for your humility and never taking anything or anyone for granted. Least of all your success and your millions of fans around the world.

Thank you for your endless consideration, always putting others first, ahead of your own needs.

Thank you for your inordinate generosity. Never letting me pay for your crab cakes and espresso coffees at your restaurant. Never letting me pay for air tickets to accompany you on locations. And never charging me rent for any of my sojourns on your hotel sofas.

And thank you for your trust, which I always cherished and never betrayed.

Above all, thank you for your laughter. The laughter you prompted in us and the laughter that came from deep inside your soul. I like to think of you cackling up there above the clouds and keeping everyone around you in gales of laughter in the next world. It is a sound that continues to echo in my ears today.

For all this, and for so very much more . . . thank you.

Barbra

Acknowledgements

My thanks first to the nearly three hundred people who contributed birthday letters for Dudley, a hundred of which are included in this book. They lifted his spirits at a time when he most needed it.

My thanks also to all those who gave interviews for my original biography, from which much is included here. So very many people who gave their time generously out of their love for Dudley.

Thanks go to his sister, Barbara Stevens, friends Teifion Griffiths and Jim Johnson and school music teacher Peter Cork who filled in so much of the teenage years. To Suzy Kendall and Brogan Lane for their overwhelming frankness about their former husband who remained their friend until his untimely death. And to Dudley's son, Patrick, whose reflections were at times painful for him.

Among Dudley's friends of more than thirty-five years, I am indebted particularly to Peter Bellwood for his untiring input about both Dudley and Peter Cook, Francis Megahy, Alys Kihl and choreographer Dame Gillian Lynne. Thanks also to Lou Pitt, Dudley's close friend and loyal agent, to Susan Anton for her refreshing insight, to Celia Hammond, Dudley's first girlfriend and to Liza Minnelli for her special reminiscences.

Jonathan Miller, Alan Bennett and John Bassett were invaluable in recalling the *Fringe* years, while John Dankworth, Cleo Laine, Vic Lewis and Joseph McGrath filled in so much of Dudley's early working life.

Leslie Bricusse and Blake Edwards shed enormous insight on Dudley's inner self, and Tom Leahy, Dudley's former majordomo and Else Blangsted in Switzerland were unusually perceptive about the man they loved.

A deep gratitude belongs to Rena Fruchter and her husband Brian Dallow, the most giving and solid influence in the latter years of Dudley's life. And his greatest support in embracing him as one of their family.

Thanks too to Tony Luke, my former BBC radio producer who raided the BBC and BFI archives in London, and to my brother Simon, who elicited other research in London during the hours that I was (rarely) asleep in Los Angeles.

My appreciation to Barbra Streisand who graciously allowed me to be present with Dudley during the early days of filming *The Mirror Has Two Faces*. And my thanks to Lin Cook who talked openly if painfully about the turbulent relationship Peter Cook shared with Dudley.

Special thanks to Angie Dickinson and Dyan Cannon for their inspiration and friendship.

My deepest thanks to Andy Halmay for his constant encouragement and suggestions throughout the writing of this book. And to my friend and colleague, Michael Pointon, for his insightful reviews of Dudley's music and his enthusiastic embrace of this project.

And to John Blake for making it all possible.

There now follows a complete alphabetical list of those people who, in Britain, Hollywood, New York, Switzerland, Italy, Germany and Australia, shared memories or thoughts about the man they revered:

Tony Adams, Julie Andrews, Ken Annakin, Susan Anton, John Bassett, Peter Bellwood, Alan Bennett, Marsha Berger, Tony Bill, Jacqueline Bisset, Else Blangsted, Paul Bloch, Marshall Brickman, Leslie Bricusse, Ray Brown, Tita Cahn, Charles Champlin, Chevy Chase, George Christy, Dick Clement, Sir Michael Caine, Kate Capshaw, Alexander Cohen, Lin Cook, Peter Cork, Brian Dallow, Rod Daniel, John Dankworth, Amelia David (the Duplex), Bo Derek, Phyllis Diller, Stanley Donen, Carol Doumani, Susie Dullea, Blake Edwards, Ahmet Ertegun, Bryan Forbes, Ruth Forman, Patricia Foy, Rena Fruchter, Kenny G, Patrick Garland, Sir John Gielgud, Dr Martin Gizzi, Dave Green, Teifion Griffiths, Celia Hammond, Goldie Hawn, Peter Hemmings, Jonathan Hewes, Arthur Hiller, Sir Peter Hall, Eric Idle, Chris Ingham, Terry Jones, Jim Johnson, Nastassja Kinski, Dennis Koch, Chris Karan, Suzy Kendall, Alys Kihl, Dr Louis Kwong, Cleo Laine, Brogan Lane, Thomas Leahy, Vic Lewis, John Lithgow, Tony Luke(BBC), Peter Lydon (BBC), Dame Gillian Lynne, Elizabeth McGovern, Joseph McGrath, Robert Mann, Francis Megahy, Jonathan Miller, Sir John Mills, Liza Minnelli, Barbara Moore, Mary Tyler Moore, Patrick Moore, Sir Roger Moore, Peter Morgan, Nicole Moore, Laraine Newman, Nanette Newman, Anthony Page, Jerry Pam, Itzhak Perlman, Oscar Petersen, Michael Pointon, Bronson Pinchot, Lou Pitt, Carl Reiner, Ann Reinking, Paul Reiser, Dr Bernard Rose, George Schlatter, Ned Sherrin, Dr Evelyn Silvers, Sir George Solti, Mary Steenburgen, Barbara Stevens, Brenda Vaccaro, Bruce Vilanch, Jan Wallman, Aileen (Jo) Weld, Robin Williams, Linda Yellen, Bud Yorkin, Howard Zieff, Pinchas Zukerman. And the following: AFI, AMPAS, BFI, Boston Globe, London Records.

Most of all, my greatest debt and thanks in memoriam belong

to Dudley, not only because after years of being pursued by my colleagues he allowed mine to be the only biography he ever authorised, but for opening up to me in the most extraordinary way. I had thought, after sixteen years of interviewing him for the BBC and other media outlets, that I knew him well but, like most of his friends, it turned out I had known only one side of him.

Through writing his biography and in the years beyond, I came to know him closely and to be greatly touched by his friendship and the depth of his soul. The time he gave me, the endless hours he endured while my birds perched on his gentle shoulders and preened his eyelashes or fell asleep on his chest, were incalculable. His candour, generosity and grace under fire (not to mention a few avian offerings) affirmed my belief that he had the hugest heart on the planet.

He was a very special man who finally, in his latter years, was able to find the peace and happiness that had eluded him most of his life and which he so richly deserved.